D1503182

Planning and
politics: uneasy
partnership.

OCT 12 '77

OCT 17 1984

DEC 12 1996

MAY 07 1999

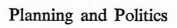

Planning and Politics

Planning and Politics: Uneasy Partnership

Edited by

THAD L. BEYLE and GEORGE T. LATHROP

University of North Carolina at Chapel Hill

The Odyssey Press   New York

Acknowledgment

Many of the papers included in this book were sponsored by grants from the Institute on State Programming for the 70's, University of North Carolina, Chapel Hill. The Institute, directed by former governor of New Mexico, Jack M. Campbell, was an independent, nonprofit organization created in January, 1967, to strengthen state government by stimulating comprehensive, long-range planning activities in all the states. The Institute was funded by a grant from the Carnegie Corporation of New York. The statements made and views expressed are solely the responsibility of the authors and do not necessarily represent the views of the Institute.

The authors are grateful to the following for permission to use the materials listed below.

The American Political Science Association: "The Diffusion of Innovations among the American States" by Jack L. Walker in the *American Political Science Review,* LXIII, no. 3 (September, 1969), 880–99.

Journal of the American Institute of Planners: "New Directions in State Planning" by Thad L. Beyle, Sureva Seligson, and Deil S. Wright in the *Journal of the American Institute of Planners,* XXXV (September, 1969), 334–39.

Copyright © 1970 by Western Publishing Company, Inc.

Published by The Odyssey Press

A Division of Western Publishing Company, Inc.

All Rights Reserved

Printed in the United States

Library of Congress Catalog Card Number: 76–124346

Contents

Preface

Suddenly, the words "public planning" are becoming acceptable—even respectable. I suspect the reason to be that most of us realize that it really didn't have to be this way. We must now know that if we can place man on the moon and photograph Mars at close range with less than a decade's work, then we should have been able to avoid or at least minimize pollution and poverty and congestion and other social problems. The trouble is that we failed to anticipate and direct social change. We failed to "plan." Some tried, but in most cases the planning was not really relevant and therefore was not politically feasible or acceptable. Our cities and their problems are an example.

When we talk about cities, or more properly, areas of population concentration, we are talking about the manifestation of almost all of our social problems. It may be correct to say that unless we quickly find ways to slow down the mass migration from rural areas to cities, create new designs for our central cities properly relating them to suburbia, develop social systems by using new techniques and technologies, break the white noose around the center cities and relieve the pressures of poverty, improve transportation and housing, and reduce pollution, then our American society not only as we have known it in the past, but as we have hoped and dreamed it would be, is doomed.

We really need not look long at the past. Observation of the explosive results of recent hot summer nights convinces us that we have in the past made frightening mistakes which we have not yet begun to attack seriously. Let us look just at the sheer numbers—numbers of people and growth rates. Present estimates are, that, despite the "pill," there will be well over three hundred million people in the United States by the year 2000—an increase of over one hundred million people, and that is only 30 years from now. Further, since two-thirds of the people who will be living then are living now, we are talking of our own crowding and not some future generation. Eighty percent, or about two hundred fifty million of these three hundred million people will be living in four giant megalopolises—on the Atlantic seaboard; around the lower Great Lakes; in Florida; and in California—on 11 percent of the land area in the continental United States. Others will live in outlying regions or in particular population concentration spots like Dallas, Houston, St. Louis, Kansas City, Albuquerque, Phoenix, Tucson, Denver, Portland, Seattle, and the Piedmont area of the Carolinas and Georgia.

Quite obviously, if we permit it, this hyper-concentration of people can cause even more social and environmental problems, such as inferior health conditions, more traffic congestion, lack of open space for recreation and relaxation, air and water pollution, even greater racial tensions, and so on and on. These problems are not new. We are experiencing their awful backlash now, but contemplate their seriousness if we insist on continuing the traditional planning and development techniques and patterns for urban growth which we have used in the past, if indeed we can dignify past practices by implying any orderly planning and development.

The blunt truth is that we are failing—to the point that our social structures are about to crash down upon us. It is no longer a question of whether we should be planning, but rather a question of whether our plans will be wise enough and put into effect soon enough to avoid catastrophe. This concern led me, in 1967, to accept the position of Chairman of the Institute on State Programming for the 70's, a Carnegie Corporation funded project with headquarters at the University of North Carolina at Chapel Hill.

During the life of this Institute we examined the public planning process in this country, particularly in state government. We worked with public officials at all jurisdictional levels, with academics and with leaders in the technological industries, such as aerospace, communications, and electronics. We sought a new focus on planning for the future. I suppose if there was a key discovered it was "relevancy"—relevancy to the real-life problems, relevancy to the political decision-makers. From this came several recurring themes.

First: Planning must be "people-oriented." Design must be built around *Man,* his desires, his hopes and aspirations, his convenience, his happiness. In the past, planning has been directed toward physical things. Giant skyscrapers built without much thought of the drudgery of a lifetime of work in them or how to get to and from them; bridges placed over rivers, with too little concern for where people want to cross and why; areas zoned with greater consideration for economic advantage than the desires of people; airports situated with no thought of convenient access to the city; the list seems endless. Facility planning is essential but we must consider the impact of these facilities upon Man's life. It has been wisely suggested that we should stop calling our population center the metropolis or the megalopolis or the cosmopolis and call it instead the "anthropolis." So, in short, we must be determined to plan and develop for Man, not just for things.

Second: We must plan innovatively and boldly. We must not become the helpless victims of the established way of doing things or of our "conventional wisdom." Urban planning and development, at any level of government, simply will not respond to conventional political approaches. We must be prepared to experiment with new methodology, new kinds of structures and organizations, greater participation on a broader and more representative basis. We must be willing to work across jurisdictional barriers to create new political structures. Planning, of necessity, deals with the uncertain and the unknown. The acceleration of change and the uncertainties of the future challenge us to be creative in what we undertake to constructively direct that change. Few of us *now* know what we want for ourselves and society. What a challenge to shape our rural areas, cities, states, and regions, in fact our society and environment, for the wants of people twenty-five or fifty years from now.

Third: We must plan "comprehensively," an awesome word but a significant one. Let me try to explain what I mean. A city cannot plan in a vacuum. It must plan with full cooperation within its own bureaucracy and in conjunction with other governmental jurisdictions, that is, surrounding communities, the county, and the state. This is not easy. Politically elected officials and bureaucracy do not respond well to coordinated effort. But unless there is comprehensive planning both horizontally across functional agencies of government and vertically between levels of government, the effectiveness of planning is seriously reduced. Those who make decisions and those who plan must recognize the interrelationships and interactions between the federal, state, and local levels of government, as well as between the areas of housing, education, recreation, industrial development, transportation, taxation, and welfare. To plan for one without considering effects upon the others is wasted planning. One of the reasons for the tragic conditions in our major cities of America is this unwillingness to plan comprehensively. It's one of the reasons, for example, that one could cross Manhattan Island in New York City several miles an hour faster in 1906, before the automobile, than one can cross it now.

Fourth, and finally: plans must be made for the purpose of implementation. Plans alone are not enough. They must be relevant, they must be practical, they must be acceptable to the decision-makers and to the public. Executive desks all over America are covered with beautifully prepared documents called "plans," public and corporate. But, to be meaningful, plans must be associated with action, and if they are public plans, with the political process. Responsibility simply must not stop with decisions or even with setting programs in motion. There must be monitoring, evaluation and assessment, feedback of information on results and on changing conditions, and then adjustment by successive rounds of decision-making. There can be no routine administration of worthwhile programs.

These then are four guidelines which must be followed if plans for the future are to be relevant and meaningful. The work involved in developing such a process and the constant leadership necessary to carry it out can become quite discouraging. Patience is not one of our society's virtues. We act on a short-term basis, reacting to crisis. Our leadership is consumed with putting out brush fires. Deep down, most of us just don't want to worry about the future—particularly the long-term future. Our governmental and business institutions are short-term by their nature. Governors and legislators and city commissioners have, in most cases, a short political life span. Our corporate executives are attuned to the *annual* financial report and stockholders meeting. None of these executives, quite understandably, wishes to assume the responsibility for decisions which will not produce visible results during his executive tenure. Our universities, although they too change (as we have witnessed), are in a unique position, as institutions, and can make a great contribution in the long-term effects of planning. If we can get the right mix of government, private enterprise, and academic resources and if we can involve people at all economic levels with varying cultural backgrounds then it just might work. At least, it will be better than the haphazard, fragmented efforts of the past.

In this book the individual authors take a look at the uneasy marriage between planning and politics. Some concern themselves with where planning has been and its effect on where we are now. Others are concerned with the techniques of planning and how we might better them and in the process better ourselves. Still others raise basic questions about the assumptions on which we have based previous planning and governmental activities. With some there is a suggested roadmap, with others not. No matter what the perspective and the argument, we at the Institute are pleased to be able to bring these articles together so these voices and arguments might be added to the debate on how we may best prepare for the future.

JACK M. CAMPBELL

Santa Fe, New Mexico

I: THE FRAMEWORK

Planning and Politics:
On Grounds of Incompatibility?

THAD L. BEYLE and GEORGE T. LATHROP

Planning may well be impossible within the American governmental and political system. It has always been very difficult and there do not appear to be any major signs on the horizon which portend any changes in the situation. Not that politicians and planners don't plan. Both do, but there is a gap between what the politicians *do* and the planning that planners *talk* about when long-range, comprehensive planning is the subject.

Planning is impossible because of the very nature of our governmental system—fragmented both in structure and power. There have been several interpretations of how our governmental system operates: the three-tiered or layer cake model, the cooperative federalism model, the marble-cake model, the picket fence model, and the harlequin ice-cream model.[1] The underlying dynamics of each of these models are: an increasing realization that our governmental system is complex; that all levels of government—federal, state, and local—are involved to some extent in most government activities; that problems are so closely interrelated that they do severe damage to the niceties of governmental organization charts; that professionalism and self-interest have made autonomy and functional communication the key goals rather than integrated activity and system-wide communication; and that politics and politicians may be the only controls (and poor ones at that) over rampant protected and isolated bureaucracies.

Planning is impossible because there is a basic dichotomy between

[1] See Morton Grodzins' *The American System* (Chicago, 1966), pp. 17–57, and "The Federal System" in *Goals For Americans* (Englewood Cliffs, N.J., 1960), pp. 265–82; Terry Sanford, *Storm Over The States* (New York, 1967), pp. 69–96; and U. S., Congress, Senate, Committee on Government Operations, Subcommittee on Intergovernment Relations, *The Federal System as Seen by Federal Aid Officials,* 89th Cong., 1st sess., 1965, pp. 93–102 for discussion of these models. There are several other kitchen models tied to reform which have not made their way into the general literature. One, the Angel cake model, suggests that only the Federal government with its fiscal resources and programs can solve our problems. A second, the devils-food cake model, asserts that nobody can solve our problems, and anyone who tries has had it politically.

1

the political and the governmental administrative roles. The latter, represented by the various bureaucracies throughout the three levels of the federal system, actually *do* the things we think government does. They build our roads, educate our young, provide for our elderly, protect us, and collect our money to pay for these goods and services. And each of them develops individual styles, procedures, and communication patterns. Seldom does overlapping occur between these functional areas. In fact, each agency best represents its function and wants to make sure its seat at the government boarding table is kept in place if not substantially improved. Thus centralization around functional goals is sought and desired so that each "unit" in the system can call on its cohorts elsewhere for aid and protection.

Yet it is the former role, that of the political system, which actually *authorizes and pays for* the governmental goods and services. Styles, procedures, and communication patterns certainly vary with the levels of local, state, and federal government, as well as with chief executives, legislators, and judges. But these actors have completely different representational bases—a varying mix of people, interests, and geographic areas. And, in the nature of our political system, the trend is toward decentralization and dispersal of power toward the lowest levels of the system on a geographic base. Actors in the political system may have favorite agencies and programs which are followed closely, but the very nature of their roles forces on them a broader view or at least a need to grasp a wider range of responsibility.

Planning is impossible because our lower levels of government rarely, if ever, have sufficient funds to meet the expenditures necessary to keep them going. There is seldom enough money to make major commitments to large-scale investments for long-term results. The increasing pressure on local and state tax revenues promises no substantial change in this situation, unless the ever increasing amounts of federal grant money filtering down through the governmental system reduce this obstacle to planning. Federal grant money has been filtering down for many years,[2] along with planning requirements, yet no one would say that the present state of our society, structures, and environment was consciously planned.

Planning is impossible because we have made sure that the political system must change, especially in the executive and the legislative branches, so that continuity in political leadership is (at best) impaired and continuing support for particular "planning" activities is uncertain. On the one hand there are the planners who want to remain free and

[2] Daniel J. Elazar, *The American Partnership* (Chicago, 1962); Grodzins, *The American System*, pp. 60–71; and Deil S. Wright, *Federal Grants-in-Aid: Perspectives and Alternatives* (Washington, D.C., 1968), pp. 25–34.

autonomous. On the other hand there is a very uncertain marriage—uncertain since there is no assurance that the political partner will be in residence after the next election.

Planning is impossible because we have thrust the planner into the untenable middle. We have asked him to straddle the fence between the administrator and the decision-maker politician, telling him that he must be concerned with comprehensiveness and the long view, but that, at the same time, he must be responsive to the decision-maker and, in fact, must concern himself with shorter range policy issues and decisions which are the bread and butter of the elected official. These issues may be, and frequently are, the major source and manifestation of his official power, which he guards zealously.

BUT THERE HAS BEEN PLANNING

In the face of all these "impossibilities," planning has continued; most planning is carried out at the local and state government level. And the planners have created their own view of the goals of planning and the role of planning over the past seventy-five years. Conscious planning in this country is traditionally said to have its roots in the Chicago World's Fair of 1895. There, out of the work of the architects and landscape architects, came an ideal which captured the imagination of many socially, aesthetically, and culturally conscious people in the United States. Those too, who had seen Europe's monumental urban architecture, were eager to transform the often hurriedly built and squalid cities of the United States into places of the serenity and beauty of Paris, Rome, and the Chicago World's Fair.[3]

There followed a period in which the city planner was an architect for the whole city, designing grand boulevards, siting impressive public buildings and magnificent parks and designing entryways and arches to grace the approaches to the "city beautiful." The results of this period are not to be minimized. Much of the open space in our cities comes from the dreams of these city planner-architects. In many instances their clients were the city governments and in others, the city's elite: the merchants and the rich men who comprised the upper-class.

The end of this era is difficult to pinpoint, but certainly it continued through the twenties and in some senses is still with us. The great depression of the thirties and the mixed results of the "city beautiful" movement, the coming of the automobile and continuing population and

---

[3] Like all generalities, this is subject to challenge and exception. Washington, D.C., a notable example, and other cities were "planned" at their inception. In *most* instances earlier planning amounted to a map of streets and boulevards. Moreover, while the street plans were often followed for central areas, they rarely extended or were extensive enough to contain the proliferation of suburbs that occurred by the latter part of the nineteenth century.

urban growth as the economy changed in the twenties and thirties, all this shifted the emphasis from the "city beautiful" to a broader goal, one that might be termed the city beautiful and healthy, or the city beautiful and efficient. The public works and other programs of the New Deal emphasized new goals for American society—to provide decent housing, jobs, and general welfare—and inevitably altered the goals of city planning.

Out of this broadened concern came the concept (later to be called environmental determinism) that many of the social ills of the urban population could be alleviated by decent environmental conditions. Before this movement could gain impetus, World War II erupted, and there was a lull in city planning. During the forties and early fifties, environmental determinism lost favor, primarily in the face of evidence that an overly simplistic solution, such as it was, could not cure the complex problems of urban America.

The concept which replaced the "city beautiful" as the general goal of planning was the "comprehensive plan." During the period of physically oriented planning (with the city beautiful and the environmental determinism movements), the physical planners had become increasingly aware of many of the interdependencies of the urban system. At first the phrase "comprehensive planning" was used for programs in which one physical element of a city would not be planned independently of another or other physical elements. But the continued practice of straightforward physical planning, even more comprehensive physical planning, made the inadequacies of that planning more and more painfully obvious, until the concept of comprehensiveness gained new and broader dimensions.

While the goals of planning in general remained the same, that a beautiful and functional city or urban environment be consciously created, the city's technical, social, economic, and political complexities forced "planners" into increasing specialization and, at the same time, forced recognition of the fact that many "non-planners" were doing planning.

Two streams emerged. One was that of increasing specialization, which, in turn, gave the profession two sorts of planners. On the one hand, planners developed specialized interests in transportation, social planning, urban design, health, and similar functional areas. On the other hand, as the planning profession recognized, many were planning and moving into planning *per se* who were not grounded in the traditional fields of architecture and engineering.[4]

⁴ In the period 1965–67, the Committee on Restatement of Institute Purposes (American Institute of Planners) recommended widening the Institute's definition of planning in recognizing practitioners for admission. As the chairman, Louis Wetmore, put it (quoted in the AIP *Newsletter,* April, 1966): "The language (of

While functional specialization appeared, new problem-solving techniques, refined during World War II and the years following, presented both opportunities to analyze and philosophies within which to view the urban phenomenon and its various facets, functions, and activities as systems. Variously known as systems analysis, systems engineering or, more specifically, as operations research, this approach to urban problems borrowed heavily from economic, business, and strategic decision theory.

In the sixties, as the condition of the poor and the black in America was starkly highlighted by the general level of prosperity, one group of planners became particularly concerned with the representation of and expertise available for these groups. Davidoff called the new movement "advocate planning" and envisioned the advocate planner in terms of a legal advocate who, by providing his services to a client group, was completely removed from the traditional government or power structure clientele of the planners' past.[5]

Planners became extremely self-conscious. A significant body of literature began to appear in the fifties, reviewing the past, examining failures, rearranging administrative structures, and then using decision and organization theory in an attempt to find an answer to the problem of performing effective planning.

A PLANNER'S AUTHORITY BASE

Where does the planner fit in our governmental structure? Theoretically he is there to intervene, to do something that is not being done through the behavior of other actors and forces. Where does he get the authority to intervene? And, again theoretically, if he legitimately has and uses this authority, his answers should prevail!! Why don't they?

Rein describes the planner's source of authority in a four-part taxonomy: expertise, bureaucratic position, consumer preference, and professional values.[6] "Expertise" means that the planner brings to his planning and subsequent intervention a special wisdom and knowledge which endows his plan with a level of quality such that it, and he, will prevail. To paraphrase, the planner and his solutions succeed on the strength of

---

the draft of the report) has been revised to make clear that the intent is to extend the scope of AIP professional planning from a sharp focus on physical elements, just as the scope was extended in 1938 away from a sharp focus on the city . . . the aspirations of the AIP are for a comprehensive planning approach in which social development and economic development are integral with but not independent from physical development."

[5] Paul Davidoff, "Advocacy and Pluralism in Planning," *Journal of the American Institute of Planners,* XXXI (November, 1965), 333–38.

[6] Martin Rein, "Social Planning: The Search for Legitimacy," *Journal of the American Institute of Planners,* XXXIII (July, 1967), 333–44.

their merit. When stated so baldly the notion may appear naive, but this same attitude pervades in other professions. Who questions the medical doctor? And if he is questioned, it is generally to another medical doctor (a more "expert" expert!) that the questioner turns!

The planner's bureaucratic position gives him some of the authority of those who direct the bureaucracy and who are, in turn, either politicians or politically responsive appointees. The assumption in this concept of role and authority is that the planner becomes a staff agent to whom attention is paid because he is doing a job that is directly connected with a decision-maker politician who has a need for the planning services he can provide. The crux of this sort of assumption and hypothesis probably lies in the political reform movement which advocated the separation of politics and administration, and it is subject to all the flaws of that movement.

An increasing number of planners respond to the call of the consumer. For example, many transportation planners have planned and urged the construction of more and more elaborate highway and expressway systems. While there have been many vocal objectors, transportation planners have pointed to the market behavior of consumers who are buying more and more automobiles and driving them farther and farther each year. Still others have attempted to rely on public opinion polls, public hearings, and the voices of pressure groups, both the well-financed and recognized ones and those whose voices have been heard rarely in the past, to legitimize their solutions. They claim to be responsive to the public interest in one way or another, and the debate over the means of determining the *public* interest, even when accepted as a legitimate clientele for planning, has become nearly fratricidal.

Finally, the planning profession has its own set of values for many issues and it proposes policies and plans which arise from them, from the professional consideration of what is "right." While this orientation is obviously that of the middle-class, because of the background of most planners, the profession's self-consciousness has urged it to have sympathy, if not empathy, with a wide range of social and economic groups in urban society.

But a taxonomy of the sources of authority and legitimacy for the planner remains an effort to analyze the more fundamental question of how planners and their efforts relate governmental policies and programs to a relatively long-range and rational objective set. For decades an overriding concern of planners has been their allegiance to the "public interest," and it has been the widening of that "interest" and the planners' perception of where it lies, what it is, and how their own values affect their concepts of the "public interest," that has brought them to the broad concerns of the present.

Despite these broadened interests and concerns, and despite the various theories describing his roles and relationships, the fact remains that if the planner is planning, and not administering or advocating, he must, in the end, communicate effectively with the individuals who make the final allocative decision—politicians in either the legislative or executive branches. In this effort to communicate and, more importantly, to sell, convince, or persuade the politician, it is true that the context is of over-riding importance, regardless of the logic of the academic discussion of the planners' source of legitimacy or authority.

THE ROLE OF REFORM

What of the context? Are there signs pointing to trends in activities and relationships which may aid the planner in his search for his place in the system?

The argument is made that our governmental and political systems have been going through several waves of reform, each guided by a certain value orientation.[7] They are the values of representation, neutral competence, and executive leadership. Each arises from the concept of responsibility and the question of who ultimately should be responsible for the activities of government.

For many years in our early history the trend was to invest ultimate responsibility in the legislative branch under the guise of broad representation for the people. Basically a reaction to the abuse of the imposed colonial governors, this soon gave way, however, to a drive to make our administrative branches of government freer of "political" domination by making them neutral in their administering activities. This came about as the result of the growing evidence of corruption in government, the seeming inability of the legislatures and councils to govern, and the need for more professionalism in government. Civil service and merit systems began to replace the "to the victors belong the spoils" system. The goal was to replace "who you know" with "what you know."

The purpose of many of these changes was to place some governmental functions and agencies outside "normal" politics. The net effect was to further dilute executive control over personnel and certain parts of the governmental structure, while developing a new type of politics around these personnel systems and the newly established "independent" agencies. The heritage of such "neutral competence" today lies in agencies free of executive restraint, and in lock-step personnel systems which often seem unable to be moved with the needs of the day.

[7] Herbert Kaufman, "Emerging Conflicts in the Doctrines of Public Administration," *American Political Science Review* (December, 1956), 1057–73 and "Administrative Decentralization and Political Power," *Public Administration Review,* XXIX (January, 1969), 3–15.

The third movement, toward the assertion of executive leadership, has been growing in importance in the twentieth century at all levels of our federal system. It is apparent in the increasing power of the executive in the budgetary area; in reorganization along functional lines of antiquated governmental structures resulting in stronger ties with the chief executive; increasing the tenure potential and administrative power of our governors and mayors (although some may argue that the former are becoming more powerful in their domain than are the latter in theirs); and in the increasing political power each chief executive has within his own geographical domain. Now Kaufman suggests that these trends are cyclical rather than a straight line development so that representation is being reasserted in the form of maximum feasible participation of those being served by the governmental programs and agencies.[8]

Some suggest that the drive for executive leadership and the reassertion of the drive for representation are clashing. The many fights between chief executives and community action program boards and other representative bodies would seem to uphold this view. However, this may be only a temporary phenomenon, with the Mayor Lindsay-New York City Board of Education fight serving as a harbinger of a future alliance between those espousing the rise of executive dominance in our governmental structure and those calling for additional and more effective representation in all aspects of governmental activity by those being served. It may actually mean that executive leadership and representation actually can work together, and must, to gain control over the remaining value, neutral competence, which seems to have gained such great control of our governmental system. The important facts here are that neutral competence is administrative in character while the other two are political—again the dichotomy—and that the conflict is much broader than the fight between trends in a developmental sequence. It is the basic conflict over who is ultimately responsible for governmental activities in our system—politicians or bureaucrats?

With this in mind, we should also note a very real change in the role of the chief executive in our lower levels of government. The political and governmental roles have broadened from that of mayor, county executive, governor (with the textbook roles of chief administrator, chief legislator, chief party officer, etc.), to that of chief federal systems officers within the geographical territory they represent. They command (or try to command) not only the resources available at their particular level of government, but also have much to say about how the resources of the other levels of government are used within their domain.

In fact, this role may be the most significant one in our system to-

[8] Kaufman, "Administrative Decentralization."

day. It is grinding, with day-in, day-out responsibility and cannot be compartmentalized into the neat categories of bygone textbook descriptions. It is a bit of all roles, but more; and it is a major source of power for our chief executive—just as it is the source of some of his major constraints. This role is the key to effective governmental action as we move into the 1970's for there is the promise of more funds filtering down through the system and more areas with which government will be concerned. (Concern in government style means money and program and not necessarily a plan of attack.)

Reform is needed, as always, and the planners and the planning function may be in the forefront of reform. For planning must be moved out of its good-government economy and efficiency mold. Planning must be perceived as a political weapon, to be placed at the disposal of the politicians. The greatest reforms needed today are those that focus power where it should be rather than dissipate it. In a few words, let the mayors and governors govern. The check and balance for unwise use of power is to combat power with power rather than to fragment power, which makes many of our proposed solutions to problems ineffectual.

The focusing of executive power is ameliorated by the concomitant increase of the representative function, be it in the legislature, the city council, the courts, or the community action boards. Again, in a few words, let the people who are served be represented. Representation has been increasingly placed within the bureaucracies, as they have been able to withstand vicissitudes of political change, and they have been able to ensure the most adequate representation of their particular function or interest (which may or may not have anything to do with those being served). The solution should be found in politics.

WHITHER PLANNING?

Currently, planning is too often the captive of the bureaucracy, with its reports and data reflecting biases of past decisions and protection for the agency and the program in the future. In a sense, planning is one of the most conservative influences on government decision-making.[9] The key to the rise of planning in the governmental and political firmament lies in its becoming politicized as a function and in the planners becoming more political. By political, we mean that planning must shake off the shackles of the past and of specialized professionalism, and become, as it should, continually critical, brooding, and involved.

But by what means can the planners achieve this? Peter Drucker's notion that government should be "the conductor" of activities for the

[9] See Ira Sharkansky, "State Government Expenditures 1903–1965: The Continuing Influence of The Past," *Spending In The American States* (Chicago, 1968), pp. 35–53.

society and not "the doer" opens a possible role for the planner.[10] Then to extend the analogy the planner would set the score and aid in orchestrating the activity to be carried out by others. Yet this analogy has been rightly criticized as moving too far away from the real world experience and therefore from the causes of many of our predicaments and dilemmas.[11] Certainly the history of such changes in direction and reforms is not one to make us comfortable with the results.

Each time the reformers develop a new technique to gain control over the governmental world, it seems to be subverted and turned against the goals of reform. Probably the best and most recent example is the advent of the Planning, Programming, Budgeting System under the Kennedy-Johnson administrations. Following Secretary of Defense McNamara from the world of big business into the world of big government, PPBS became the darling of the organizational reformers as it appeared instrumental in bringing the several dynasties in the Department of Defense under seemingly tight civilian control. And it should not surprise presidential observers that President Johnson, a most political president, should attempt to use this new tool to gain even more control over the myriad of government agencies—and the lower levels of the federal system. Now it appears that there are signs that agencies have learned how to use PPBS for their own benefit, to reassert some degree of autonomy in certain relationships.[12] Initially developed for management and then used as a political tool to gain control over the bureaucracy, PPBS, like many other reforms, could become a bureaucratic weapon used to further agency demands on governmental and political systems.

To look for a viable plan for reform is to look to the real world of government and politics. We have posited the newly developing role of our state and local government executives as the chief federal systems officers within their domains. Perhaps the broad "conductor" analogy is overdrawn, but certainly something closely akin to it would appear to be possible and necessary. Planners should aspire to be advisors to these chief executives—the mayors and the governors. For it is here that key decisions are made and actions are taken and where the best of advice is needed. Probably the crux of the situation is whether we want decisions made with conscious planning or whether we want decisions made on

[10] Peter F. Drucker, "The Sickness of Government," *The Age of Discontinuity* (New York, 1968), pp. 212–42.

[11] "Dr. Drucker: The Great Healer," *Public Administration Review*, XXIX (July–August, 1969), 386–88.

[12] William M. Capron, "Advantages and Strengths of PPBS" (Address before the Twenty-fourth Annual Meeting of the National Association of Budget Officers, San Antonio, Texas, August, 1968, on pp. 18–19 of the proceedings from the conference.

an *ad hoc* basis with no conscious overall plan or set of priorities. Many of our current problems and dilemmas flow from the latter approach to handling crises (on the volunteer fire department model). The answer, then, is obvious.

Several trends which are converging suggest the directions to be taken. First, the call for planning at the lower levels of our system is immense. One official estimated that "there are more than thirty planning assistance programs being administered by eighteen (federal) executive branch organizational units. There are nine separate (federal) programs which assist the comprehensive planning of social services, and five separate planning programs directed to urban development."[13] In a study of planning grants, at the state level, it was estimated that "Nearly 100 grant-in-aid programs relate to state planning or have requirements for a 'state plan'."[14] While the caliber of these plans is not necessarily high, as noted earlier, their presence demands that certain procedures, products, and processes be undertaken—under the rubric of planning. Therefore, demand for people called planners is high.

Second, as some of the selections in this volume indicate, the chief executives in our state and local governments are pulling the planners closer to them structurally and are working closely with the chief planner. Planning there will be, but who will be the planners—professionals trained in the art or political appointees of unknown quality?

Third, an entirely new form of patronage in our political system has been developing over the past few decades. Instead of jobs being rewarded to the faithful, we now find that grants, projects, and programs are the reward. Some jobs are still available and attractive, but much more attractive is a major facility, or service, or program which will help a community, be it town, county, multi-county, state, or multi-state. Thus, the old style of patronage has declined in its relative importance to governing, and the provision of goods and services, government style, has become the trading card. It is the planners and the chief executives who develop and pass on the mode of dispensing these rewards. For these new rewards are keyed to a plan and something called a planning process. It is not surprising that a new role has been added in the mayors' and governors' offices—that of the grantsman—the person who makes sure that all monies and programs possible are brought into the particular unit of government. And it is the person who fills this role who

[13] Statement of Richard C. Van Dusen, Under Secretary, Department of Housing and Urban Development, before The Subcommittee on Intergovernmental Relations of the House Committee on Government Operations, on The Grant Consolidation Act of 1969, and the Intergovernmental Cooperation Act of 1969, August 6, 1969.

[14] The Council of State Governments, *State Planning and Federal Grants* (Chicago, 1969), p. 25.

attempts to match need with program. It is this grantsman who, because of the rewards he can promise, negotiates with recalcitrant legislators and councilmen on the executive program.

Since plans or a planning process are called for by statute and guideline, does this mean that it is the planner who becomes the new political grantsman? Or is his role more as the advisor who sets the process in motion and provides the broader planning inputs which allow the what, where, and when of this patronage to be made on other than crass "votes delivered" criteria?

The roles seem self-evident and, in the continuing process of self-definition, the challenge is to the planner, for the executive needs the aid and will turn elsewhere for staff if those called planners do not produce. Planning there must and will be, and it will be a politicized planning responsive to its client and stripped of many of the liabilities of bureaucratization. The client may well be the mayor or governor. But it may well be that responsiveness to and empathy with the client is what advocate planning is all about! Could the various planners and the political scientists be saying the same thing???

II: EVIDENCE OF UNEASY ACCEPTANCE

INTRODUCTION

If it may be said that the relationship between planning and politics is uneasy and ill-defined, then an observation of planning activity at various levels of government and in various organizational structures should reveal a confused and fluid situation. This is seen in the three selections that follow, as the authors examine the changing and expanding role of planning at the state government level, attempt to measure the spread of program innovation among the states, and scrutinize the perceived and actual relationships of planners and city administrators to policy-making in the urban environment.

As the introductory chapter indicates, the conflicts in the interests and perceived roles of the planner and politician apparently raise a paradoxical situation which is virtually impossible to resolve. In the continuing need to look ahead, to plan, and to anticipate the consequences of their actions, politicians turn to planners in some instances and the planners, in their quest to define their role, stand ready to offer some assistance. Yet the relationship of the seeker and the sought descends all too often to a hackneyed attempt to revise the administrative structure, searching within that structure for a remedy for lack of communication.

In the first selection in this section, Thad Beyle, Sureva Seligson, and Deil Wright review some of the evidence of an increase in planning activity at the state level; this review grew out of their work with the Institute on State Programming for the 70's. It is clear from their findings that *formal* state planning activity is increasing and that it is generally moving closer to the governor, the chief politician. The unanswered question is the extent to which: (1) governors are availing themselves of the advice and abilities of the planners, and (2) planners in the state planning offices are doing what the planning profession considers to be planning. Unfortunately, these two points are not as easily measurable as are administrative arrangement and staffing.

Walker's broader view of innovation in state activity departs from the usual picture of vertical communication between state and local or federal government by documenting the extent to which new programs have appeared in state government as a function of regional grouping, as well as other indicators of communication. Not only is planning one of these activities; many of the others that Walker lists are the sorts of innovations popular with planners. Again, many questions are raised by the material: To what extent is innovation affected by planning? To what extent is planning just another new program seized upon for its political capital? To what extent is vertical communication, in the form of Federal requirements, forcing the hand of state government?

In the final selection, Deil Wright analyzes the activities and attitudes of city managers, mayors, and city planners in their respective roles as policy advocates to city executives and to city councils. Both of these professionals, in theory removed from the political arena, reflect the confusion noted above with the added dimensions of confusion between each of their roles as well as between the political and professional roles.

The picture derived from the three empirical examinations of the current relationship between planning and politics is an adapting and changing one, with individual circumstances and situations playing a strong part in any given relationship.

New Directions in State Planning*

THAD L. BEYLE, SUREVA SELIGSON, and DEIL S. WRIGHT

The state planning process is on trial. It is not yet clear to what extent planners and state planning agencies can fulfill their responsibility to contribute to more efficient and effective state government. The need for a state planning process that identifies rational and efficient uses of government resources is clear. The relevance, structure, and activities of state planning have been extensively discussed.[1] Comprehensive, coordinated, long-range, broad-based, integrated socioeconomic and political goals have become part of the vocabulary of state government as well as of state planning. But are they now or will they become a workable part of the state planning function?

State planning has been in flux since it became a part of the reform-

* Reprinted by permission of the *Journal of the American Institute of Planners* (Vol. XXXV, no. 5, September, 1969).
[1] See in particular U.S. Natural Resources Board, *State Planning, A Review of Activities and Progress* (Washington, D.C., 1935); John E. Ivey, Jr., "State Planning: Experiments in the American Planning Process" (unpubl. Ph.D. diss., University of North Carolina, 1945); Harvey S. Perloff, *Education for Planning: City, State, and Regional* (Baltimore, 1957); American Institute of Planners Committee on State Planning, "State Planning: Its Functions and Organization," *Journal of the American Institute of Planners*, XXV (November, 1959), 207–14; and Thomas J. Anton, "State Planning, Gubernatorial Leadership and Federal Funds: Three Cases," in Institute of Government and Public Affairs, *The Office of Governor* (Urbana, Ill., May, 1963), pp. 63–79, for discussion of the history and proposed role of state planning.

er's package in the series of economy and efficiency reforms suggested in the thirties. It stayed fluid in the recommendations of various "Little Hoover Commissions" in the fifties and in numerous piecemeal reform efforts during the mid-sixties. As long as it is a viable function of government, planning will change, making it difficult to write a fixed definition of state planning or a static job description for a state planner. The activities of planners and agencies provide the best definition of the state planning process. At a time when states are inundated with local problems and national responsibilities, and almost every federal program calls for a state plan or an effective planning process, the general measure of "effectiveness" must be the extent to which state planners and their offices contribute to sound state government.

RECENT SURVEY FINDINGS

Two recent studies indicate that state government is not well served by state planners and state planning agencies. The first evaluation was in conjunction with "A Study of American States" conducted by former North Carolina Governor Terry Sanford.[2] In October, 1965, each state's governor was asked: "What powers, both formal and informal, do you lack which could aid you significantly in effecting your programs?"[3]

Responses from thirty-nine states (thirty-two from governors and the remainder from immediate gubernatorial aides) indicated that in only two states was state planning perceived as a missing element that governors needed to carry out their programs. Governors felt most restrained in their appointive power, reorganization power, veto power, tenure potential, and legislative relations. Planning was either not perceived as lacking, or it was not considered a particularly significant tool for governors to add to their arsenals.

This was clarified by the second study, "A Survey of the Present Status, Effectiveness and Acceptance of State Planning and Advance Programming in State Government," conducted by the Institute on State Programming for the 70's during the summer of 1967.[4] It concludes:

[2] "A Study of American States" was a two–year study (1965–67) of the present condition and future potential of the American States. It was funded by joint grants from the Ford Foundation and the Carnegie Corporation and had headquarters at Duke University. See Terry Sanford, *Storm Over The States* (New York, 1967) for the report, recommendations, and activities of the study.

[3] See Thad L. Beyle, "Gubernatorial Power: A View from the Governor's Chair," *Public Administration Review,* XXVII (November–December, 1968), 540–45, for a presentation of these data.

[4] The collection, tabulation, and analysis of data for the survey were supervised by the authors. The survey was conducted under a U.S. Department of Housing and Urban Development, Urban Planning and Research Demonstration contract awarded under the provisions of Section 701(b) of the Housing Act of 1954, as amended. Its components included: (1) field interviews with eighteen governors and 677 persons involved in charting and reporting on the direction of all fifty

"This survey suggests that there is an urgent need to broaden the concept of state planning and to strengthen the ability of the states to assume an aggressive, imaginative and creative role in the federal system. It indicates that the states neither view nor utilize the planning process as providing a rational basis for decision making."[5]

The Institute survey examined four central components of the state planning process: (1) gubernatorial commitment; (2) legislative intent; (3) legislative and executive branch involvement; and (4) the level of state planning agency support and performance. The major conclusions drawn from the survey findings are:

There is a strong gubernatorial commitment to state planning. Most governors are aware of the potential of the planning process and of the programs and activities of state planning agencies.

State legislatures are not consistent in defining the objectives of the state planning process or the role of state planning agencies.

The legislative branch is neither deeply involved nor firmly committed to state planning.

There is no strong commitment to state planning throughout the executive branch although many administrative agencies are involved in the planning process.

State planning agencies are not receiving strong financial or operational support. Their activities are hindered by inadequate funding and staffing, a lack of cooperation from both executive and legislative branches, and a climate of government that views planning as unnecessary or impossible.

The performance of state planning agencies is inconsistent and inadequate. Their programs and activities are not relevant to the decision-making process and do not discharge the responsibilities assigned to them by legislative and executive authority.[6]

The results of this survey not only identified the state planning agency itself as "an obstacle to effective state planning" (in seventeen states), but only twenty-three state planning agencies—less than half—were viewed as "relevant to the decision-making process."

A Shift in Location

Despite these readings on how those in state government view the process and impact of state planning, the agency still remains a visible and necessary portion of most state government reform packages. More

---

state governments; (2) a detailed content analysis of enabling legislation for officially designated state planning agencies; and (3) supplementary questionnaires designed to verify and expand information supplied by state planning agency officials.

[5] Institute on State Programming for the 70s, "State Planning: A Quest for Relevance" (Chapel Hill, N.C., 1968), p. ii.

[6] "State Planning: A Quest for Relevance," pp. ii–iii.

Table 1: Location of State Planning Agency

LOCATION	1960	1965	1967	1969
Governor's office	3	11	18	20
Department of administration or finance	2	2	6	7
Department of community affairs	0	0	2	3
Department of commerce, development, or planning and development agencies	23	27	15	13
Independent planning agency	5	7	6	5
Other agencies	4	1	2	2
Total state planning agencies	37	48	49	50

importantly, evidence indicates that state planning agencies now have a greater opportunity than ever before to aid decision-makers at the highest levels in state government, partially due to their new locations closer to the action.

Since 1960, there has been a dramatic shift in the organizational status of planning in state government. Table 1, Location of State Planning Agency, presents data from four recent years, 1960, 1965, 1967, and 1969. These data were obtained through a content analysis of each state's enabling legislation during the period.

The table indicates that, between 1960 and 1969, thirteen states added state planning agencies; thirty-one states changed the location of their agencies; and only eleven maintained existing arrangements.

In line with current theory, the trend is to place the function as close to the governor and his fiscal and management arm as is possible. Considerable residue remains, however, from the practice of the 1940's and 1950's of placing planning in development agencies. In 1960, only five states had their planning agencies located in or close to the governor's office; by 1969, twenty-seven states had such an arrangement.

The beginnings of a corollary trend, establishing planning agencies in departments of community or urban affairs, was evident between 1965 and 1969, as three states opted for such an arrangement. These new departments are usually closely tied to the governor both in personnel, programs, style, and power, and therefore appear to be serving as key gubernatorial agencies.[7]

At the same time, the more traditional pattern of locating planning

[7] These states are Missouri, New Jersey, and Washington. The relationship between the department and the governor is especially close in New Jersey. The political rationale for this kind of relationship is fairly evident as governors are increasingly becoming urban or metropolitan oriented. Robert C. Wood discussed this point in his unpublished 1949 doctoral dissertation, "The Metropolitan Governor," for the Department of Government, Harvard University.

agencies in departments of commerce or development, or as independent agencies entirely, was followed by twenty-eight states in 1960, thirty-four in 1965, followed by a marked shift back to eighteen by 1969. The moves were most significant in departments of commerce or development, which housed twenty-seven planning offices in 1965 and only thirteen by 1969. The rapid growth in the number of state planning agencies that are gubernatorial staff services has been accompanied by a concomitant decrease in the number of agencies located outside direct gubernatorial control.

The Legislative Mandate

Table 2, Legislative Intent and Planning Agency Activity, indicates how few agencies are meeting their legislative charge. Data are based on the Institute's analysis of state planning agency enabling legislation and reports from field interviews.

The gaps between those responsibilities assigned and those actually executed are especially apparent in certain areas. Despite enabling legislation mandating the activities, twenty-one state agencies are not providing information or research services, eighteen are not preparing a comprehensive state plan or state functional plans, and seventeen are not advising governors on policy and programs. Preparing state functional plans may well be too broad a charge. Less than a third of the state agencies are assigned this type of responsibility in six to fifteen functional areas, and a third are assigned the role in as many as sixteen to twenty-five areas. Sheer numbers of programs and agencies involved would seem to preclude such an effort. Yet, in some key broad functional areas such as health planning, it may be incumbent on the state planning agency to carry out the planning function.

But laxity in the other three activities—preparing a comprehensive state plan, advising the governor on policy and programs, and providing information and research services—is a serious indictment. It bodes ill for state planning agencies because: (1) these are key areas of the state planning function, particularly when legally prescribed; (2) the credibility of any agency is impaired when it fails to meet its responsibilities; and (3) failing to perform assigned functions means they have to be carried out elsewhere in state government or not at all. The many problems confronting the states suggest that these functions are not being carried out in systematic fashion.

Table 2 also supports the observation that state planning agencies find it easier to cope with coordinating activities and local (or regional) planning than with goals and policy development. The high number of agencies (thirty-three) coordinating various state line agency programs and the low number (six) ignoring that assigned responsibility indicate

Table 2: Legislative Intent and Planning Agency Activity, Summer, 1967
(by Number of States)[a]

ACTIVITY	(A) Those assigned the activity by legislation	(B) Those assigned and performing the activity	(C) Those *not* assigned but *are* performing the activity	(D) Total state agencies performing the activity (B plus C)	(E) Those assigned but *not* performing the activity (A minus B)
Providing information or research services	43	22	3	25	21
Preparing a comprehensive state plan	36	18	5	23	18
Preparing state functional plans	30	12	3	15	18
Advising the governor on policy and programs	39	22	3	25	17
Local planning assistance	40	32	3	35	8
Regional planning assistance	29	21	10	31	8
Coordinating state functional agency programs	28	22	11	33	6

[a] Totals do not equal fifty as figures reflect information from forty-six states in five activity areas and from forty-seven states in two activity areas.

that planning offices are willing to make coordination a positive part of their programs. On the positive side, coordination performs a necessary service in governmental systems that are highly complex, interrelated, and frequently confusing. To the various agencies seeking to maintain their autonomy, coordination could provide the mechanism and framework that an autonomous agency needs to define its role within the larger political system. State planning agencies performing the coordination activity are probably aware of its practical necessity for agency survival, above and beyond its status as a "good government" reform goal. Whatever the agency view on coordination may be, this activity can make a contribution to the goal of better state government. In the long run, it may not be fair to consider state planning agencies' failures to fulfill a particular set of legislative mandates as weaknesses when a larger goal is a practical possibility.

Table 2 also suggests that new trends of training and socialization in planning schools might alleviate problems for state planning agencies. The break between relatively high and low levels of nonperformance occurs between advising the governor on policy and programs and local and regional planning and assistance (columns D and E). In addition to the coordination function, the highest performance levels (column D) are in local and regional planning assistance, the areas in which professionally trained planners have been schooled. The new demands of providing adequate and accurate information, developing a more comprehensive view of state government activities, and advising the governor on policy and programs may well call for not only new styles in curricula, but also a different type of person to be a planner.

SOURCES OF SUPPORT

Contact and Receptivity

Two series of data collected by the Institute help determine which parts of state government rely on the state planning agency: (1) 1967 field interviews indicated which parts of state government were most receptive to the concept of planning, and (2) a 1968 mail questionnaire to each chief state planning officer asked with whom his agency had frequent contacts.[8]

The data identify areas of receptivity and frequent contact by major areas of state government:

AREA OF RECEPTIVITY	No. of States	AREA OF FREQUENT CONTACT	No. of States
Governor and staff[9]	20	Administrative agencies	35
Administrative agencies	9	Governor and staff[9]	30
Legislature	9	Legislature	17
None indicated	12	None indicated	3

Receptivity and contact with the executive branch far outweigh legislative branch involvement, underlining the basic executive branch bias of state planning agencies. The data do not disprove the often prescribed role of planning agencies as staff aids to the executive rather than the

---

[8] Frequent contacts were defined as daily or weekly contact in carrying out official duties; infrequent contacts as monthly, seldom, or nonexistent.

[9] This category includes the governor and his immediate staff, including heads of departments of administration, finance and budget. The category of administrative agencies includes all references to agencies with functional, line activities.

legislative branch. This, of course, accords with good planning theory—placing the planning function as close as possible to the decision-makers in the executive branch—and with the current trend in locational patterns in the fifty states as shown in Table 1. On the other hand, it raises questions as to whether state legislatures will support agencies at these considerably lower levels of receptivity and contact.

Obstacles to Effective State Planning

Table 3, Obstacles to Effective State Planning, categorizes obstacles reported in fifty states by Institute field interviewers and further defines the degree of reliance upon the state planning agency by segments of state government.

The climate of government and the state planning agency are clearly identified as major obstacles, comprising more than half the obstacles mentioned in the total mentions column. While climate of government is a residual category used to pinpoint such items as obsolete structure of government, lack of concern, understanding, and cooperation in government, a feeling that planning is unnecessary, and a general anti-planning bias, it includes areas that effective state planning can move to combat. According to these data, state planning has a poor image; either people are ignorant of the job these agencies have done or the agencies

Table 3: Obstacles to Effective State Planning, Summer, 1967
(by Number of States)[a]

Nature of obstacle	Only obstacle mentioned	One of two obstacles mentioned	Total mentions
Climate of government[b]	8	12	20
State planning agency	12	5	17
Other administrative agencies	5	6	11
Legislature	3	5	8
Governor	1	6	7
Partisan conflict	0	4	4
Total	29	38	67

[a] These data were obtained by field interviews in each state during the summer of 1967. All but two states were identified as having obstacles to an effective state planning process: twenty-nine were identified with one and eighteen with two obstacles. Some were noted with more than two, but only those indicated as primary obstacles were included.

[b] This category includes those states for which obsolete structure of government: lack of concern, understanding, and cooperation throughout government; a feeling that planning is unnecessary; and general anti-government and anti-planning biases were cited as obstacles.

have failed to do the job. The fact that seventeen state planning agencies themselves are cited as major obstacles to an effective state planning process strongly suggests the latter.

Other administrative agencies, the legislature, and the governor, when grouped, make up 40 percent of the total mentions of obstacles to an effective state planning process. These are the three institutions in state government with which the state planning agency must work closely and from which the agency must receive adequate support if the planning process is to be successful. Eighteen of twenty-six obstacles identified in this group lie in the executive branch—the specific segment of state government the planning agency is designed to serve as staff, both by intent and location.

It is interesting to note that "partisan conflict" is not identified as a major obstacle to the state planning process. It was never mentioned as the single most important obstacle and appears as one of the two obstacles mentioned in only four states.

The figures do not paint a pretty picture. When one obstacle is mentioned, that obstacle is the planning agency in 40 percent of the cases. When two obstacles are mentioned, the agency is one of them in 13 percent of the cases. In seventeen out of forty-eight states (35 percent), the state planning agency itself was a significant obstacle to an effective planning process. Either state planning agencies are not conducting activities that contribute to sound planning or too many state government officials feel this is the case. In either event, it is not an encouraging commentary on several decades of effort.

THE ROLE OF LOCATION

The location of the planning agency, a long debated question, appears to be settled by locational shifts during the 1960's. The following two tables examine the relevance, performance, and financial support levels of state planning agencies located in and outside of the governor's office or his department of administration, finance, or budget. In some cases the data were incomplete, but they represent the best available information on the agencies.

Table 4, The Role of Location: The Governor's Arm, demonstrates that while access to the governor's office does not guarantee significant levels of performance or relevance to decision-making, it does relate positively to these two indicators of effort. Less than half (twenty-three) of the state planning agencies are considered relevant to the decision-making process and fourteen of these are located under the governor's direct control. Only four of the sixteen agencies considered not relevant to the decision-making process are actually located close to the governor.

Table 4: The Role of Location: The Governor's Arm—
Relevancy and Average Performance[a]

State planning agency relevant to the decision-making process[b]	In governor's office or department of administration, finance, or budget		Outside governor's office or department of administration, finance, or budget		Totals	
	Number[c]	Average performance[d]	Number	Average performance	Number	Average performance
Yes	14	5.0	9	3.1	23	4.3
No	4	3.0	12	3.9	16	3.7
Not adequately determined	6	4.0	4	3.5	10	3.8
Totals	24	4.4	25	3.6	49	4.0

[a] Data obtained from enabling legislation as of 1967. All states, except Arizona which had no legislation, are included.
[b] Data obtained from field interviews in each state during summer, 1967.
[c] The number of states within that category.
[d] Average performance of the states within the particular category as measured by the state planning agencies fulfillment of legislative intent. (See also Table 2.) The seven areas in which performance was measured were: preparing state functional plans; advising governor on policy and programs; preparing a comprehensive state plan; providing information or research services; local planning assistance; regional planning assistance; and, coordinating state agency programs. The highest possible value would be seven, if the legislation assigned and the agency were fulfilling each. Data obtained from enabling legislation and field interviews.

The average performance level is highest (5.0) for agencies that are close to the governor and considered relevant. Performance level is lowest (3.0) for agencies that are close to the governor but not viewed as relevant. Average performance for "relevant" agencies is about the same as for nonrelevant agencies in the governor's office. Those outside of direct gubernatorial control and judged not relevant are at the midpoint (3.9) in agency performance.

These data suggest that there is a connection between location in the governor's office, higher level of agency performance, and a greater tendency to be relevant to the decision-making process. This provides reform advocates with some tangible evidence that placing state planning agencies close to the governors can lead in the direction of desired results.

Extending the discussion further, Table 5, which is based on information about thirty-one states, presents partial yet intriguing data. In this table, planning agency location is related to the judged relevancy of the agency in the decision-making process as well as to the average fiscal

Table 5: The Role of Location: The Governor's Arm—
Relevancy and Average Support[a]

State planning agency relevant to the decision-making process[b]	In governor's office or department of administration, finance, or budget		Outside governor's office or department of administration, finance, or budget		Totals	
	Number[c]	Average support[d]	Number	Average support	Number	Average support
Yes	6	.60	4	2.00	10	1.2
No	3	.33	10	.80	13	.69
Not adequately determined	6	.66	2	.50	8	.63
Totals	15	.60	16	1.06	31	.84

[a] Data obtained from enabling legislation as of 1967. All states, except Arizona which had no legislation, are included.
[b] Data obtained from field interviews in each state during summer, 1967.
[c] The number of states within that category.
[d] Average support score for states within that category. Individual scores obtained by dividing total general state expenditures into state planning agency expenditures for the fiscal year 1965–66. To categorize these percentages, a *three* was assigned to the one state where the percentage was above .25 percent; a *two* was assigned to six states where the percentage ranged between .15 percent and .25 percent; a *one* was assigned to the eleven states where it ranged between .05 percent and .14 percent; and a *zero* was assigned to thirteen states where it was below .05 percent. Data on state government expenditures were developed from U.S., Census Bureau, *Government Finances in 1965–1966* (Washington: U.S. Government Printing Office, 1967), Chart 18; and, the data on state planning agency expenditures were developed from American Society of Planning Officials, *ASPO Planning Advisory Service* (Chicago: ASPO, April, 1967), Report No. 221, Table 17. Data on the latter were available on only thirty-one states. Numbers indicated by category.

support of the agency. An initial suggestion is that agencies deemed relevant to the decision-making process have an expenditure support level nearly double that of other state planning agencies.

Yet more to the point may be the suggestion that location outside the governor's immediate control seems to be related to a much higher expenditure support level. One interpretation of this unexpected result is that those agencies furthest removed from gubernatorial control have more freedom to develop additional expenditure support, especially under the various federal grant-in-aid programs that support state planning activities.

The implication from data in Tables 4 and 5 is that location is of paramount importance. When located in or near the governor's office, state planning agencies are more apt to carry out their legislative mandates, to be relevant to the decision-making process, and to operate at lower levels of expenditure. Conversely, location outside gubernatorial control tends to be associated with a lower level of performance in fulfilling legislative mandate, a lesser degree of relevance to the decision-making process, and a higher level of expenditure.

In other words, fiscal support is less important than location and performance. This may jar those calling for higher levels of support to upgrade this function. But it is a happy finding for those advocating, both in theory and practice, that state planning is a staff function which should be close to the top decision-makers in state government.

STATE PLANNERS: A NEW BREED?

We have considered several important formal and organizational features relating to the status of state planning—legislative mandate, location, and obstacles to and support for state planning activities. In addition to these aggregate variables it seems natural and appropriate to examine characteristics of the directors of state planning agencies. For this purpose, we consider three types of planner-related variables: personal, positional, and interactional characteristics of the state planning directors.

Personal Characteristics

The educational attainment of state planners is high. Twenty-four of the forty-five state planning directors (53 percent) had advanced degrees—nineteen Master's degrees in various fields including planning, and public administration and five Ph.D.'s. Thirty-eight percent of those with advanced degrees received them in planning (nine out of twenty-four); which means that only 20 percent of all respondents (nine out of forty-five) had an advanced degree in planning per se.[10] A formal educational background in planning has not then been a prime factor in selecting planning directors.

Instead, experience in government appears to be more significant. Twenty-nine of the forty-five respondents (64 percent) had previous experience in appointed (twenty-nine) or elected (seven) positions in federal, state, county, or city governments.[11] Most had served at the local (seventeen) and state (fifteen) levels; only four had been appointed to federal positions. The positions held immediately prior to becoming state planning director are varied: thirteen were subordinates within their agency while seven worked in the same state government but not in the state planning agency. Thus, only 45 percent (twenty out of forty-five)

[10] If we add those receiving a Master's degree in public administration to this total, assuming that these are sister professions requiring somewhat similar training and goals, the percentages become 50 (twelve out of twenty-four) and 27 (twelve out of forty-five).

[11] Because these are not mutually exclusive categories, the numbers overlap.

were drawn from their state's government. Of the remainder, three were in agencies in other states, and eleven entered the planning agency from the private sector.

While these data present a mixed picture, they do show that the state planning director most likely has made a vertical move upward from local government or a lateral one within state government. There are few state planning directors from federal agencies; there are some from outside the government.

Positional Characteristics

In terms of the directors' own mode of appointment, analysis of the enabling legislation of forty-seven states indicated that appointments were made by the governor in fifteen states; required at least the governor's acquiescence in the appointment in nine states; did not involve the governor in the selection process in nine states; and did not stipulate the appointment style in fourteen other states.

Turning to the planning director's administrative role, we found that they were relatively free from personnel constraints. Thirty-three directors replied that they did not need "clearance" from the governor's office prior to appointing staff members. Only six directors' jobs in forty-four reporting states were covered by a civil service system (14 percent). Agency staffs, on the other hand, were more enmeshed in the protection afforded by personnel systems, as nineteen state agencies were totally covered by civil service regulations, nine others were partially covered, and seventeen state agencies had no such coverage.

As a result, we found planning directors essentially free of civil service constraints, but subject to some political pressures from the governor. Conversely, agency staff were relatively free of gubernatorial political pressures, but more subject to civil service constraints. Political pressures push from the top down, while bureaucratic pressures move laterally, buffering the agency from the political pressures—no different from the cross pressures experienced by most governmental agencies.

Interactional Characteristics

With whom do the state planner and his agency interact? How often does he have contact with other state officials?[12] There is a significant break in the answers of the forty-five responding state planning directors. Nearly 90 percent (forty out of forty-five) indicated they had daily or weekly contact with the governor or his immediate staff. The figure is slightly lower (thirty-eight out of forty-five) for contact with administrative agencies. However, only seventeen of the forty-five directors had frequent contact with the state legislature.

[12] See footnote 8 above.

Because we were unable to obtain any measure of the quality of the contact or of the frequency of contact at a prior point in time, generalizations must be limited. However, we can see that, as the physical location of the state planning agency moves closer to the governor and his staff, planners interact with executives at a relatively high frequency. This is a qualitative change of some significance. Planners are being given a chance to be part of the governing process. The data that follow provide some insight into what they do with that opportunity. Conversely, there is a low rate of interaction of planners with the legislature because the planning function is more closely tied to the executive. But this raises severe problems in soliciting legislative support.

PLANNERS, PROFESSIONALISM, AND POLICY

In this section we relate the above characteristics of the state planning director to two agency variables: (1) location within the state governmental structure; and (2) the relevancy of the state planning agency's activities to the decision-making process. The first is structural and the second relates to agency performance.

Education Level

Looking at the educational variable (respondents who attended college, obtained college degrees, or had graduate training), no significant relationship was found to location of agencies (within or outside of the governor's office);[13] nor did the educational level of the director appear related to the relevancy of agency activities—but, the four directors who do not hold college degrees were supervising agencies deemed relevant. Agencies directed by individuals with college educations or higher degrees were almost equally spread as to their relevancy or non-relevancy. Despite this, we must conclude that the number of years in school has little effect on the activities of state planners or planning agencies.

Type of Education

The type of educational background of the directors is directly related, however, to the location of the agency (Table 6). Those without graduate training were more likely to head agencies outside the governor's office (fourteen out of twenty-five), and those with advanced degrees were more frequently in charge of agencies within the governor's office (sixteen out of twenty-four). This is accentuated by the fact that those with degrees in public administration (all three) and in planning (six out of nine) were located in or close to the office of the governor.

No matter how appealing these findings may be to those who train planners and public administrators and who urge governors to recruit

---

[13] This category includes the governor and his immediate staff, including heads of departments of administration, finance, and budget.

Table 6: Agency Location and Type of Director's Education

	LOCATION OF PLANNING AGENCY			
	Within Gov.'s Office	Outside Gov.'s Office	Not applicable	Total
Type of Education				
No Advanced Degree	9	14	2	25
Planning Degree	6⎫	3⎫	0	9⎫
Public Administration Degree	3⎬16	0⎬8	0	3⎬24
Other Advanced Degree	7⎭	5⎭	0	12⎭
Total	25	22	2	49

from their schools, it must be noted again that educational achievement had *no* relationship to the agency's performance in terms of the relevance of the state planning agencies' activities to the decision-making process. Again, formal education appears not to be significant in explaining the performance of state planning activities.

Occupational Background

When state planning directors were asked to give their main occupation previous to their present position, replies were categorized as: planner (seventeen); business, administration, or management (six); public administration, finance, or city management (six); other occupations (sixteen) (Table 7).[14]

However, the directors who had a background in business, management, or public administration were most frequently working within the governor's office (nine out of twelve); while those who had been planners (seven out of seventeen) or specified other backgrounds (six out of sixteen) were supervising offices outside of immediate gubernatorial control. Similarly, those with a business, management, or public administration background were much more likely to be directing agencies deemed relevant to the decision-making process of the state government. Those with planning or other occupational backgrounds reversed this relationship and were much less likely to be directing agencies that conduct relevant activities.

These data highlight the importance of a management background in helping to make a state planning agency relevant to decision-making.

[14] The term "planner" used in this context is to be differentiated from that term used earlier in the discussion of type of education. Whereas earlier the term reflected the type of educational degree received, this refers to the director's perception of his main occupation regardless of degrees attained.

Table 7: Occupational Background, Agency Location, and Relevancy

	LOCATION				RELEVANCY			
Occupational Background	Within Gov.'s Office	Outside Gov.'s Office	Not applicable	Total	Relevant	Not relevant	Not adequately determined	Total
Planner	7	9	1	17	6	8	3	17
Business Adminis., Mgt.	5	1	0	6	5	0	1	6
(Business + Public Ad.)	9	3		12	9	1	2	12
Public Administrator	4	2	0	6	4	1	1	6
Other	6	9	1	16	6	6	4	16
Total	22	21	2	45	21	15	9	45

Because respondents with an explicit planning background were more frequently placed outside the governors' purview, it is not altogether surprising that their activities were not viewed as relevant. But these data indicate that the director's background, as measured by his professed occupation, is significantly related to the relevancy of his state planning agency's performance. The implications for those seeking criteria in selecting state planners are abundantly clear.

Political Background

To determine "political background," directors were asked whether they had ever held an elective or appointive position in any governmental unit previous to their present position. Twenty-nine had and sixteen had not. Six had held elective offices at either the state or local level.

There were strong relationships between a director's political background, the location of his agency, and the relevancy of the agency's performance (see Table 8). The political background of a director is highly related to his being located close to or within the governor's office and also to his agency's performance of relevant activities. Conversely, a non-political background is highly related to placement in a location outside the governor's immediate area of control and is strongly associated with an agency's conducting non-relevant activities.

Again the findings are clear: a political background for a state planner is a significant variable in relation to an agency's performance. We

Table 8: Political Background of Director, Agency Location, and Relevancy

		LOCATION				RELEVANCY			
		In Gov.'s Office	Outside Gov.'s Office	Not applicable	Total	Yes	No	Not adequately determined	Total
Background	Political	17	11	1	29	16	8	5	29
	Not Political	5	10	1	16	5	7	4	16
	Total	22	21	2	45	21	15	9	45

cannot posit a cause and effect relationship in relating occupational or political backgrounds with relevancy. Which comes first? Does the fine performing agency attract certain types of personnel, or do the fine performing personnel create a specific kind of agency? But the nexus of the variables is clear: management and/or political experience and a high rating on agency performance. Conversely, apolitical planners have a lower rating on state planning activities.

Administrative Freedom: Mode of Appointment[15]

The final analysis concerns the relative administrative freedom of the director to conduct the activities of the agency he heads. We explored his mode of appointment—by or with the consent of the governor or outside of gubernatorial influence—to find that there were significant relationships between both the location and relevancy of the agency and the mode of selecting its director (see Table 9).

Directors of agencies located close to or within the governor's office were more likely (sixteen out of twenty-four) to be gubernatorial appointments than the directors of agencies outside the governor's office (nine out of twenty-three). But, more to the point, directors whose appointments involved the governor were much more likely (fifteen out of twenty-four) to direct agencies deemed relevant than were non-gubernatorial appointments (seven out of twenty-three). This echoes the findings presented in Table 4, but adds a significant variable—gubernatorial involvement in the appointment process—which is associated with agency performance.

Administrative Freedom: Type of Staff

Two points regarding planning agency staffs merit mention. Because staff attributes constrain or enhance the ability of its director

[15] Because these data were developed from a content analysis of enabling legislation, the sample size is different.

Table 9: Mode of Appointment, Agency Location, and Relevancy

		LOCATION				RELEVANCY			
		In Gov.'s Office	Outside Gov.'s Office	Not applicable	Total	Yes	No	Not adequately determined	Total
Appointment	Governor Involved	16	8	0	24	15	6	3	24
	Governor *Not* Involved	9	14	0	23	7	10	6	23
	Not Ascertained	0	0	2	2	1	0	1	2
	Total	25	22	2	49	23	16	10	49

to conduct business, we were interested in whether planning staffs were covered by civil service and therefore somewhat insulated from political intrusion; whether the director had a cadre of professionally trained planners at his disposal; and, how both these factors related to the activities of the agency.

Coverage of state planning agency staff by civil service regulations is related only to location: the higher the civil service coverage, the greater the tendency to be located within the governor's office (eleven out of nineteen); non-coverage was associated more with locations outside the governor's purview (seven out of seventeen); and agencies with only some coverage were evenly spit as to location (four and four).

The nature of this "professionalism" is an open question but could be more a measure of tenure and longevity than specific trained competence, e.g., experience over education. The data cannot test this, but we can venture an informed guess, supported by earlier findings regarding directors' background, that as state planning agencies attract more "mobile management" and "political-type" directors, the staff tends to be more professional. As leadership becomes more politically attuned, staff professionalism increases.

When the actual number of professional planners on the staff of the agency was related to location and relevancy, two trends emerged (see Table 11).[16] The first suggests that there is no significant relationship between the number of planners in an office and its location outside the governor's office, but that location within the governor's office is strongly

[16] The cut-off points in Table 11 of five professional planners for agency location and ten professional planners for agency relevancy were selected solely to indicate at what point the data contained significant relationships. Therefore, no prior assumptions or theories are being tested.

Table 10: Civil Service Coverage and Agency Location

	LOCATION			
	In Gov.'s Office	Outside Gov.'s Office	Not applicable	Total
Staff Coverage Yes	11	7	1	19
Some	4	4	1	9
No	7	10	0	17
Not Ascertained	3	1	0	4
Total	25	22	2	49

related to a sizeable number of planners. This tends to support the findings in Table 10 and our view that political direction and staff professionalism are concomitant developments in state planning.

The second finding gives pause, however, as the data indicate that when there are more than ten professional planners in an agency there is a startling reversal in the relevancy of the agency's performance. The lower the number of planners, the more likely that the agency's activities are relevant; conversely, the more planners, the less likely it is that there will be relevant performance. Therefore, higher numbers of planners may be associated with closer gubernatorial supervision, but they are not associated with state planning agencies which have greater relevancy to the decision-making process. In fact, the reverse is suggested.

Administrative Freedom: Directors' Mobility

Probably the most significant implications of the data appear when tenure of the agency director is related to agency performance (see Table

Table 11: Number of Professional Planners, Agency Location and Relevancy

	LOCATION				RELEVANCY				
No. of planners	In Gov.'s Office	Outside Gov.'s Office	Not applicable	Total	No. of planners	Yes	No	Not adequately determined	Total
Less than five	6	11	2	19	Less than ten	17	6	8	31
More than five	19	11	0	30	More than ten	6	10	3	19
Total	25	22	2	49		23	16	11	50

Table 12: Tenure of the State Planning Director, in the State
Government, in the Agency, as Director

	LOCATION				RELEVANCY			
	Within Gov.'s office	Outside Gov.'s Office	Not appli-cable	Total	Yes	No	Not adequately determined	Total
Length of Director's employment within the particular state government								
Less than two years	13	7	0	20	13	3	4	20
More than two years	9	14	2	25	8	12	5	25
Not Ascertained	3	1	0	4	2	1	2	5
Total	25	22	2	49	23	16	11	50
Length of Director's employment within the agency he now heads								
Less than two years	15	8	1	24	14	3	7	24
More than two years	7	13	1	21	7	12	2	21
Not Ascertained	3	1	0	4	2	1	2	5
Total	25	22	2	49	23	16	11	50
Length of Director's tenure in present position								
Less than two years	18	10	1	29	17	4	8	29
More than two years	4	11	1	16	4	11	1	16
Not Ascertained	3	1	0	4	2	1	2	5
Total	25	22	2	49	23	16	11	50

12). Regardless of how tenure is defined—amount of time working in a particular state government, in the state planning agency, or as planning director—the results are the same: the shorter the director's tenure, the more likely his agency to be located under the governor's direct control *and* performing relevant activity!

Common sense would suggest that the closer one is to the governor or to the chief political leaders, the more tenuous the job security. But surprisingly, it is precisely this job insecurity and mobility—more than any other variable—which relates most to relevancy. Job security and tenure are associated with agencies which are not involved in the decision-making process.

Again, it appears that the job of directing a successful planning agency at the state level is closely tied to politics and political timetables. The implications are clear: no agency will be a part of the decision-making process unless its director is politically attuned and tackles his job with a short-term perspective. Both governors and state planning directors are involved in decisions which have obvious political overtones. This very fact can make the hard decisions easier, for job protection is politically impossible and therefore not a constraint in the decision-making process. Decisions, then, have governmental and political, not personal, impact. And this is as it should be.

SUMMARY—PLANNERS AND CONSEQUENCES

Certain attributes of state planning directors—their background and their office—are correlated with the relevant performance of state planning activities. Their level of education appears to be irrelevant; the type of education is only slightly related; but their career background is highly significant, especially in terms of prior work in management, political experience, and mobility. And the closer the relationship of the director and the governor, the more likely is the agency to be performing relevant activities.

These conclusions do not enhance the prospect of seeing state planning become a science which can be learned in school. They suggest an art which must be learned by experience. The problem, as in so many fields, is how to marry education and experience. But, in this area, we suggest that the impetus must come from the educators simply because the politicians are always in the process of change and occupied with defining and meeting immediate goals.

Politics and mobility emerge as key variables in explaining just what makes state planning successful. We would suggest that the vagaries of politics enhance the ability of the planning function to contribute to the decision-making process and to become an essential part of state government. Agencies and directors that shrink from the political are, in reality, avoiding their responsibility to state government and to the profession.

NEW DIRECTIONS

State planning is still young. It is maturing as a staff function, rapidly moving closer to the chief decision-makers in the states. When it is so located, evidence indicates that the chances for successful performance of the agency are greater than when it is located elsewhere.

Yet, there are disquieting signs. Liaison with legislatures—fulfillment of legislative intent, receptivity to planning by the legislature, legislator-planner contact—is low. At least one state planning director in a major midwestern state recognized this problem when he indicated at a 1967 meeting that "I spend a lot of time 'working the legislature,' showing them what we are about and helping them. Sure it's politics, but I'm building support for my agency." This view should prevail in more state planning efforts.

We would conclude that the many obstacles to effective state planning—whether they be governors, administrative agencies, the planning agencies themselves, or the general "climate of government"—can be overcome. In fact, they must be, for they form the crux of the state planning process—access and acceptability.

The key lies in state planners and agency fulfillment of its broad role. State planners should look to staff needs in the decision-making process and fill the gaps in their assigned responsibilities. This means creating a climate of opinion that makes the planning process not only acceptable, but an integral part of state government activities. Planners, in other words, must educate state government about their own utility.

For those who train planners, we see a call to broaden the perspectives and capabilities of their students. Special techniques and a particularistic disciplinary view of planning will no longer suffice. A sense of policy, politics, and management must become part of the curricula because it is so necessary in the practical activities of planners. As state leaders call for an increased input from state planning to their decision processes, professional planners must respond, or new sources of planning counsel will be sought.

The Diffusion of Innovations among the American States* †

JACK L. WALKER

We are now in the midst of a notable revival of interest in the politics of the American states. During the last decade many studies have been conducted of the social, political, and economic determinants of state policy outcomes.[1] Several of these writers have argued that the relative wealth of a state, its degree of industrialization, and other measures of social and economic development are more important in explaining its level of expenditures than such political factors as the form of legislative apportionment, the amount of party competition, or the degree of voter

* Reprinted by permission of the *American Political Science Review* (Vol. LXIII, no. 3, September, 1969).

† Thanks are due to the Social Science Research Council, The Carnegie Corporation, the Michigan Legislative Intern Program, and the Rackham Faculty Research Fund of The University of Michigan for grants which made this study possible.

[1] Beginning with Richard E. Dawson and James A. Robinson, "Inter-Party Competition, Economic Variables, and Welfare Policies in the American States," *Journal of Politics,* XXV (May, 1963), 265–89, there have been numerous articles and books on the subject. The most recent summary is John H. Fenton and Donald W. Chamberlayne, "The Literature Dealing with the Relationships Between Political Processes, Socio-economic Conditions and Public Policies in the American States: A Bibliographical Essay," *Polity,* I (Spring, 1969), 388–94.

participation.[2] It has been claimed that such factors as the level of personal income or the size of the urban population are responsible *both* for the degree of participation and party competition in a state, *and* the nature of the system's policy outputs. By making this argument these writers have called into question the concepts of representation and theories of party and group conflict which, in one form or another, are the foundations for much of American political science.[3]

There is a growing awareness, however, that levels of expenditure alone are not an adequate measure of public policy outcomes. Sharkansky has shown, for example, that levels of expenditure and levels of actual service are seldom correlated; presumably, some states are able to reach given service levels with much less expenditure than others.[4] Besides establishing the appropriate level of expenditure for a program, policy-makers must also decide about the program's relative scope, provisions for appeal from administrative orders, eligibility requirements, the composition of regulatory boards and commissions, and many other matters which have little to do with money. Before we can evaluate the relative importance of structural and political factors as determinants of policy, therefore, we need to investigate decisions outside the budgetary process. In order to advance that object this study will focus on one of the most fundamental policy decisions of all: whether to initiate a program in the first place.

States have traditionally been judged according to the relative speed with which they have accepted new ideas. Wisconsin, because of its leadership during the Progressive period and its early adoption of the direct primary, the legislative reference bureau, and workmen's compensation, gained a reputation as a pioneering state which it has never lost. Reputations of this kind are usually based only on random impressions and they

[2] For examples see Herbert Jacob, "The Consequences of Malapportionment: A Note of Caution," *Social Forces,* XLIII (1964), 260–66; the chapters by Robert Salisbury, Robert Friedman, Thomas Dye, and Dawson and Robinson in Herbert Jacob and Kenneth Vines, eds., *Politics in the American States: A Comparative Analysis* (Boston, 1965); Richard I. Hofferbert, "The Relation Between Public Policy and Some Structural and Environmental Variables in the American States," *American Political Science Review,* LX (March, 1966), 73–82; and Thomas Dye, *Politics, Economics and the Public: Policy Outcomes in the American States* (Chicago, 1966).

[3] For an evaluation of the significance of this literature and its implications for political science see Robert Salisbury, "The Analysis of Public Policy: A Search for Theories and Roles," in Austin Ranney, ed., *Political Science and Public Policy* (Chicago, 1968), pp. 151–78.

[4] Ira Sharkansky, "Government Expenditures and Public Services in the American States," *American Political Science Review,* LXI (1967), 1066–77. Sharkansky also identifies important political variables in his "Economic and Political Correlates of State Government Expenditures: General Tendencies and Deviant Cases," *Midwest Journal of Political Science,* XI (May, 1967), 173–92.

may be inaccurate or misleading, but, if it is true that some states change more readily than others, a study of the way states adopt new ideas might lead to some important insights into the whole process of political change and development.

This essay is primarily an exercise in theory building. My aim is to develop propositions which might be used as guides to the study of the diffusion of innovations and which might also apply to budgeting and other forms of decison-making.[5] Limitations in the data I have collected do not allow empirical testing of all the explanations I propose; the currently untestable propositions are presented in the hope that they may help in preparing the ground for future research. The study begins with an effort to devise a measure of the relative speed with which states adopt new programs. Once a measure of this phenomenon is created efforts are made to discover its principal demographic and political correlates. The article concludes with an effort to devise an explanation for the adoption of innovations based on insights gathered from studies of decision making, reference group theory, and the diffusion of innovations. The major questions being investigated are: (1) why do some states act as pioneers by adopting new programs more readily than others, and, (2) once innovations have been adopted by a few pioneers, how do these new forms of service or regulation spread among the American states?

DEFINITIONS AND DISTINCTIONS

Several terms have already been used here which have ambiguous meanings and it is important to make clear just how they are to be defined. The most important, and potentially misleading, is the term "innovation." An innovation will be defined simply as a program or policy which is new to the states adopting it, no matter how old the program may be or how many other states may have adopted it. Even though bureaucratic innovations or new departures by regulatory commissions or

[5] There is a well established body of research on the diffusion of innovations from which I have drawn many insights. For general reviews of this literature see Everett M. Rogers, *Diffusion of Innovations* (New York, 1962) and Elihu Katz, Martin L. Levin, and Herbert Hamilton, "Traditions of Research in the Diffusion of Innovations," *American Sociological Review,* XXVIII (1963), 237–52. For early attempts to study the American states from this perspective see Ada J. Davis, "The Evolution of the Institution of Mothers' Pensions in the United States," *American Journal of Sociology,* XXXV (1930), 573–82; Edgar C. McVoy, "Patterns of Diffusion in the United States," *American Sociological Review,* V (1940), 219–27; and E. H. Sutherland, "The Diffusion of Sexual Psychopath Laws," *American Journal of Sociology,* LV (1950–51), 144–56. Also see Torsten Hagerstrand, *Innovation Diffusion as a Spatial Process* (Chicago, 1967) and Robert Mason and Albert N. Hatter, "The Application of a System of Simultaneous Equations to an Innovation Diffusion Model," *Social Forces,* XLVI (1968), 182–93.

courts may be mentioned in the course of the discussion, the data used to measure the relative speed of adoption of innovations consist exclusively of legislative actions, simply because the data were readily available only in that form.

We are studying the relative speed and the spatial patterns of adoption of new programs, not their invention or creation. Invention, or bringing into being workable, relevant solutions to pressing problems, is an important activity and has been the subject of fascinating research.[6] We will concentrate on the way in which organizations select from proposed solutions the one which seems most suited to their needs, and how the organizations come to hear about these new ideas in the first place.[7] We are not trying to specify the circumstances under which new ideas or programs will be conceived or developed; we are studying instead the conditions under which state decision-makers are most likely to adopt a new program.

The object of this analysis is the process of diffusion of ideas for new services or programs. Sometimes new legislation is virtually copied from other states. The California fair trade law, adopted in 1931, "was followed either verbatim or with minor variations by twenty states; in fact, ten states copied two serious typographical errors in the original California law."[8] No assumption is being made, however, that the programs enacted in each state are always exactly alike or that new legislation is written in exactly the same way by every legislature. It is unlikely that the highway department established in Wisconsin in 1907 had the same organizational format as the one adopted by Wyoming in 1917, or that the council on the performing arts created in New York in 1960 bears an exact resemblance to the one created by Kentucky in 1966. In each case, however, a commitment was made to offer a new service, establish a new principle of regulation, or create an agency which had never existed before. Our concern is the origin and spreading of the idea to provide public subsidies for the arts, not the detailed characteristics of institutions created in each state to implement the policy.

No ideological bias was employed in selecting issues for study. The

---

[6] For example see Gary A. Steiner, ed., *The Creative Organization* (Chicago, 1965) and Tom Burns and G. M. Stalker, *The Management of Innovation* (London, 1961).

[7] There is much confusion over this distinction in the literature on diffusion. For an excellent discussion of the problem see Lawrence B. Mohr, "Determinants of Innovation in Organizations," *American Political Science Review,* LXIII (1969), 111–26.

[8] Once the mistake was discovered, the Arkansas statute, which reproduced a model prepared by the National Association of Retail Druggists, was copied either verbatim or with minor changes by seventeen states. See Ewald T. Grether, *Price Control Under Fair Trade Legislation* (New York, 1937), pp. 19–20.

patterns of diffusion for each issue have been treated equally, and no effort was made to develop any method of determining the relative importance or desirability of the programs.[9] Programs are sometimes enacted
only to provide symbolic rewards to groups within the population and
once created are left with inadequate funds or otherwise disabled.[10]
Oklahoma's legislature, for example, emulated other states by creating a
state civil rights commission, but once the commission was established,
only $2,500 was appropriated for its operation.[11] For the purposes of
this study, however, all adoptions are equal. My goal is to provide an
explanation of the relative speed of adoption and the patterns of diffusion of innovations; I am not interested in the effectiveness of
Oklahoma's civil rights commission. The questions to be answered are,
first, where did the legislature get the idea to create such a commission
and, second, why did it act when it did.

THE INNOVATION SCORE

First our aim is to explain why some states adopt innovations more
readily than others. I am assuming that the pioneering states gain their
reputations because of the speed with which they accept new programs.
This study must begin, therefore, with an attempt to devise an innovation
score that will represent the relative speed with which states adopt innovations.

The innovation score is based on the analysis of eighty-eight different programs (see the Appendix for a list) which have been enacted by
at least twenty state legislatures prior to 1965, and for which there was
reliable information on the dates of adoption. In order to make the collection of programs as comprehensive and representative as possible, I
adopted a list of basic issue areas similar to the one employed by the
Council of State Governments in its bi-annual reports included in the
Book of the States. I tried to study six to eight different pieces of legislation in each of these areas: welfare, health, education, conservation,
planning, administrative organization, highways, civil rights, corrections
and police, labor, taxes, and professional regulation. In the course of my
analysis I studied issues ranging from the establishment of highway departments and the enactment of civil rights bills to the creation of state
councils on the performing arts and the passage of sexual psychopath

---

[9] In later work I will report the results of comparisons of the diffusion patterns of
issues from different subject matter areas. Preliminary efforts at such comparisons, however, have not revealed significant variations. There does not seem to
be much difference in the diffusion patterns of issues of different types.
[10] For a discussion of this phenomenon see Murray Edelman, *The Symbolic Uses of
Politics* (Urbana, Ill., 1964), pp. 22–43, 172–87.
[11] Duane Lockard, *Toward Equal Opportunity* (New York, 1968), p. 23.

laws. Most of the programs were adopted during the twentieth century, but sixteen of them diffused primarily during the latter half of the nineteenth century.

Once the eighty-eight lists of dates of adoption were collected they were used to create an innovation score for each state. The first step was to count the total number of years which elapsed between the first and last recorded legislative enactment of a program. Each state then received a number for each list which corresponded to the percentage of time which elapsed between the first adoption and its own acceptance of the program. For example, if the total time elapsing between the first and last adoption of a program was twenty years, and Massachusetts enacted the program ten years after the first adoption, then Massachusetts received a score of .500 on that particular issue. The first state to adopt the program received a score of .000 and the last state received a 1.000. In cases in which all the states have not yet adopted a program, the states without the program were placed last and given a score of 1.000.[12] The innovation score for each state is simply 1.000 minus the average of the sum of the state's scores on all issues. The larger the innovation score, therefore, the faster the state has been, on the average, in responding to new ideas or policies. The issues may be divided into groups according to subject matter areas or time periods, and separate scores can be created for these smaller groupings of issues by following the same procedure. The results of this scoring procedure, using all eighty-eight issues, are presented in Table 1.

A note of caution should be sounded before the results of this exercise are analyzed. We are endeavoring to measure a highly complex process in which an enormous number of idiosyncratic influences are at work; an official with an unusually keen interest in a particular program, a chance reading of an article or book by a governor's aide, or any number of other circumstances peculiar to any one issue might lead to the rapid adoption of a piece of legislation by a state which is usually reluctant to accept new programs. Mississippi, which has the lowest average score and ranks last among the states in relative speed of adoption, was nonetheless the first state to adopt a general sales tax.

If this reservation is kept in mind, the data in Table 1 provide us with a crude outline of the standard or typical pattern of diffusion of new programs or policies among the American states. The states at the top of the list tend to adopt new programs much more rapidly than those at the bottom of the list. Having provided a preliminary measurement of this

[12] The beginning point for the existence of each state was the date upon which it was officially organized as a territory. Using this system, Oklahoma is the last state to come into being, having been organized in 1890. If a program began its diffusion before a state came into existence, that issue was not included in figuring the innovation score for the state.

Table 1: Composite Innovation Scores for the American States[18]

New York	.656	New Hampshire	.482	Idaho	.394
Massachusetts	.629	Indiana	.464	Tennessee	.389
California	.604	Louisiana	.459	West Virginia	.386
New Jersey	.585	Maine	.455	Arizona	.384
Michigan	.578	Virginia	.451	Georgia	.381
Connecticut	.568	Utah	.447	Montana	.378
Pennsylvania	.560	North Dakota	.444	Missouri	.377
Oregon	.544	North Carolina	.430	Delaware	.376
Colorado	.538	Kansas	.426	New Mexico	.375
Wisconsin	.532	Nebraska	.425	Oklahoma	.368
Ohio	.528	Kentucky	.419	South Dakota	.363
Minnesota	.525	Vermont	.414	Texas	.362
Illinois	.521	Iowa	.413	South Carolina	.347
Washington	.510	Alabama	.406	Wyoming	.346
Rhode Island	.503	Florida	.397	Nevada	.323
Maryland	.482	Arkansas	.394	Mississippi	.298

phenomenon, we must now try to explain it. Why should New York, California, and Michigan adopt innovations more rapidly than Mississippi, Wyoming, and South Dakota?

THE CORRELATES OF INNOVATION

Demographic Factors

After studying the acceptance of technological innovations by both individuals and organizations, several writers have concluded that the decision-maker's relative wealth, or the degree to which "free floating" resources are available, are important determinants of the willingness to adopt new techniques or policies.[14] If "slack" resources are available, either in the form of money or a highly skilled, professional staff, the decision-maker can afford the luxury of experimentation and can more easily risk the possibility of failure.[15] Other studies, especially in the areas of agriculture and medicine, have also shown organizational size to be a strong correlate of innovation.[16] Given these results from prior studies in

---

[13] Alaska and Hawaii were omitted from the analysis because data for their years of adoption were often missing.

[14] Everett M. Rogers, *Diffusion of Innovations* (New York, 1962), pp. 40, 285–92. Also see S. N. Eisenstadt, *The Political System of Empires* (New York, 1963), pp. 27, 33–112.

[15] For a discussion of "slack" resources and innovation see Richard M. Cyert and James G. March, *A Behavioral Theory of the Firm* (Englewood Cliffs, N.J., 1963), pp. 278–79.

[16] Rogers, *Diffusion*, Mohr, "Determinants"; and also Edwin Mansfield, "The Speed of Response of Firms to New Techniques," *Quarterly Journal of Economics*, LXXVII (1963), 293–304; Jerald Hage and Michael Aiken, "Program Change and Organizational Properties: A Comparative Analysis," *American Journal of Sociology*, LXXII (1967), 516–17; and Richard J. Hall, S. Eugene

Table 2: Correlations Between Innovation Scores and Social
and Economic Variables, by Time Periods

SOCIAL-ECONOMIC VARIABLES	INNOVATION SCORES*			
	1870–1899	1900–1929	1930–1966	Composite Score
Percent Population Urban:	.62**	.69	.62	.63
Total Population:	.52	.40	.50	.59
Average Income, Per Capita:	***	.62	.50	.55
Value Added Per Capita by Manufacturing:	.46	.55	.57	.66
Average Value, Per Acre, of Farms:	.70	.52	.52	.54
Percent Population Illiterate:	−.58	−.44	−.12	−.23
Median School Years Completed:	***	***	.24	.26

* In order to insure that the innovation score and the social and economic variables came from comparable periods, separate innovation scores were calculated for three time periods: 1870–1899, 1900–1929, and 1930–66. In constructing this table each innovation was placed in the time period during which the first ten states adopted it. Thus, if a program was adopted by only four states during the 1890's, and completed its diffusion during the 1900's, the program is placed in the second time period: 1900–1929, even though its first adoptions took place during the nineteenth century. Social and economic data are taken from the years 1900, 1930, and 1960. The composite score is correlated with social and economic data from 1960.
** The table entries are Pearson product-moment correlations.
*** Measures of these phenomena corresponding with these time periods do not exist.

other fields we might expect to find that the larger, wealthier states, those with the most developed industrial economies and the largest cities, would have the highest innovation scores. It would seem likely that the great cosmopolitan centers in the country, the places where most of the society's creative resources are concentrated, would be the most adaptive and sympathetic to change, and thus the first to adopt new programs.

In order to test these assumptions several measures of social and economic development were correlated with the innovation score. As we can see in Table 2, there is evidence that the larger, wealthier, more industrialized states adopt new programs somewhat more rapidly than their smaller, less well-developed neighbors. Fairly strong relationships exist between the innovation score and the value added by manufacturing, the average per acre value of farms, the size of the urban population, and the average per capita income. These relationships remain virtually unchanged in all time periods. In fact, the only relationship which changes

Haas, and Norman J. Johnson, "Organizational Size, Complexity and Formalization," *American Sociological Review,* XXXII (1967), 903–12.

substantially with time is that between innovation and the percentage of illiterates in the population, which percentage declines steadily across the three time periods. This declining relationship and the low correlation between innovation and the median school year completed is caused primarily by the states in the Rocky Mountain region which have the highest rankings on median school years completed and yet are among the slowest to adopt new programs.[17] The median of educational attainment in the states with the highest innovation scores is pulled down by the presence of a large, poorly educated lower class, living primarily in the inner cities. The highly industrialized states with large urban concentrations are characterized by great inequality of social status and attainment. It would seem, however, that the elements necessary to foster innovation are present in these states even though they do not have highest average level of educational achievement.

Political Factors

Although students of policy-making have begun to doubt the importance of the political system as an independent determinant of the behavior of decision makers, it seems likely that both the degree of party competition and a state's system of legislative apportionment would affect its readiness to accept change. It would seem that parties which often faced closely contested elections would try to outdo each other by embracing the newest, most progressive programs and this would naturally encourage the rapid adoption of innovations. Lowi argues that new departures in policy are more likely at the beginning of a new administration, especially when a former minority party gains control of the government.[18] If

---

[17] Regional affects of this kind appear frequently in analyses of data from the American states. In many studies, especially those which involve measures of political participation or party competition, strong relationships appear which are actually only a result of the distinctive nature of the Southern states. In order to insure that the correlations in this analysis were not merely a result of the social and political peculiarities of the South, the eleven states of the Confederacy were removed from all distributions. Since the Southern states do not cluster at one extreme of the innovation scale, no great changes occurred in correlation coefficients based upon data from the thirty-nine states outside the South. Within the eleven Southern states, however, almost all the relationships were substantially reduced in size. Because only eleven states are involved, this fact is difficult to interpret, but will be treated more fully in a later work. For an example of this problem discussed in another context see Raymond Wolfinger and John Osgood Field, "Political Ethos and the Structure of City Government," *American Political Science Review*, LX (1966), 306–26. For a more extensive discussion of the methodological implications see the discussion of "interaction effects" in Hugh Donald Forbes and Edward R. Tufte, "A Note of Caution in Causal Modelling," *American Political Science Review*, LXII (1968), 1261–62 and the communications from Dennis D. Riley and Jack L. Walker, *American Political Science Review*, LXIII (1969), 890–92.

[18] Theodore Lowi, "Toward Functionalism in Political Science: The Case of Inno-

this tendency exists it would also seem likely that state political systems which allow frequent turnover and offer the most opportunities to capture high office would more often develop the circumstances in which new programs might be adopted.[19]

Another prerequisite for the rapid adoption of new programs might be a system of legislative apportionment which fully represented the state's urban areas and which did not grant veto power to groups opposed to change. Such a system might be expected to allow consideration and debate of new policies and programs in all areas. Some recent findings, such as Barber's study of legislators in Connecticut,[20] lead us to speculate that representatives from newly developing urban and suburban areas would be more cosmopolitan, better informed, and more tolerant of change. If nothing else, urban legislators would probably be more willing to deal with problems of sanitation, planning, transportation, and housing peculiar to large metropolitan areas.

No matter what the composition of the legislator's constituency, however, it would seem that the presence of competent staff, superior clerical facilities, and supporting services would allow him to give serious consideration to a large number of new proposals. Several studies of the diffusion of technological innovations have demonstrated that the best informed individuals are most likely to pioneer in the use of new techniques or tools,[21] and so the states which provide the most extensive staff and research facilities in their legislatures ought to pioneer in the adoption of new programs.[22]

In Table 3 efforts to test some of these hypotheses in different time periods are displayed. Measures of political variables are usually based

vation in Party Systems," *American Political Science Review*, LVII (1963), 570–83. Evidence which seems to confirm Lowi's theory may be found in Charles W. Wiggins, "Party Politics in the Iowa Legislature," *Midwest Journal of Political Science*, XI (1967), 60–69 and Frank M. Bryan, "The Metamorphosis of a Rural Legislature," *Polity*, I (1968), 181–212.

[19] Joseph A. Schlesinger has developed an index of the "general opportunity level" in each state. The index measures the relative number of chances which exist in each state to achieve major political office. See *Ambition and Politics: Political Careers in the United States* (Chicago, 1966), pp. 37–56.

[20] James D. Barber, *The Lawmakers: Recruitment and Adaptation to Legislative Life* (New Haven, 1965). For testimony from legislators about the importance of reapportionment see Frank M. Bryan, "Who is Legislating," *National Civic Review*, LVI (December, 1967), 627–33 and Allan Dines, "A Reapportioned State," *National Civic Review*, LV (February, 1966), pp. 70–74, 99.

[21] Rogers, *Diffusion*. Also see: Mansfield, "Speed of Response"; James S. Coleman, Elihu Katz, and Herbert Menzel, *Medical Innovation: A Diffusion Story* (Indianapolis, 1966); and John W. Loy, Jr., "Social Psychological Characteristics of Innovators," *American Sociological Review*, XXIV (1969), 73–82.

[22] For a somewhat different view see Norman Meller, "Legislative Staff Services: Toxin, Specific, or Placebo for the Legislature's Ills," *The Western Political Quarterly*, XX (June, 1967), 381–89.

Table 3: Correlations Between Innovation Scores and Measures
of Political Variables, by Time Periods

POLITICAL VARIABLES*	INNOVATION SCORES			Composite Score
	1870–1899	1900–1929	1930–1966	
Party Competition for Governorship:	.36	.02	.14	.24
David-Eisenberg Index of Malapportionment:	**	.07	.55	.65

* The Index of party competition used in this table is the percent of the total vote going to the gubernatorial candidate coming in second, times 2. This yields a scale from 0 to 100. It was created by Richard Hofferbert. The apportionment Index appears in Paul T. David and Ralph Eisenberg, *Devaluation of the Urban and Suburban Vote* (Charlottesville, Va.: Bureau of Public Administration, University of Virginia, 1961).
** Measures of this phenomenon corresponding with this time period do not exist.

on evidence only from contemporary periods because data are seldom available on state and local elections or the operation of legislatures in earlier decades. Measures are available, however, for the degree of party competition and the extent of legislative malapportionment.[23] As we can see in Table 3, party competitiveness does not seem to be consistently related to the innovation score, at least as it is measured here.[24] Legislative apportionment is not correlated with the innovation score in the 1900–29 period but is related in the 1930–66 period. Since legislatures steadily became less representative of urban populations after 1930, it may be that we have here some empirical evidence of the impact of malapportionment on policy-making in the states.

Recent studies of state expenditures have shown that the explanatory effects of political variables could be eliminated if statistical controls for social and economic variables were applied. Therefore, in Table 4 I have presented both the zero-order correlations of the composite innovation score with measures of party competition, turnover in office, legisla-

[23] There is one other index in existence which deals with political phenomenon: Rodney Mott's Index of Judicial Prestige. The Mott index measures the degree to which state supreme courts were used as models by the legal profession. It is based on a study of citations in federal Supreme Court decisions and all state supreme court decisions, the number of cases reprinted in standard textbooks, and the opinion of a panel of prominent legal scholars; it covers the period 1900 to 1930. The Mott index and the innovation score from the same time period are correlated at .62. This finding might be interpreted to mean that emulative behavior in the judicial arena is not much different from that in the legislative arena. For details of the Judicial Prestige Index see Rodney L. Mott, "Judicial Influence," *American Political Science Review*, XXX (1936), 295–315.
[24] Data for this table was derived from Richard Hofferbert's collection, "American State Socioeconomic, Electoral, and Policy Data: 1890–1960," which he has graciously allowed me to use.

Table 4: Relationships Between the Composite Innovation Score and
Measures of Legislative Apportionment and Party Competition

		PARTIALS				
	Zero-Order	Value added manu-facturing	Percent urban	Total population	Per capita income	Four factors combined
Apportionment						
David-Eisenberg Index	.65	.47	.64	.67	.60	.58
Schubert-Press Index	.26	.12	.34	.31	.26	.21
Party Competition						
Hofferbert Index	.54	.35	.34	.50	.26	.12
Riley-Walker Index —Gov.	.40	.33	.22	.47	.09	.17
Riley-Walker Index —Legis.	.31	.24	.17	.34	.04	.07
Turnover in Office						
Schlesinger Index of Opportunity	.53	.40	.39	.32	.34	.24
Legislative Services						
Grumm's Index of Legislative Professionalism	.63	.38	.33	.41	.51	.11

tive apportionment, and legislative professionalism,[25] and also partial correlations with four social and economic variables controlled. The control variables are value added by manufacturing, percent urban population, total population size, and per capita personal income, all of which earlier proved to be independently related to the innovation score. In Table 4 the effect of each control variable is displayed separately along with the combined impact of all four. The results tend to corroborate earlier analyses which minimize the independent effects of these political vari-

[25] The sources are Richard Hofferbert, "Classification of American State Party Systems," *Journal of Politics*, XXVI (1964), 550–67; Dennis Riley and Jack L. Walker, "Problems of Measurement and Inference in the Study of the American States," (Paper delivered at the Institute of Public Policy Studies, University of Michigan, 1968); David and Eisenberg, *Devaluation;* Glendon Shubert and Charles Press, "Measuring Malapportionment," *American Political Science Review*, LVIII (1964), 302–27, and corrections, 968–70; Schlesinger, *Ambition and Politics;* and John Grumm, "Structure and Policy in the Legislature" (Paper presented at the Southwestern Social Science Association Meetings, 1967).

ables on policy outcomes. The Schlesinger index of opportunity, which measures the difference among the states in the average number of times major offices have changed hands, and the Hofferbert index of inter-party competition seem to have some independent impact on innovation, although it is greatly weakened when all four control variables are combined. This finding lends some credence to Lowi's argument that turnover in office fosters change.

Certainly, the most important result depicted in this table is the consistent strength of the correlation between innovation and the David and Eisenberg index of urban representation.[26] Earlier studies, using expenditures as a measure of policy outcomes, have consistently found that apportionment has little importance as an explanatory variable.[27] Our findings indicate that apportionment does make a difference where innovation is concerned. Although the other political factors do not have great independent impact on innovation, the clear implication arising from data presented in Tables 3 and 4 is that those states which grant their urban areas full representation in the legislature seem to adopt new ideas more rapidly, on the average, than states which discriminate against their cities.

Given the results of this correlational analysis, we might conclude that New York, California, and Michigan adopt new programs more rapidly than Mississippi, Wyoming, and South Dakota primarily because they are bigger, richer, more urban, more industrial, have more fluidity and turnover in their political systems, and have legislatures which more adequately represent their cities. Although these findings are important, they leave many important questions unanswered. The political system does not react automatically in response to the growth of manufacturing industries or to the increase in the percentage of the population living in cities. Developments of this kind obviously cause problems which public officials might try to solve, but the mere presence of such a stimulant does not cause public officials to act, nor does it determine the form the

[26] Although much simpler than the Schubert and Press measure, the David and Eisenberg index seems to have more relevance to political outcomes. Thomas Dye had the same experience. See Dye, *Politics, Economics and the Public,* pp. 19–20, 63–69, 112–14, 146–48, 174–77, 236–37, 270–81.
[27] Herbert Jacob, "The Consequences of Malapportionment: A Note of Caution," *Social Forces,* XLIII (1964), 260–66; Thomas R. Dye, "Malapportionment and Public Policy in the States," *Journal of Politics,* XXVII (1965), 586–601; Richard I. Hofferbert, "The Relation Between Public Policy and Some Structural and Environmental Variables in the American States," *American Political Science Review,* LX (1966), 73–82; David Brady and Douglas Edmonds, "One Man, One Vote—So What?" *Trans-action,* IV (March, 1967), 41–46. A recent article calls some of the conclusions of this research into question: Alan G. Pulsipher and James L. Weatherby, Jr., "Malapportionment, Party Competition, and the Functional Distribution of Governmental Expenditures," *American Political Science Review,* LXII (1968), 1207–19.

solution will take, nor does it indicate which state might act first to meet the problem. Our analysis has provided us with evidence that change and experimentation are more readily accepted in the industrialized, urban, cosmopolitan centers of the country, but we have not improved our understanding of the institutions and decision-making processes which cause strong statistical relationships between industrial output and innovation. Also, we have not explained the way innovations spread from the pioneering states to those with lower innovation scores. In order to develop explanations of these processes we must go beyond the search for demographic correlates of innovation and develop generalizations which refer to the behavior of the men who actually make the choices in which we are interested.

POLITICAL SCIENCE AND INNOVATION

In one form or another, interest group theories, based on self-regulating systems of countervailing power, are at the heart of much of the recent research into American politics.[28] Studies of the legislative process in the United States, for example, have been strongly influenced by theories which emphasize the importance of the group basis of politics. Beginning with the efforts of A. Lawrence Lowell,[29] political scientists have worked to discover the basic factions within the legislature and have striven to develop operational definitions of power or influence.[30] Extensive efforts have been made to isolate and measure the various influences which come to bear on the individual legislator and motivate him to join one or another legislative bloc: what is a legislator's most important source of cues; is it a lobbyist with whom he has close connections, his party leaders, members of his constituency, the governor, or members of his own family? What impact on his attitudes does the legislative institution itself have; do its informal rules and traditions affect the legislator's decisions, and if so, in what way?[31] Great emphasis has been placed on the analysis of roll-call votes and several sophisticated research tech-

---

[28] Examples of this general approach to policy-making are David B. Truman, *The Governmental Process* (New York, 1960); Edward Banfield, *Political Influence* (New York, 1961); and Richard E. Neustadt, *Presidential Power* (New York, 1960). For an excellent critique of theories which employ concepts of power as a major explanatory variable see James G. March, "The Power of Power," in David Easton, ed., *Varieties of Political Theory* (Englewood Cliffs, N.J., 1966), pp. 39–70.

[29] A. Lawrence Lowell, "The Influence of Party Upon Legislation," *Annual Report of the American Historical Association* (1901), pp. 321–543.

[30] The best example is Robert Dahl, "The Concept of Power," *Behavioral Science,* II (1957), 201–15.

[31] For the best general review of the results of research on the legislative process, see Malcolm E. Jewell and Samuel C. Patterson, *The Legislative Process in the United States* (New York, 1966).

niques have been developed to pursue this work, ranging from Beyle's cluster block analysis and Guttman scaling to the more complex, computerized routines presently in use.[32] But all this machinery is useful only in studying those roll-calls which cause divisions in the house; all unanimous votes, nearly 80 percent of the total in most legislatures, are ignored. Riker has devised a technique in which he uses the percentage of the total membership which is present for the vote and the closeness of the division to determine the relative significance of roll-call votes in legislatures. The more legislators present and the closer the vote, the more significant the issue involved.[33] The full attention of the researcher is thus focused on the relatively small number of decisions which cause significant disagreements, because it is assumed that these are the most important votes; at least, they are the only ones which will provide clues to "the conflicting forces and pressures at work in the legislative system,"[34] and the discovery of those forces and pressures, according to the group theory of politics, is the principal object of political science.

One of the main purposes in this study is to develop an approach to governmental policy-making which will serve as a guide in the analysis of *all* legislative decisions, the unanimous as well as the contested ones, and which will lead as well to a better understanding of decisions made by bureaucrats, political executives, and other governmental officials. Rather than focus upon the patterns of conflict among factions within the legislature or the administrative agencies, I will search for the criteria employed by legislators and administrators in deciding whether a proposal is worthy of consideration in the first place. This search rests on the belief that whoever the decision-maker may be, whether administrator, lobbyist, party leader, governor, or legislator, and however controversial a particular issue may become, a set of general criteria exists in every state which establish broad guidelines for policy-making. Regardless of the interests supporting an innovation, no matter whether the decision system is primarily monolithic or pluralistic, if a proposal for change does not fall within those guidelines its chances for acceptance are slim. Many of the propositions I will develop cannot be verified until they are tested with evidence from individual decision-makers,[35] they are presented here only

---

[32] For a discussion of these techniques see Lee F. Anderson, Meridith W. Watts, Jr., and Allen R. Wilcox, *Legislative Roll-Call Analysis* (Evanston, 1966). Also see Jewell and Patterson, *Legislative Process,* pp. 528–50.

[33] William H. Riker, "A Method for Determining the Significance of Roll Calls in Voting Bodies," in John C. Wahlke and Heinz Eulau, eds., *Legislative Behavior* (New York, 1959), pp. 337–83.

[34] Jewell and Patterson, *Legislative Process,* p. 416.

[35] Thanks to a grant from the Carnegie Corporation I have been able to launch a pilot study involving interviews in several states.

as a first, tentative step toward a more comprehensive theory of governmental policy making.

EMULATION AND DECISION-MAKING IN THE STATES

We are searching for answers to three major questions: (1) why do certain states consistently adopt new programs more rapidly than other states; (2) are there more or less stable patterns of diffusion of innovations among the American states; and (3) if so, what are they? The answers to these questions will be founded, in part, on the theories of organizational decision-making developed in recent years by writers like Simon, March, Cyert, and Lindblom.[36] At the heart of these theories is the concept of the decision-maker struggling to choose among complex alternatives and constantly receiving much more information concerning his environment than he is able to digest and evaluate. An ordinary decision-maker, required to make frequent choices and faced with an inconclusive flood of reports, programs, suggestions, and memos, must simplify his task in some way. According to Simon, he does not—cannot—search in every case for the best possible solution to the problems he faces; he has neither the time nor the energy. Instead, he makes decisions by searching until he finds an alternative which he believes is good enough to preserve whatever values are important to him. The limits of rationality imposed by human capacities prevent him from maximizing his benefits in every situation; rather, he "satisfices," or chooses a course of action which seems satisfactory under the circumstances.

The individual in a complex organization, therefore, does not deal directly with all the sources of information potentially available to him, nor does he evaluate every conceivable policy option. In place of the debilitating confusion of reality he creates his own abstract, highly simplified world containing only a few major variables. In order to achieve this manageable simplicity he adopts a set of decision rules or standard criteria for judgment which remain fairly stable and which guide him in choosing among sources of information and advice. A decision-maker decides both where to look for cues and information and how to choose among alternatives according to his decision rules; these rules also embody the current goals and aspirations of his organization, or the values which the organization is designed to advance and protect. Hence, if we wish to predict the decision-maker's behavior, we should try to discover these rules of thumb, or "heuristics" as they are sometimes called, which shape his judgment. His choices could then be explained in terms of the

[36] Herbert Simon, *Administrative Behavior,* 2nd ed. (New York, 1957); Richard M. Cyert and James C. March, *A Behavioral Theory of the Firm* (Englewood Cliffs, N.J., 1963); and Charles E. Lindblom, *The Intelligence of Democracy* (New York, 1965).

alternatives he considers, his knowledge of each alternative, the sources of his knowledge, and the standard decision rules he applies in cases of this kind.[37]

Taking cues from these theories of human choice and organizational decision-making, our explanation of the adoption of innovations by the states is based on the assertion that state officials make most of their decisions by analogy. The rule of thumb they employ might be formally stated as follows: *look for an analogy between the situation you are dealing with and some other situation, perhaps in some other state, where the problem has been successfully resolved.*[38]

We are looking to what has been called the "inter-organizational context,"[39] or the *horizontal* relationships among the states within the federal system, for the principal influences which regulate the speed of adoption and the patterns of diffusion of innovations. Most of the existing work on inter-governmental relations and federalism concentrates on the question of centralization within the American system of government. In line with the general interest of most political scientists in the factors which affect the access of organized groups and the lines of authority within a political system, many writers are concerned with the virtues of centralization or decentralization and try to determine how much of either exists in the system. They have studied primarily the *vertical* relationships among national, state, and local governments, and have usually identified the party system and its demands as the institutional influence most responsible for maintaining the present, decentralized, federal relationships.[40] I want to focus attention on the mutual perceptions and relationships among state governments and to show how these relationships affect the behavior of state decision-makers.[41]

[37] For a comprehensive review of the literature on decision-making see Donald W. Taylor, "Decision Making and Problem Solving," and Julia Feldman and Herschel E. Kanter, "Organizational Decision Making," in James G. March, ed., *Handbook of Organizations* (Chicago, 1965), pp. 48–86, 614–49. Also see W. Richard Scott, "Theory of Organizations," in Robert E. L. Faris, ed., *Handbook of Modern Sociology* (Chicago, 1964), pp. 485–529.

[38] Decision rules of this kind are mentioned in both Taylor, "Decision Making and Problem Solving," pp. 73–74; and Cyert and March, *Behavioral Theory,* especially pp. 34–43.

[39] William M. Evan, "The Organization-Set: Toward a Theory of Inter-Organizational Relations," in James D. Thompson, ed., *Approaches to Organizational Design* (Pittsburgh, 1966), pp. 173–91.

[40] Some recent examples are William Anderson, *The Nation and the States, Rivals or Partners?* (Minneapolis, 1955); M. J. C. Vile, *The Structure of American Federalism* (London, 1961); William Riker, *Federalism: Origin, Operation, Significance* (Boston, 1964); Daniel J. Elazar, *American Federalism: A View From the States* (New York, 1966); Morton Grodzins, *The American System* (Chicago, 1966). For a general critique see A. H. Birch, "Approaches to the Study of Federalism," *Political Studies* (1966), pp. 15–33.

[41] This is not the first study to discover the important role of emulation and compe-

One of the most common arguments used in state legislatures against raising taxes or passing measures designed to regulate business is the fear that such measures might retard industrial development or force marginal plants to leave the state. Lawmakers often are called upon to deal with the problems which arise when one or two states establish extremely permissive standards for the granting of licenses, such as the corporation laws in New Jersey and Delaware, or the divorce laws in Nevada. However, interstate competition does not always drive standards down; it has a positive side as well. State decision-makers are constantly looking to each other for guides to action in many areas of policy, such as the organization and management of higher education, or the provision of hospitals and public health facilities. In fact, I am arguing that this process of competition and emulation, or cue-taking, is an important phenomenon which determines in large part the pace and direction of social and political change in the American states.[42]

Uncertainty and the fear of unanticipated consequences have always been formidable barriers to reform. Proponents of new programs have always had to combat the arguments of those who predict dire consequences if some innovation is adopted. Even though American history is full of cases where the opponents of change have later had to admit that the dangers they feared never materialized, inertia and the unwillingness to take risks have prevented a more rapid rate of change.

Inertia can more easily be overcome, however, if the proponent of change can point to the successful implementation of his program in

---

tition in the development of public policy. Richard Hofferbert in "Ecological Development and Policy Change in the American States," *Midwest Journal of Political Science*, X (1966), 485; and Ira Sharkansky in "Regionalism, Economic Status and the Public Policies of American States," *Southwestern Social Science Quarterly*, LXIX (1968), both mention the influence of other states in the calculations of state decision-makers. Several earlier students of local government complained that sparsely populated, arid Western states had blindly copied from the heavily populated Eastern states forms of local government which were inappropriately suited for the conditions prevailing in the Great Plains. See A. Bristol Goodman, "Westward Movement of Local Government," *The Journal of Land and Public Utility Economics*, XXXVI (1944), pp. 20–34 and Herman Walker, Jr. and Peter L. Hansen, "Local Government and Rainfall," *American Political Science Review*, XL (1946), 1113–23. Robert L. Crain has recently used emulation as a principal explanatory variable in his study of the spread of water fluoridation programs among American cities in "Fluoridation: The Diffusion of an Innovation Among Cities," *Social Forces*, XLV (1966), 467–76, as did Thomas M. Scott in his: "The Diffusion of Urban Governmental Forms as a Case of Social Learning," *The Journal of Politics*, XXX (1968), 1091–1108.

[42] This set of hypotheses is consistent with more general theories concerning the manner in which human beings formulate judgments and establish expectations in all areas of life. See Leon Festinger, "A Theory of Social Comparison Processes," *Human Relations* (1954), pp. 117–40 and Robert Merton, *Social Theory and Social Structure*, rev. ed. (New York, 1957), pp. 225–420.

some other similar setting. If a legislator introduces a bill which would require the licensing of probation officers, for example, and can point to its successful operation in a neighboring state, his changes of gaining acceptance are markedly increased. As Harsanyi has asserted:

. . . it is not an overstatement to say that a very considerable part of the social values of most societies is based on sheer ignorance. . . . One of the reasons why other persons' example is so important in encouraging changes in people's values and behavior lies in the fact that it tends to dispel some groundless fears about the dismal consequences that such changes might entail. Another reason is of course that people can more easily face the possible hostility of the supporters of the old values if they are not alone in making the change.[43]

In fact, once a program has been adopted by a large number of states it may become recognized as a legitimate state responsibility, something which all states ought to have. When this happens it becomes extremely difficult for state decision-makers to resist even the weakest kinds of demands to institute the program for fear of arousing public suspicions about their good intentions; once a program has gained the stamp of legitimacy, it has a momentum of its own. As Lockard found in studying the passage of Fair Employment Practices laws, the actions of other states are sometimes key factors in prompting reluctant politicians to accept controversial programs:

Pressure mounted in New Jersey during 1944 and 1945 for some stronger policy, and when New York passed its FEP law certain key politicians in New Jersey decided to act. Governor Walter E. Edge concluded, apparently reluctantly, that he had to commit himself to such a law. "As the session drew to a close," Edge wrote in his autobiography, "minority racial and religious groups pressed for adoption of an antidiscrimination program. While it was a subject which I would have preferred to give greater study, politically it could not be postponed because New York had passed a similar measure and delay would be construed as a mere political expedient."[44]

For similar reasons there have been numerous efforts to enact a program of homesteading in Hawaii as a way of disposing of its arable public lands even though the circumstances there are quite different from other states where homesteading was successfully introduced.[45] And in Connecticut one of the most powerful arguments in favor of introducing the direct

---

[43] John C. Harsanyi, "Rational Choice Models v. Functionalistic and Conformistic Models of Political Behavior" (Paper delivered at American Political Science Association Meeting, 1967), p. 17.

[44] Duane Lockard, *Towards Equal Opportunity* (New York, 1968), pp. 20–21.

[45] Allan Spitz, "The Transplantation of American Democratic Institutions," *Political Science Quarterly*, LXXXII (1967), 386–98,

primary system during the 1950's was simply that all the other states had adopted one.[46]

The Connecticut case neatly illustrates some of the generalizations we are developing. Lockard points out that the leaders of both political parties privately opposed the introduction of a primary system but felt that an endorsement of the idea had to be put into their platforms to avoid having their opponents charge them with "bossism." Demands for the primary came for the most part from small groups in the state's suburban areas which were interested in the issue as "a consequence of the influx of migrants from states with primaries."[47] Speaking as a professional political scientist as well as a legislator, Lockard was well suited to counter the extreme fears expressed by the party leaders who predicted that party organizations would be completely destroyed if primaries were introduced. Lockard reasoned by analogy to the experience in other states both in countering the opponents of change and in shaping his own moderate position:

I expressed my considerable doubts about the effect of party primaries on party organization. From observations of politics in some of the most thoroughgoing party primary states, [however,] it seemed that the party organizations had been shattered with many undesirable consequences. In my campaign I expressed support only for a limited form of a primary and not one calculated to wreck the party system.[48]

Events like these illustrate the way in which the agenda of controversy in a state is determined, at least in part, by developments in other states, and they also show how experiences and examples from outside the system help to overcome the natural reluctance of any institutional structure to risk the consequences of change. The constituent units of any federal system are under considerable pressure to conform with national and regional standards or accepted administrative procedures. These norms result primarily from the processes of emulation and competition we have described, and also from the efforts of nationally organized interest groups. They are affected also by the growth and development of professional organizations and other forms of communication among state administrators, and the natural circulation of active, politically involved citizens among the states, such as the Connecticut suburbanites who began agitating for a primary system in their adopted political home.

[46] Duane Lockard, *Connecticut's Challenge Primary: A Study in Legislative Politics*, Eagleton Case #7 (New York, 1959).

[47] Lockard, *Connecticut*, p. 2.

[48] Lockard, *Connecticut*, p. 22.

REGIONAL REFERENCE GROUPS AND STANDARDS OF EVALUATION

Nationally accepted standards or norms provide a convenient measure which can be used by interested citizens or political leaders to judge the adequacy of services offered in their own states. But, these norms have an ambiguous influence on the performance of state governments. On the one hand, the existence of national standards probably encourages *higher* performance among the *poorer* members of the federation than we could expect if functions and service levels were established independently within each unit of government, solely as a result of internal demands. An example of this tendency was discovered by May in his study of Canadian federalism:

Newfoundland chose for a long time to remain outside the Canadian federation, thus not subjecting itself to the forces of national reorientation, and when, after joining the Dominion, a royal commission reported on its financial position, the commission observed that Newfoundland's public services were very backward in relation to those of the other provinces, including even the maritimes. . . .[49]

In the United States, Mississippi, Vermont, and North Dakota are good examples of relatively poor states which are making unusually large efforts to bring their public services into closer approximation of national standards. But, on the other hand, national standards and norms can have a *conservative* impact, especially in the *richer,* industrial states which are able to provide services somewhat above the national averages with relatively little effort.[50] Hansen complains of this tendency when he points out that:

Some northern states fall considerably below their northern neighboring states in public service standards. . . . Their fiscal problems arise not because they are poor but because their tax levels are low by northern standards. This is notably true for example of a tier of large industrial states—Illinois, Indiana, Ohio and Pennsylvania . . . . These states are not excessively hard pressed by tax burdens relative to the country as a whole.[51]

This statement by Hansen is drawn from an essay in which he expresses disapproval of what he considers the inadequate public services

[49] Ronald J. May, "Financial Inequality Between States in a Federal System" (unpublished doctoral dissertation, "Nuffield College, Oxford University, 1966), p. 168.

[50] For a somewhat similar argument concerning government spending see Anthony Downs, "Why the Government Budget is Too Small in a Democracy," *World Politics,* XII (July, 1960), 541–63.

[51] Alvin H. Hansen, *The Postwar American Economy: Performance and Problems* (New York, 1964), pp. 30–31.

of large industrial states which have relatively low tax burdens. But the statement we have cited contains several ambiguities. For example, Hansen charges that "some northern states fall considerably below their northern neighboring states in public service standards," but then he specifically points as examples to Illinois, Indiana, Ohio, and Pennsylvania, states which border on each other. It is not clear whether we are being asked to compare these states to their neighbors, to other northern states with higher tax burdens, or to "the country as a whole." Within Illinois, however, the state's decision-makers are probably comparing their own performance with their counterparts in Indiana, Ohio, Pennsylvania, or New Jersey. Officials in Illinois may know of the procedures and performance levels in New York or California, but they are unlikely to think of events in these states as legitimate guides to action.[52]

When examining the public policy of any state, therefore, it is important to discover in which "league" it has chosen to play. For example, Salisbury, in a statement much like Hansen's, reasons by analogy in arguing that Missouri does not provide as much aid for its schools as its potential resources might warrant. He points out that in 1959 the "state ranked 18th in per capita income but 38th in per capita expenditure for local schools."[53] This relatively low level of support seems to result from the correspondingly low aspirations of the officials of the Missouri State Teachers Association who, according to Salisbury, "have chosen to get what they can with a minimum of agitation or conflict rather than attempt broader public campaigns in behalf of larger objectives."[54] The officials of MSTA "are fully conscious of the gap between the Missouri school aid level and that of, say, neighboring Illinois," but they are quick to point out "that by comparison with other neighboring states—Arkansas, Oklahoma, or Nebraska, for example—Missouri's record is much more impressive."[55] It would seem from this example that Missouri's leaders, at least those concerned with public education, are emulating and competing primarily with the states to their south and west, rather than with the Great Lakes states to their north and east, or the Rocky Mountain states, the Deep South or the Far West. The choice of relatively poor states like Arkansas and Oklahoma as the principal, legitimate reference groups establishes an upper limit of aspirations which is

---

[52] For evidence of this perspective see Thomas J. Anton, *The Politics of State Expenditure in Illinois* (Urbana, 1966), p. 263.

[53] Nicholas A. Masters, Robert Salisbury, and Thomas H. Eliot, *State Politics and the Public Schools* (New York, 1964), p. 12.

[54] Masters, Salisbury, Eliot, *State Politics*, p. 25.

[55] Masters, Salisbury, Eliot, *State Politics*, p. 21. For a similar discussion of the importance of aspirations in determining the speed with which innovations are adopted see Rufus P. Browning, "Innovative and Noninnovative Decision Processes in Government Budgeting," in Robert T. Golembiewski, ed., *Public Budgeting and Finance* (Itasca, Ill., 1968), pp. 128–45.

considerably below that which might exist if Missouri's accepted basis for comparison were the public services of Illinois, Wisconsin, or Michigan.

Regional Groupings among the States

We have come far enough in our analysis to see that our original presentation of the innovation scores in Table 1 as a linear distribution masked some pertinent information. A more useful representation of the data, which would conform more closely to the actual patterns of diffusion, would have to be in the form of a tree. At the top of the tree would be a set of pioneering states which would be linked together in a national system of emulation and competition. The rest of the states would be sorted out along branches of the tree according to the pioneer, or set of pioneers, from which they take their principal cues. States like New York, Massachusetts, California, and Michigan should be seen as regional pace setters, each of which has a group of followers, usually within their own region of the country, that tend to adopt programs only after the pioneers have led the way. For example, Colorado, which ranks ninth in Table 1, might be seen as the regional leader of the Rocky Mountain states. The rest of the states in that region are found much further down the list: Utah is twenty-second, Idaho is thirty-third, Arizona is thirty-sixth, Montana is thirty-eighth, New Mexico is forty-first, Wyoming is forty-sixth, and Nevada is forty-seventh. All of these states, with the possible exception of Utah, which may share in the leadership of the region, might be seen as Colorado's followers, who usually pick up new ideas only after the regional pioneer has put them into practice.

If we are right about the general patterns of competition and emulation, we should discover in our data some evidence of the existence of regional clusters among the states. In an effort to find such groupings, a varimax factor analysis was performed, using a matrix of pair-wise comparisons of all state innovation scores on all eighty-eight issues. If states in the same region are adopting programs in a similar order or pattern over a period of time, a factor analysis should uncover several underlying dimensions in the matrix along which all states would be ordered according to their responses to the programs upon which the innovation score is based. The results of the factor analysis are presented in Table 5.

As we can see, the regional groupings we expected to find do exist, although the patterns are not as neat and clear as we might have hoped. To produce each factor I recorded all loadings which were over .400. The five factors which result bring the states into generally recognizable, contiguous groupings. The states with the largest loadings in each region are not necessarily those with the highest innovation scores. Instead, they are states like Connecticut, Florida, or New Mexico whose innovation

Table 5: Varimax Factor Analysis of Innovation Scores
for Forty-Eight States

FACTOR I (South)	
Factor Loading	*State*
.756	Florida
.711	Tennessee
.663	Alabama
.661	Virginia
.656	Georgia
.630	Mississippi
.621	Delaware
.600	North Carolina
.590	South Carolina
.576	Arkansas
.543	Texas
.517	Nebraska
.464	West Virginia
.460	Louisiana
.459	Iowa
.454	South Dakota
.433	Nevada

7.8   *Total Factor Contribution*

FACTOR II (New England)	
Factor Loading	*State*
.795	Connecticut
.766	Massachusetts
.758	New Hampshire
.659	Rhode Island
.536	New York
.512	Vermont
.434	Maine
.404	Pennsylvania

4.1   *Total Factor Contribution*

Table 5 (*continued*)

FACTOR III (Mountains and Northwest)

Factor Loading	State
.791	New Mexico
.719	Idaho
.702	Montana
.694	Utah
.638	Washington
.620	North Dakota
.610	Wyoming
.569	Oklahoma
.516	Louisiana
.503	South Dakota
.432	Oregon
.419	Maryland
.410	Arkansas
.407	West Virginia

6.7   *Total Factor Contribution*

FACTOR IV (Mid-Atlantic and Great Lakes)

Factor Loading	State
.795	New Jersey
.637	Wisconsin
.605	New York
.577	Minnesota
.536	Illinois
.516	Pennsylvania
.451	Indiana

4.0   *Total Factor Contribution*

FACTOR V (Border, Great Lakes, and California)

Factor Loading	State
.698	California
.610	Missouri
.584	Kentucky
.577	Michigan
.548	Ohio
.515	Nebraska
.458	Illinois

4.1   *Total Factor Contribution*

scores are closer to the average for their regions. The presence of Nebraska, Iowa, and South Dakota on Factor 1, which otherwise identifies Southern states, may indicate that more than one regional cluster is being identified on that factor.

There are several ambiguities in the data. For example, New York, Pennsylvania, West Virginia, Arkansas, and Illinois are loading on more than one factor. The easiest explanation of this may be that the states actually have connections with more than one region. This is especially true of New York, the state with the highest innovation score, which displays fairly strong connections in this analysis with the New England, Mid-Atlantic, and Great Lakes states. I believe that this finding reflects the fact that New York actually serves as a model for states in all three areas. Certainly New York is formally involved in interstate compacts with all three regions, and, if nothing else, enjoys a perfect geographical position from which to carry on relations over such a large area. If the findings concerning New York seem explainable, those concerning California do not. I cannot explain why California loads on Factor V, especially since many of its neighbors load on Factor III. These ambiguous findings concerning New York and California might be merely a reflection of ambiguity in the data. Factor analysis will identify regional groupings in the data only if the regions respond to new programs as a unit, adopting some new ideas with haste and lagging behind on others. Since New York and California consistently lead the country in the adoption of new programs, they may not be members of any cohesive regional group or "league" of states, a fact which may prevent their neat categorization through factor analysis.

There is no accounting at all in this analysis for the behavior of three states: Arizona, Colorado, and Kansas. Both Colorado and Arizona load at the .300 level on Factor III, the one which includes most of the rest of the Rocky Mountain states. Colorado and Nevada both load strongly (.577 and .485 respectively) on a separate factor which was not reported since no other state scored higher than .300 on the factor and its contribution score was only 1.7. The same is true for Kansas which was the only state loading strongly (at .658) on a factor whose contribution score was only 1.9.

Specialized Communications among the States

Our analysis has provided evidence that a continuum exists along which states are distributed, from those which are usually quick to accept innovations to those which are typically reluctant to do so; we also know something about the correlates of innovation and have evidence of regional groupings among the states; but it is not always easy to identify a regional pioneer or to know exactly which states make up each "league" or sub-system of cue-taking and information exchange. Some states seem to have connections with more than one region and may regularly receive cues from states in both groupings. As the American political system has developed, an increasing number of specialized communication systems have been created which cut across traditional regional lines and bring officials from many different regions into contact with each other and with federal and local officials, journalists, academic experts, and administrative consultants.

There are several organizations now in existence such as the Council of State Governments, the Advisory Commission on Intergovernmental Relations, and the recently established Citizen's Conference on State Legislatures whose primary function is to improve communications among the states. Most important of these specialized communications networks are the professional associations of state officials, such as the National Association of State Budget Officers, or the National Association of State Conservation Officers. Associations of this kind were first created late in the nineteenth century and more seem to be forming each year. There were only five formed prior to 1900, but by 1930 there were approximately thirty-one, and by 1966 there were at least eighty-six in existence.[56]

These groups serve two general purposes: first, they are sources of information and policy cues. By organizing conferences or publishing newsletters they bring together officials from all over the country and facilitate the exchange of ideas and knowledge among them, thus increasing the officials' awareness of the latest developments in their field. Second, these associations serve as "occupational contact networks" which expedite the interstate movement or transfer of personnel. Through the efforts of these groups officials become aware of desirable job openings in other states and are able to create professional reputations that extend beyond the borders of their own states.[57]

By rapidly spreading knowledge of new programs among state officials and by facilitating the movement of individuals to jobs in other states, professional associations encourage the development of national standards for the proper administration and control of the services of state government. Just as in other sectors of American life such as the business, the military, and the academic world, as individuals increase their mobility, their role perceptions are likely to change; they are likely to adopt a more cosmopolitan perspective and to cultivate their reputa-

[56] Unpublished memo from the Council of State Governments, Chicago, Illinois.
[57] For a discussion of the role of professional organizations in determining career lines see Fred E. Katz, "Occupational Contact Networks," *Social Forces,* XXXVI (1958), 52–58. Also see Jack Ladinsky, "Occupational Determinants of Geographic Mobility Among Professional Workers," *American Sociological Review,* XXXII (1967), 253–64.

Table 6: Average Elapsed Time of Diffusion in Years
for Innovations in Three Time Periods

Time periods	For all adoptions	First twenty adoptions
1870–1899:	52.3	22.9
1900–1929:	39.6	20.0
1930–1966:	25.6	18.4

tions within a national professional community rather than merely within their own state or agency.[58]

Since general awareness of new developments is achieved much more quickly now than ever before, we would expect that the time which elapses from the first adoption of an innovation by a pioneering state to its complete diffusion throughout all the states would be greatly reduced. Certainly, several recent innovations, such as educational television or state councils on the performing arts, have diffused rapidly. In Table 6 we have measured the average speed of diffusion in years for three periods of time: 1870–99, 1900–29, and 1930–66. The results shown in the first column of this table make it very plain that the speed of diffusion has been constantly increasing as time has passed. This measurement, however, is somewhat misleading. The second column of the table indicates the average number of years it took the first twenty states to adopt the programs in each time period. The same trend towards increased speed of diffusion is evident here, but the differences among the three time periods are much smaller.[59] This evidence suggests that the pioneering states, those with high innovation scores, adopted new programs about as quickly in the early part of this century, prior to the development of many specialized communication links, as they did in the 1960's. The total elapsed time of diffusion, however, has decreased primarily because the laggard states, those with low innovation scores, are now reacting more quickly to pick up new programs adopted by the pioneers. This development results partly from the efforts of the federal government to stimulate state action through grants-in-aid, and partly from the increas-

[58] Merton, *Social Theory.* Also see Alvin W. Gouldner, "Cosmopolitan and Locals: Toward an Analysis of Latent Social Roles," *Administrative Science Quarterly,* II (1957), 281–306 and Harold L. Wilensky, *Intellectuals in Labor Unions* (New York, 1956).

[59] A small portion of the difference between the two columns in Table VI is an artifact of measurement. Since not all the programs in this analysis have been adopted by all forty-eight states, laggard states sometimes remain. As time passes and programs receive widespread acceptance these laggard states slowly fall into line and adopt the programs. Since the programs in the first two time periods have been around longer, they have more likely completed their spread among the states and thus, given our scoring procedure, are also more likely to have a longer period of diffusion.

ing professional development in state government. Both these tendencies seem to have had a larger impact on the behavior of the more parochial states than the more cosmopolitan, pioneering states.

CONCLUSIONS

This essay began as an effort to explain why some states adopt innovations more rapidly than others, but, in order to explain this aspect of American federalism, we have had to make a more extensive investigation of the complex system of social choice by which we are governed. The approach to policy-making which has emerged from our investigation is founded on the perceptions and attitudes of individual state decision-makers. Of course, as I have already mentioned, the theory cannot be fully elaborated or put to a test until data can be gathered directly from legislators, bureaucrats, governors, and other officials in several states, on a comparative basis. Enough evidence has been presented already, however, to make apparent the major theoretical and practical implications of this approach.

The theory presented here directs our attention to the rules for decision employed by policy-makers, rather than to their formal group affiliations or to their relative power or authority, and thus useful explanations of all policy decisions, can be offered not merely of those which generate controversy. Emphasis is placed on those factors which lead to the establishment of parameters or guidelines for decision, not on the groups or interests supporting one policy over another. In Figure 1 the outlines of the diffusion process are depicted as it operates in a single state. There are undoubtedly many other influences on the level of agitation for change than the ones presented here, and many other secondary effects stemming from the enactment of new programs; this simple diagram is only meant to summarize the fundamental process operating in most cases of diffusion. Relationships are characterized by plus and minus signs but no effort has been made to estimate their relative importance in the system.

The process we have been describing is extremely complex; many influences shape decisions to adopt innovations and no two ideas diffuse in exactly the same way. In all cases, however, the likelihood of a state adopting a new program is higher if other states have already adopted the idea. The likelihood becomes higher still if the innovation has been adopted by a state viewed by key decision-makers as a point of legitimate comparison. Decision-makers are likely to adopt new programs, therefore, when they become convinced that their state is relatively deprived, or that some need exists to which other states in their "league" have already responded.

Before states may respond to new programs adopted in other states

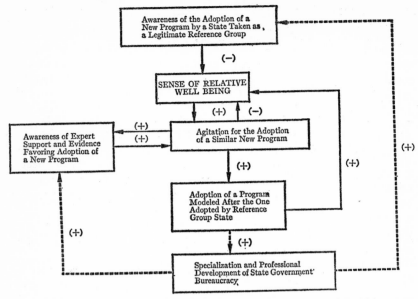

Figure 1. Factors affecting the adoption of innovations*

* Secondary effects depicted by broken lines.

their political leaders must be aware of these developments, so interstate communications are an important factor in the process of diffusion. We have mentioned that many specialized systems of communication among the states have grown up during the last thirty years, mainly through the creation of professional associations of state administrators. These new information networks are spreading into all the states, but even today the isolation of some state capitols from the major cosmopolitan centers of the country is a major obstacle to the adoption of new ideas.[60]

Emerging from this study is the picture of a national system of emulation and competition. The states are grouped into regions based on both geographical contiguity and their place in the specialized set of communication channels through which flow new ideas, information, and policy cues. Through this nationwide system of communications a

[60] See Alan L. Clem's description of the isolation of Pierre, the capitol of South Dakota, in his *Prairie State Politics: Popular Democracy in South Dakota* (Washington, D.C., 1967), p. 137 and Norton E. Long's emphasis on the importance of information sources in his "After the Voting is Over," *Midwest Journal of Political Science* (1962), pp. 183–200. For a general review of communications theory and its application to politics see Richard R. Fagen, *Politics and Communication* (Boston, 1966), especially pp. 34–69, 88–106. Also see Karl W. Deutsch, *The Nerves of Government*, 2nd ed. (New York, 1966), especially pp. 145–256.

set of norms or national standards for proper administration are established. This system links together the centers of research and generation of new ideas, national associations of professional administrators, interest groups, and voluntary associations of all kinds into an increasingly complex network which connects the pioneering states with the more parochial ones. Because of the limitations of the data presently available we can only outline each regional grouping of states, and cannot yet construct an elaborate theory of the interactions among professional associations, federal officials, private interest groups, and political leaders in setting the agenda of politics within a state. Normative questions arise, which cannot be considered here, concerning the responsiveness of this system and the degree to which it is subject to the control of democratic, representative institutions.[61] Much more investigation will be necessary before we can gain a full understanding of this system and its function as a device for controlling the pace and direction of policy development in the American states. Once we know more, it might be possible to prescribe with confidence some changes in the decision-making system, or the creation of some new governmental institutions, which might accelerate or redirect the process of innovation.

[61] Questions of this kind have been raised already in Daniel P. Moynihan, "The Professionalization of Reform," *The Public Interest*, no. 1 (1965), pp. 6–161; Theodore J. Lowi, "The Public Philosophy: Interest Group Liberalism," *American Political Science Review*, LXI (1967), 5–24; and Philip Green, "Science, Government, and the Case of RAND: A Singular Pluralism," *World Politics*, XX (1968), 301–26.

APPENDIX

NOTE: Following are the eighty–eight programs upon which the innovation score is based.

1. Accountants Licensing
2. Advertising Commissions
3. Agricultural Experiment Stations
4. Aid for Roads and Highways
5. Aid to the Blind (Social Security)
6. Aid to Dependent Children (Social Security)
7. Aid to Permanently and Totally Disabled (Social Security)
8. Air Pollution Control
9. Alcoholic Beverage Control
10. Alcoholic Treatment Agencies
11. Anti-Age Discrimination
12. Anti-Injunction Laws
13. Architects Licensing
14. Australian Ballot
15. Automobile Registration
16. Automobile Safety Compact
17. Beauticians Licensing
18. Board of Health
19. Budgeting Standards
20. Child Labor Standards
21. Chiropractors Licensing
22. Cigaret Tax
23. Committee on the Aged
24. Compulsory School Attendance
25. Conservation of Oil and Gas
26. Controlled Access Highways
27. Council on the Arts
28. Court Administrators
29. Debt Limitations
30. Dentists Licensing
31. Direct Primary
32. Education Agencies
33. Education Television
34. Engineers Licensing
35. Equal Pay for Females
36. Fair Housing—Private
37. Fair Housing—Public Housing
38. Fair Housing—Urban Renewal Areas
39. Fair Trade Laws
40. Fish Agency
41. Forest Agency
42. Gasoline Tax

43. Geological Survey
44. Highway Agency
45. Home Rule—Cities
46. Human Relations Commissions
47. Initiative and Referendum
48. Integrated Bar
49. Junior College—Enabling Legislation
50. Juveniles Supervision Compact
51. Labor Agencies
52. Legislative Pre-Planning Agencies
53. Legislative Research Agencies
54. Library Extension System
55. Mental Health Standards Compact
56. Merit System
57. Migratory Labor Committee
58. Minimum Wage Law
59. Normal Schools—Enabling Act
60. Nurses Licensing
61. Old Age Assistance (Social Security)
62. Parking Agencies—Enabling Act for Cities
63. Park System
64. Parolees and Probationers Supervision Compact
65. Pharmacists Licensing
66. Planning Board—State Level
67. Development Agency
68. Police or Highway Patrol
69. Probation Law
70. Public Housing—Enabling Legislation
71. Real Estate Brokers—Licensing
72. Reciprocal Support Law
73. Retainers Agreement
74. Retirement System for State Employees
75. Right to Work Law
76. School for the Deaf
77. Seasonal Agricultural Labor Standards
78. Slaughter House Inspection
79. Soil Conservation Districts—Enabling Legislation
80. Superintendent of Public Instruction
81. Tax Commission
82. Teacher Certification—Elementary
83. Teacher Certification—Secondary
84. Urban Renewal—Enabling Legislation
85. Utility Regulation Commission
86. Welfare Agency
87. Workmen's Compensation
88. Zoning in Cities—Enabling Legislation

Governmental Forms and Planning Functions: The Relation of Organizational Structures to Planning Practice*

DEIL S. WRIGHT

"Forms of government . . . fools contest"—Alexander Pope's pronouncement has formed the fulcrum for many debates weighing the relative merits of structure versus content, process versus substance, and means versus ends. The shape and focus of these debates have ranged from Plato's *Republic* (the earliest known comprehensively planned community) to the recurrent controversy over the optimum positioning of the planning function for effective impact on the policy process. This selection is addressed to the long-standing concern of both the planning profession and political scientists: what is the relationship between structural features of government and the conduct of public programs?

The first section treats descriptively the results of a survey that gathered data on five dimensions dealing with the conduct and content of city planning. The five dimensions are: (1) structure, (2) personnel, (3) performance, (4) perceptions, and (5) preferences of chief executives and local planning directors. With the descriptive findings in hand attention will shift to the explanatory and analytic aspects of structure as it relates to the remaining four dimensions.[1]

RESEARCH ON LOCAL PLANNING

Recent research on planning with a broad-based empirical bent has tended to focus on the personal and professional norms of individuals in or about to enter planning positions. Emphasis has been placed on socialization processes, technical competencies, and personal motivations. Research contexts have ranged from enrollees in planning schools (and the schools' curricula) to on-the-job planners examined by in-depth studies, interviews, or mail questionnaires.[2]

* The author is indebted to several sources of support and assistance in the conduct of this study. Support from the School of City and Regional Planning and the Institute of Environmental Health Studies at the University of North Carolina is gratefully acknowledged. Funds from the National Science Foundation under a Science Development grant to the University of North Carolina permitted the hiring of research assistants for data analysis. The data were originally collected with the partial support of funds from the Graduate College at the University of Iowa.
[1] For a conventional but clearly drawn distinction between descriptive and explanatory (causal) research see Claire Selltiz, *Research Methods in Social Relations*, rev. ed. (New York, 1960), pp. 65–143.
[2] Francine F. Rabinovitz and J. Stanley Pottinger, "Organization for Local Plan-

Two complementary themes appear in the findings of this research. First, a distinct anti-political bias exists among planners. Second, and closely related to the first, is the observation that as professional planning norms become more pervasive there is a consequent atrophy in the planners' capacity to affect public policy. This view is described by Rabinovitz: "If planners avoid the hard [political] choices required, they may begin to find that as respect for their profession grows, its utility as a mechanism for affecting urban development is withering."[3]

The extent to which there is a direct trade-off between political roles and professional planning norms has been challenged, at least implicitly, by Alan Altshuler. Starting with a different substantive focus, a process orientation, and employing contrasting methodology (large-city case studies), Altshuler questions whether planners (and the activity called planning) can ever gain access to objective norms confirming their professional status.[4] Altshuler's reservations stem largely, if not exclusively, from the political content and context of planning. This formulation alters the professionalism versus politics dichotomy by questioning the applicability of the former in view of the latter. This explains why Altshuler's attention is focused more on planners' strategies, planning structure, and policy substance than on socialization, professionalization, and norms.

The main thrust of two recent studies has been an effort to connect elements of the norm-related research with a larger set of organizational and system variables.[5] Professor Rabinovitz explores aspects of planning effectiveness in relation to planner role norms, organizational structure, and political systems features. Professor Ranney posits a technical, rational core at the heart of planning and spells out a varied set of political and governmental variables operative on that core. The research reported here is in the mode initiated by these two authors.

The focus of this essay is on both city planners and municipal chief executives in medium-sized United States cities.[6] Perhaps its most dis-

ning: The Attitudes of Directors," *Journal of the American Institute of Planners,* XXXIII (January, 1967), 27–32 and Francine F. Rabinovitz, "Politics, Personality, and Planning," *Public Administration Review,* XXVII (March, 1967), 18–24, plus references cited in these two articles.

[3] Rabinovitz, "Politics, Personality, and Planning," p. 24.

[4] Alan A. Altshuler, *The City Planning Process: A Political Analysis* (Ithaca: Cornell University Press, 1965), esp. Ch. VII.

[5] Francine F. Rabinovitz, *City Politics and Planning* (New York, 1969), and David C. Ranney, *Planning and Politics in the Metropolis* (Columbus, Ohio, 1969).

[6] The survey was conducted in the spring of 1967 by a graduate seminar at the University of Iowa under the general direction of the author and faculty colleagues. The survey's focus was on cities that had, in 1960, populations of 25,000 to 250,000. The rationale for this size spectrum was both substantive and methodological. On the substantive side we were interested in considering cities in which there is or will be the greatest population growth. We were also interested

tinctive feature is the effort to explore and link simultaneously the responses of chief executives (mayors and city managers) with those of city planners. The underlying rationale for this focus is purely and simply comparative. To gain a better comprehension of where the planner stands in relation to the policy process, it seemed desirable, if not mandatory, to have a criterion group against which to judge the planners' responses. What better comparison group could be found than officials formally positioned to function at the nexus for local policy formulation—municipal chief executives?

Our survey of executives and planners generated approximately a 40 percent response rate, varying with type and size of city. Unfortunately, the number of responses from the executive and planner in the same city (joint responses) was only about half this rate. Both the descriptive and explanatory sections rely on the gross replies which include the joint as well as non-joint responses.[7]

The various aspects of the survey are divided into the five major data dimensions mentioned above. The general outlines of each dimension and its question content are summarized in Table 1. In most cases identical questions were asked of both the chief executive and the planner. In a few instances, however, it was necessary to alter the wording of questions with similar intent in order to recognize the different formal positions of the respondents. In other instances it was desirable to ask questions of one set of respondents that were entirely inappropriate for the other set. These differences will become evident in the subsequent tabular presentations and descriptive discussion.

The rationale for the selection of these data dimensions and research strategy can be briefly summarized. The substantive dimensions fit a Parsonian-type scheme for the analysis of social systems.[8] The existence

---

in avoiding municipal entities which, while presenting great challenges to the capacity of man to plan, pose problems of scale politically, economically, and socially.

We settled for an upper limit on size that would yield a substantial number of returns and make possible comparisons among city size groupings. By omitting cities over 250,000 we excluded only 51 incorporated cities. The 625 cities included in the purview of our interest contained 51 percent of the 80 million people residing in incorporated urban places over 25,000 in 1960.

In retrospect, we probably should have included some cities over 250,000. In the context of the research "moment," however, we opted to spread our limited resources more broadly by sending questionnaires to all municipal executives and planners in 256 cities between 50,000 and 250,000 and to a 50 percent sample of 350 cities with populations between 25,000 and 50,000. In all, we mailed 862 questionnaires to municipal chief executives and planners in 431 cities. The response rate was 42 percent from executives, 36 percent from planners.

[7] Further analysis of the eighty joint (same-city) responses is in progress. Preliminary analysis shows no substantial differences from any of the results presented and discussed in this paper.

[8] Talcott Parsons, *The Social System* (New York, 1951); see also Talcott Parsons, *Structure and Process in Modern Societies* (New York, 1960).

Table 1: Data Set Outline: Chief Executives and Planners

A. Structural Variables

1. Form of city government
2. Type of planning organization structure (independent or executive staff)
3. Planner appointment and removal

B. Personal Variables

1. Age
2. Education
3. Length of residence
4. Prior positions

C. Performance Variables

1. Planning activities performed
2. Executive-planner interaction
3. Planner deviation from prescribed procedures

D. Perceptual-Evaluative Variables

1. Most important planning activity
2. Evaluation of present planning organization structure
3. Primary function of plan commission
4. Evaluation of plan commission accomplishment
5. Influence on planning activities
6. Executive support of planning
7. Planner's support base

E. Preference Variables

1. Who should present planning proposals to the city council
2. Desire for change in planning responsibility
3. Policy orientation of planning
4. Definition of planning

---

of and interaction between social structures (institutional patterns) and personal career (life pattern) variables form the conceptual basis for data dimensions (A) and (B). Variables identified in the performance category (C) are aimed at measuring actions or activities for the specific scenes in which the individual structural interaction occurs. These might be more adequately and accurately described as "behavioral" variables in the less restrictive sense of the term.

Categories (D) and (E) in the outline correspond closely and respectively to Parsons' concepts of cognition and moral evaluation. A more operational and specific elaboration of these dimensions has been made in terms of attitude measurement by employing the frequently used cognitive-affective distinction.[9] The major feature of the former category is

[9] Harry S. Upshaw, "Attitude Measurement," in *Methodology in Social Research,* ed.

the knowledge-awareness-judgment component present in the question stimuli and expected responses. Replies are presumed to be anchored in the rational and deliberative thought structures of the respondents as they perceive and judge real-world phenomena. The affective dimension (preference variables) on the other hand, is intended to elicit the normative or moral orientations of the respondent. The variables attempt to assess desired end-states, aims, and goals of the respondent by posing questions that permit the expression of sentiments about what should or ought to be the character of reality.

EXECUTIVES AND PLANNERS: DESCRIPTIVE COMPARISONS

Structural Variables

The percentage distributions under Form of City Government in Table 2 indicate the relative response rates for the executives and planners by the type of city government. Compared with the nationwide distributions of forms of city government, the two distributions displayed are not radically different from national proportions nor from each other. The comparable national figures for cities of 25,000 to 250,000 are 53 percent for council manager, 36 percent for mayor-council, and 11 percent for commission.[10] The two response distributions slightly over-represent the manager form and under-represent the other two types of city governing structures. The evident but modest bias is introduced because of the greater tendency of respondents in manager-governed cities to reply to mail questionnaires. It bears repeating, however, that the separate distributions are neither grossly misrepresentative nor markedly different from each other.[11]

An important planning-related structural feature of city government is the organizational status of the planning function. While data on several aspects of planning organization have been published they do not

---

Hubert M. Blalock and Ann B. Blalock (New York, 1968), esp. pp. 69–74. For an analogous three-category set dividing actions, cognitions, and values as applied to the planning field see Henry Fagin, "Perspectives on the City," *Public Administration Review*, XXVIII, no. 3 (May–June, 1968), 287–92. It should be noted that Fagin adds a fourth dimension, time, to his analysis.

[10] *Municipal Year Book, 1966* (Chicago, 1966), p. 90.

[11] Data on other political structure characteristics are being collected and merged with these data not only to assess the accuracy of our sample responses, but also for use as explanatory variables. The characteristics include at-large elections, non-partisan elections, and council appointment rather than popular election of the mayor. Other research shows that these "reform" political structures intervene and interfere with the relationship between community social cleavages and aggregate public policy outputs. These structures, it is argued, tend to dampen community conflict. See Robert L. Lineberry and Edmund P. Fowler, "Reformism and Public Policies in American Cities," *American Political Science Review*, LXI (September, 1967), 701–16.

Table 2: Percentage Response Comparisons on Structural Variables for
Municipal Chief Executives and Planning Directors in
Cities of 25,000–250,000

	CHIEF EXECUTIVES (N=180)	PLANNING DIRECTORS (N=155)
	(percentages)	
Form of City Government		
Council Manager	66	61
Mayor-Council	27	32
Commission	7	7
Planning Organization		
Staff Aide to Executive	64	64
Independent Commission	22	32
City Council	8	3
Planner Appointed By		
Chief Executive	68	62
Plan Commission	12	25
Council	11	8
Planner Removed By		
Chief Executive	63	59
Plan Commission	12	23
Council	10	10

appear to be tabulated in summary form. The three remaining data sets
in Table 2 document the predominance of the executive staff status of
the planning function. Regardless of the operational measure or the respondent, roughly three-fifths to two-thirds of the reporting units have
the local executive as the flywheel of the planning motor in city government.[12]

[12] These findings of executive dominance depart markedly from the results of the
recent survey by Rabinovitz and Pottinger. They found only 38 percent of 201
respondents (from a list of AIP members) classifying themselves as responsible
to local chief executives; another 38 percent saw their status as "independent of
the executive." The remaining 24 percent were classified as "combination planning agencies," that is, responsible to both lay boards and the chief executive.
There are at least two reasons for the discrepancy between these two surveys.
First, the sample (or populations) were substantially different. The Rabinovitz-
Pottinger survey circularized 309 names from the membership roster of the
American Institute of Planners. Contrastingly, we circularized chief executives
and the heads of planning agencies in 431 cities. As will become apparent later,
this allowed for responses from the heads of planning agencies who were not
"planners" insofar as AIP membership was concerned. The first difference, then,
was between a sample of *planners* and a sample of *cities*.

Our findings confirm the extent to which municipal governments have taken seriously Robert Walker's advocacy of planning as an executive staff process.[13] We should acknowledge, of course, that executive appointment of the planning director does not guarantee proximity, immediacy, and saliency of planning to the local executive. Although not suffi-

---

The second factor contributing to the differences disclosed by the two surveys is the question format. The Rabinovitz-Pottinger study offered the respondents only two planning structure options:

 A. Responsible to the chief executive.

 B. Independent of the executive, responsible to the city legislature through lay/professional commissioners.

Because of the apparent difficulty in choosing between these two alternatives, a substantial proportion of the planners (24 percent) circled both alternatives, indicating their feeling of responsibility to both the executive and a lay board or commission. A planning survey published in *The Municipal Year Book*, 1965 (pp. 326–37), revealed that out of nearly 700 cities with populations over 25,000 only 18 did *not* have an official planning board or commission.

Our 1967 study posed the planning status question in a somewhat different form. We asked about the organizational position of planning *and* put three options to our respondents, each option accompanied by a small organization chart with lines of authority and advice appropriately drawn. The verbal alternatives accompanying the visual schema were:

 1. Independent activity of the planning commission

 2. Staff-aide to the chief executive

 3. Policy advisor to the city council.

In this context we received higher executive-oriented responses than the former survey. The congruity of proportions between the two types of officials as well as among the three status-related measures (organization, appointment, and removal) tends to confirm our confidence in the results reported in Table 2. Of course, the among-measure similarities could be the result of either response set on the three questions and/or isomorphism between appointive power and formal organizational status.

Fortunately, a third survey provided data for independent checking and validation. These data, mentioned above, are in the *Municipal Year Book*, 1965. In lieu of city-for-city validation of the accuracy of each response we tallied by population size categories the proportions of reporting cities indicating that the planning director is appointed by the local chief executive (whether city manager or mayor). These proportions are:

City Size	Percentage	Number of Reporting Cities
Over 500,000	33	18
250,000–500,000	58	26
100,000–250,000	60	54
50,000–100,000	64	113
25,000–50,000	69	131

These proportions (60–69 percent) are sufficiently close to our survey figures to validate our results and allow us to proceed with reasonable confidence to more detailed discussion and data analysis.

[13] Robert A. Walker, *The Planning Function in Urban Government*, 2nd ed. (Chicago, 1950).

cient in and of itself, executive appointment is definitely the modal pattern for relating planning activities to executive decision processes.

Somewhat less than one-third of the executives and planners report that planning enjoys an "independent" status, a position endorsed, albeit cautiously, by Altshuler.[14] The minority position of the independent commission illustrates the evolution of function without significant change in form. The origins of independent planning commissions can be traced to what Herbert Kaufman has termed the "neutral competence" doctrine of public administration.[15] Implementation of this doctrine took policy and administrative activities in a specified sphere "out of politics" and into the hands of technical specialists, "experts," and the interest groups that were aligned with them.[16] It was against this backdrop and doctrine that Walker argued articulately and persuasively.

Recent political signs and academic commentators seem to suggest that the current function of the independent planning commission is viewed more as a vehicle for concerting power and mobilizing influence *on* public policy rather than the invention and advancement *of* policy.[17] In fulfilling interest aggregation and articulation functions the independent commission appears to have evolved as a substitute for other representational mechanisms. In this role it best characterizes current manifestation of Kaufman's doctrine of representativeness, that is, popular access to influence on policy.[18]

If these observations are accurate and the trend continues, local planning commissions, somewhat like the experimental neighborhood councils and community school boards, may become the rallying points for citizen mobilization. They may even perform political cadre functions analogous to the ward leaders in the heyday of patronage and spoils. Although the content of the rewards has changed greatly, the functional parallels seem strikingly similar. The logical extension and semi-institutionalized status of advocacy planning is in the direction of representation.

Two comments on structural features deserve mention. First, the quantitatively minute role of the local legislative body in overseeing planning activities is evident. This by no means rules out significant council

[14] Altshuler, *City Planning*, pp. 384–91.
[15] Herbert Kaufman, "Emerging Conflicts in the Doctrines of Public Administration," *American Political Science Review*, L (December, 1956), 1057–73.
[16] The practical or operational form in which neutral competence was expressed appeared in the early "model" city planning law: *Standard City Planning Enabling Act*, rev. ed. (Advisory Committee on Planning and U. S. Department of Commerce, 1928).
[17] Altshuler, *City Planning;* Edward C. Banfield, *Political Influence* (New York, 1961).
[18] Herbert Kaufman, "Administrative Decentralization and Political Power," *Public Administration Review*, XXIX (January–February, 1969), 3–15.

influence on executive- or commission-oriented planners or on planning generally. But clearly T. J. Kent's clarion call for legislative directorship of the planning function has made little headway.[19] His call for legislative dominance is reminiscent of Charles Hyneman's articulate advocacy, two decades ago, of legislative (congressional) primacy in the development and overseeing of national policies.[20] Policy-making, it appears from most evidence adduced, is still the prime province of the bureaucracy and the executive, while the concerned citizenry anxiously search for new mechanisms of impact.

The other note on structure involves an inter-level comparison. Elsewhere evidence is presented on the shift to the chief executive of planning functions at the state level.[21] Time trend data at the local level reveal the heavy attrition suffered by the independent commission during a period of nearly twenty years. In 1948 slightly over 50 percent of all full-time planning directors were formally appointed by plan commissions.[22] A 1965 tabulation for 467 cities reporting full-time directors revealed about 18 percent appointed by commissions.[23] Our survey (Table 2) shows executives reporting that 12 percent of the planners are appointed by commissions; planners report 25 percent of their numbers are so designated. The movement toward executive primacy in planning may have run its course in municipal government. The tide at the local level, however, has preceded the breaker waves among the states rushing toward an executive focus for planning. This is perhaps another instance, for good or ill, in which local innovation has preceded adoption at the state level.

Personal Variables

Considerable economy can be exercised in presenting and discussing highlights about the personal characteristics of the two groups of respondents.

Table 3 provides the precise information; here we simply call attention to prominent features and offer a few interpretive comments:

1. there is an obvious generation gap between executives and planners with about 40 percent of the former over fifty and more than half of the latter under forty

[19] T. J. Kent, *The Urban General Plan* (San Francisco, 1964). See also Kenneth L. Kraemer, "New Comprehensiveness in City Planning," *Public Administration Review,* XXVIII (July–August, 1968), 382–89.

[20] Charles Hyneman, *Bureaucracy in a Democracy* (New York, 1950).

[21] See above, Beyle, Seligson, and Wright, "New Directions in State Planning," pp. 14–35.

[22] Frederic N. Cleaveland, "Organization and Administration of Local Planning Agencies," in *Local Planning Administration,* 3rd ed. (International City Manager's Association, Chicago, Ill.: 1959), p. 55.

[23] *Municipal Yearbook,* 1965, pp. 326–37.

Table 3: Percentage Response Comparisons on Personal Variables for
Municipal Chief Executives and Planning Directors in
Cities of 25,000–250,000

	CHIEF EXECUTIVES (N=180)	PLANNING DIRECTORS (N=155)
	(percentages)	
Age		
Over 50	41	12
Under 40	19	53
Education		
B.A. Degree	29	54
Graduate Degree	41	39
Planning Degree		41
Length of Residence in Community		
Four years or less	20	51
Five to eleven years	30	29
Eleven years or more	50	20
Prior Positions Held by Planners		
Planning Consultant		30
City Planning		64
State Planning		19
Federal Planning		6
Engineering		14

2. planners, as a group, are "better" educated than their executive counterparts in terms of percentages holding undergraduate degrees, but about equal proportions of both groups hold graduate degrees (chiefly law in the former group and planning in the latter)

3. less than half of the planners in the medium-sized cities hold a planning degree

4. there is a substantial local-cosmopolitan gap between the executives and planners, although one-fifth of the planners have been residents of the community in which they work for at least ten years

5. there is a moderate to substantial variety in the types of prior positions planners held; while prior city planning experience predominates, many planners have had experience as consultants, state planners, and engineers.

These gross and generalized statements about planners in city governments produce little surprise. We would expect them to be young, mobile, and well educated, with diverse professional experience. The single figure that does signal comment is the low proportion (41 percent) of the planning respondents holding a planning degree. Here we must recall the size of the cities under scrutiny and the historical forces restricting planning education until recent years. It still seems significant, however, that planning activities in most medium-sized cities are under the guidance of "non-planners." These comments are not intended to reflect negatively upon either these persons or their programs. The comments are more appropriately directed to the planning fraternity at large. They reemphasize the substantial number of persons drawn from a wide variety of non-planning backgrounds who are doing planning. The observations are parallel to those made at the state level about the presence of non-planners in planning positions.

Performance Variables

How does the planning function operate? What is it that planners do? What is the configuration of activities that implement planning in these cities and what are the relational and behavioral patterns of the planner in performing these activities?

Three "core" items constitute the nearly universal set of activities for planning in these medium-sized cities (see Table 4). They are zoning, comprehensive (master) planning, and technical or special studies. Only the last activity shows a modest discrepancy between the two respondent types. The difference could arise from a sampling error or it could be traced to the planner's greater awareness of the performance and significance of this ad hoc intelligence activity.

A larger percentage-point difference appears for capital improvements programming. The difference exceeds sampling error and evidently arises from the contrast in perspective of the executives and planners. Planners report this assigned responsibility more often than the chief executives with whom they serve. Could it be that the capital improvements activity is the one most oriented to policy of all planning operations? Could it also be that planners tend to inflate the extent of their responsibilities in this activity?

Affirmative responses to these two questions provide one rationale for explaining the lower proportion of chief executives acknowledging planner responsibility for capital improvements programming. An alternate explanation for the divergent proportions is to attribute inaccurately low responses to the chief executives. While it is possible that executives overlook or are unaware of the location of capital improvements programming, it seems less likely than over-reporting on the part of planners.

A third and most probable explanation is the existence of slightly varying response sets by the two groups of officials. Planners may have a clearer but broader definition of what constitutes capital improvements

Table 4: Percentage Response Comparisons on Performance Variables for
Municipal Chief Executives and Planning Directors in
Cities of 25,000–250,000

	CHIEF EXECUTIVES (N=180)	PLANNING DIRECTORS (N=155)
	(percentages)	
Major Activities Performed by the Planning Agency		
Zoning	93	96
Comprehensive Plan	93	99
Technical Surveys & Special Studies	82	94
Capital Improvements Programs	58	77
Street-Highway Location	59	62
Urban Renewal	39	46
Traffic	41	11
Public Housing	21	17
Contact Between Planner and:		
Chief Executive—Daily	60	65
City Council—Daily		3
—Weekly		48
Planning Commission—Daily		2
—Weekly		24
Other Departments—Daily		35
—Weekly		21
Planner Deviation from Prescribed Procedures		
Often—Frequently		26
Occasionally		54
Seldom—Never		19

programming than is the case for executives. Planners may be more attuned to the coordinative-evaluative function of this particular activity whereas the executive sees innovative-political elements in the determination of whose streets are paved.[24]

One other notable discrepancy occurs in Table 4, i.e., for traffic-related activities. Two chief executives out of five report traffic matters as a responsibility of their planning agencies; only one planner in ten so reports. The difference is not easily explained but probably springs from the same source as the last one suggested above for capital improve-

[24] For the distinction between evaluative and innovative planning, see Altshuler, *City Planning*, pp. 333–53. For a case study of the extent to which capital improvement plans are subject to change by political considerations see William H. Brown, Jr. and Charles E. Gilbert, "Capital Programming in Philadelphia: A Study of Long-Range Planning," *American Political Science Review*, LIV (September, 1960), 659–68.

ments, namely, the differential significance or awareness levels between the two types of officials.

Moderate emphasis has been placed on the reported differences in activities undertaken by the planning agencies in these cities. Overriding the two notable contrasts, however, is a high degree of congruity in the responses for the other planning activities. Indeed, the dominant pattern for these activities as well as for several other sectors of the survey is the substantial similarity between the executive and planner responses.

This similarity is present for the one other comparison question reported in Table 4, namely, the frequency of daily contact between the planner and the executive. Both planners and executives report daily contact in about equal proportions. They report contact (face-to-face) daily in nearly two-thirds of the cities. The mere fact of contact is a weak reed on which to attach inferences about the significance of the contact or the content of the exchange. It is not easy however, to infer influence in the absence of contact. If we treat contact as a measure of proximity and involvement rather than influence, then the data support the conclusion that planners are close satellites in the orbits around executive decision processes.

Furthermore, from the planner's performance or interaction standpoint, the executive is the dominant "relevant other" among municipal agencies and officials. The planners report daily contact with other departments in only about one-third of the cities and daily contact with councilmen or planning commissioners in less than 5 percent of the cases. To the extent that an "executive centered coalition" exists in these cities, it seems reasonable to suggest that the local planner is probably a part of it.[25] Conclusive evidence on the point, however, would require more extensive performance and perceptual data than we gathered in our survey.

In addition to the activities and the interactions of the local planner we were also interested in self-assessment of the degree to which planner performance is routinized or non-routinized. The focal aspect of our inquiry can be stated in organization theory terms expressed by March and Simon in their discussion of programmed versus non-programmed decision-making.[26] We queried the planner respondents on the frequency with which they found it necessary to depart from established or prescribed procedures in order to do a more effective job. The frequency of deviation was taken as a measure of the presence of non-programmed or non-routinized action by the planner.

[25] The presence of an executive-centered coalition in American communities (or New Haven, Connecticut at least) is developed in Robert A. Dahl, *Who Governs?* (New Haven, 1961).

[26] James G. March and Herbert A. Simon, *Organizations* (New York, 1958).

The marginal distribution reported at the bottom of Table 4 lends support to the hypothesis that planning behavior for most planners involves considerable non-programmed action. Less than one-fifth of the planners report that they seldom or never depart from fixed patterns or routines in performing their jobs. This relatively small fraction pursues planning strictly "by the book." A slightly larger fraction, about one-fourth, indicates rather regular non-programmed performance. More than half of the planners, however, state that their deviation from set routines occurs with occasional or moderate frequency.

Planner behavior, as perceived and reported by the planner himself, tends to include a substantial non-programmed activity. Given the nature of the planning function and the specific activities for implementing it, this is not very surprising. On *a priori* grounds one might have expected even less programmed behavior. Since the concept of programmed behavior has seldom been measured and comparative data are not available, we limit our comments to a few speculative questions:

Is planning accomplishment related to non-programmed planner behavior?

Is the tendency toward programmed behavior essentially the same as bureaucratic or rule-oriented behavior?

Is non-programmed behavior the equivalent of policy-oriented, innovative, activist planner behavior?

Are there significant differences between real and reported non-programmed behavior, that is, between objective, researcher-defined non-routine action and subjective, respondent-perceived non-prescribed performance?

Perceptual-Evaluative Variables

The discussion of programmed behavior is related to the last question above insofar as it raises the matter of perceptions. The respondent was asked to "see through" his actions and to offer a judgment about them. In this section we expand on this cognition-judgmental aspect by presenting and discussing not only respondent perceptions but also respondent evaluations of planning activities, functions, structure, and achievement.

Among the several planning activities previously identified, comprehensive planning was ranked as the most important by both executives and planners. Table 5 indicates, however, a noteworthy difference in proportions. Nearly two-thirds of the planners rate it first; less than half of the executives give it top billing. This inter-official difference is substantial and in accord with advance expectations. Planners, more than political executives, could be expected to rank high the goal-setting function im-

Table 5: Percentage Response Comparisons on Perceptual-Evaluative Variables for Municipal Chief Executives and Planning Directors in Cities of 25,000–250,000

	CHIEF EXECUTIVES (N=180)	PLANNING DIRECTORS (N=155)
	(percentages)	
Most Important Planning Activity		
1st Choice: Comprehensive Plan	46	65
Zoning	31	21
Urban Renewal	8	5
2nd Choice: Comprehensive Plan	29	24
Zoning	22	21
Urban Renewal	4	8
Capital Improvements	14	24
Special Studies	15	15
Evaluation of Existing Planning Structure		
Excellent	18	12
Very good	35	30
Good	27	30
Fair	9	21
Poor	5	6
*Planning Commission Primary Function**		
Plan Formulation (Goal Setting)	53	64
Zoning-Related (Implementation)	39	30
Citizen Representation (Mobilization)	22	34
Evaluation of Plan Commission Accomplishment		
Very High—High	50	43
Moderate	35	43
Low—Very Low	6	11
Estimated Influence on Planning		
Strong	40	46
Moderate	39	45
Some or Little	17	6
Executive Support for Planning		
Primary	56	
Secondary	35	
Limited	8	
*Planner Support on Controversial Proposals**		
Chief Executive		43
Plan Commission		50
City Council		12

* More than one response alternative could be designated.

plicit in comprehensive planning. Executives, more attuned to the art of the possible and schooled in the virtues of compromise, would be less goal-oriented and more concerned with implementation and bargaining.

If selection of comprehensive planning does measure the importance of goals to the respondent, then 46 percent of the executives taking this option represents possibly the most noteworthy figure in the table. The prominence of explicit goals to political executives is not one of the characteristics usually attributed to such officials in either journalistic or scholarly literature. Quite to the contrary, most writing tends to emphasize that executives bargain, mediate, and compromise, roles with emphasis on short run considerations and immediate results rather than longer range goals and deferred accomplishments.[27] The other striking feature about planning activities is the similarity of the proportions for the other activities. This is the first of several demonstrations of congruity in perceptions and evaluations of planners and executives.

A shift in focus from planning activities to planning structures and functions offers additional points for comparison of executive and planner perceptions-evaluations. The two groups, for example, show only modest variations in their respective evaluations of existing organizational arrangements for planning. Dissatisfaction with planning structure, as represented by "fair" and "poor" responses, is distinctly a minority opinion. There seems to be little sentiment to support a second "organizational revolution" that would reverse the Walker-inspired shift which put planning predominately in the hands of chief executives.

One result of the shift toward the executive was not to abolish planning commissions but to leave them in existence, presumably to perform a different function. The question is: What function? To explore this question we posited three functions a commission might fulfill: goal setting (plan formulation), implementation (zoning-related), and mobilization (citizen representation). Both groups of officials were asked to designate one primary function but were allowed to designate more than one if they felt it necessary. The plan formulation (goal-setting) function was selected by a majority of both groups. This finding supports the thesis that commissions are viewed as vehicles for taking the longer, broader outlook on planning matters.

Significant segments of both groups (around one-third) see implementation as the most important function.

But, representation also constitutes an important commission function, as viewed by executives and by planners. The recognition given to this citizen mobilization aspect of the commission's role may be a precursor of larger things to come. As advocacy planning becomes an extensive and established feature of the municipal landscape we might expect in-

[27] Altshuler, *City Planning;* Dahl, *Who Governs;* Anthony Downs, *Inside Bureaucracy* (Boston, 1967); G. L. S. Shackle, *Decision, Order, and Time in Human Affairs* (Cambridge, England, 1961).

creased awareness of the representational role in planning. The process of advocacy could logically become a part of the planning commission.

Other evidence reveals the planning commission's advisory role insofar as its present functions are concerned. Goal setting and implementation are decision-oriented functions; they both have what the economists term "product effects" and what political scientists currently and fashionably label as "outputs."[28] The representational function, in contrast, is a process rather than a product oriented activity; it relates to inputs more than to outputs. The process or input sector of the local political system appears to offer the planning commission the best opportunity for greatest operational impact.

Any effort to shift the role and function of the planning commission will start from a base of substantial satisfaction not only with the existing structure (see above) but also from a similar evaluation of the commission's actual accomplishment. Only about 10 percent or less of the officials judge commission achievement as low or very low. Obstacles to further change are likely to arise less out of deep-seated opposition to proposed reforms but more from a preponderance of semi-satisfaction and inertia.

The discussion of perceptions has centered on planning activities, structure, and functions. We now turn to a topic nearer to the dynamics of the planning process, i.e., matters of influence and support. Executives and planners who estimate their influence on planning operations as "strong" are not a majority, although in both cases they hold a minute plurality over their respective colleagues who see themselves as holding moderate sway over the paths that local planning pursues.

One intriguing question raised by these data can perhaps best be expressed in a general formulation: Do executive-planner relationships tend toward a zero-sum game pattern or are these two-person relationships better characterized by an open system model in which the existence of "slack" allows for the introduction of side payments.[29] In other words, if the chief executive exerts strong influence over local planning does this mean that the local planning director exerts less (a zero-sum pattern)? The open system model would fit a situation in which both the executive and planner exerted strong influences on planning. Operation-

[28] A good discussion, by an economist, of the distinction between product effects and process effects can be found in Jesse Burkhead, *Government Budgeting* (New York, 1956), pp. 69–70. Studies by political scientists (and some economists) in the output genre are too numerous to cite. One of the most recent is Ira Sharkansky, *Spending in the American States* (Skokie, Ill., 1968).

[29] Richard M. Cyert and James G. March, *A Behavioral Theory of the Firm* (Englewood Cliffs, N.J., 1963); a brief discussion of the zero-sum problem in organizations appears in Arnold S. Tannenbaum, *The Social Psychology of Work Groups* (Belmont, Cal., 1967) and in William A. Gamson, *Power and Discontent* (Homewood, Ill., 1968).

ally this could be explored by examining whether "strong influence" executives are associated with "strong influence" planners. If the two are positively related then some doubt is cast on the zero-sum model.

We probed perceptions of support for planning from the separate positions of our two types of respondents. We assumed a high degree of general support by the planner for planning proposals. Otherwise some awkward or embarrassing queries might have been required. But executive support for planning was a crucial feature worthy of exploration. Our concern centered around the planners' perceived locus of support when "hot" planning issues arose. Who does the planner, in controversial situations, see as his chief basis of support? The response alternatives were couched in institutional terms, i.e., plan commission, chief executive, and city council.

While chief executives feel a primary obligation to support planning in more than half of the responding cases, from the planner's perspective this support level is not quite reciprocated, for 43 percent of the planners indicated executive support for volatile planning issues. Half of the planners, however, see the plan commission as a firmer political backstop than the executive. One-third (33 percent) mention the plan commission alone and one-sixth (17 percent) mention the commission in combination with the executive, the city council, or other actor. Only 12 percent mention the city council while less than half of this group designate the council as the single primary support base.

These results suggest that the planner is caught in institutional cross-fire between chief executives and planning commissions. The secular movement toward executive-centered planning has been extensively and solidly sold and executives see planning as a general function for which they have an important responsibility. But from the planner's perspective and institutional position the vestiges of independence as exemplified in a commission orientation still holds an honorable heritage.

The heritage is not only honorable but highly practical and politic. The shifting personnel and preferences among municipal executives dispose the planner to hedge his bets in terms of institutional support. The striking feature about these data is the extent to which local legislative support fails to develop or is extensively discounted by the planner. The same issue, with strongly similar results, persists at the state level. One need not concede the extremities of all points argued by T. J. Kent for legislative-oriented planning to admit that the reservoir of legislative power holds untapped support potential. Cultivation of city council support on hard issues would not be an easy matter or an unmixed blessing. Council support could compel direct trade-offs with plan commission support.

These data partially clarify the direction in which planning in the local community could go. They also offer selected perspectives on the present status of the structure, function, and support mechanisms for planning. But the results do not disclose much about how planning came to its present status. The future-oriented focus of planning does urge that some attention be given to where planning might be going and explore some predictive concerns. For observations on this matter we move to a discussion of preference variables, i.e., what respondents think the planning process ought to be like.

PREFERENCE VARIABLES

Four features of executive and planner preferences were considered in this survey. They can be summarized in the form of four questions:

1. Who should present planning proposals to the city council?

2. Should there be any change in the planning responsibilities exercised by the respondent groups?

3. How policy oriented should planning be?

4. Which one of three contrasting definitions of planning do the respondents prefer?

The first two questions deal with preferred distributions of roles in the planning process. Their process focus is evident in the character of both inquiries. Who should play the lead role in the formal "selling" of planning proposals to the local legislative body? Should executive or planner responsibility for planning be altered upward or downward? The last two questions, in contrast to the first two, center on the intrinsic content or character of the planning function. Responses were elicited on what planning is (denotative definition) and on the preferred degree of policy orientation (connotative implications).

Inspection of the tabulations in Table 6 leads to a single observation. There are striking similarities in the preferences of executives and planners on both the process and content dimensions of planning. Roughly half of each of the two groups of officials think the planner alone should present planning proposals to the city council and at least two-thirds think the planner should be involved in such presentations either alone or in conjunction with other officials. More than three-fourths of each group feel no changes should be made in their respective planning responsibilities. Clearly the planning director is the preferred leader for fulfilling the presentational role on planning proposals. In addition, only small segments of executives or planners express preferences for change in the allocation of planning roles.

On the content dimension of planning a majority believes that planning should be strongly policy oriented and two-thirds of both groups prefer a definition of planning that emphasizes a combined physical environment-economic development focus. About one-third of the planners

Table 6: Percentage Response Comparisons on Preference Variables for
Municipal Chief Executives and Planning Directors in
Cities of 25,000–250,000

	CHIEF EXECUTIVES (N=180)	PLANNING DIRECTORS (N=155)
	(percentages)	
Who Should Present Planning Proposals to the City Council		
Planner	46	55
Planner Plus Others	21	16
Plan Commission	14	14
Chief Executive	17	14
Desire For Change in Planning Responsibilities		
More Responsibility	13	17
No Change in Responsibility	79	76
Less Responsibility	6	3
How Policy Oriented Should Planning Be		
Strongly	55	63
Moderately	33	31
Slightly	8	4
Definition of Planning		
Physical (only)	6	2
Physical-Economic	68	66
Human Needs	24	32

and one-fourth of the executives define planning as centrally concerned
with human or social policy issues. Given the relative recency of the elevation of "people problems" to the center of the public policy stage, the
last proportions cited could be interpreted as showing reasonable responsiveness to some of the new scenery in which planning operates. Whether
this responsiveness is adequate in either an absolute or relative sense
cannot be ascertained objectively from these data and findings. But we
can conclude that both municipal chief executives and planners exhibit
notable concern for the policy relevance of planning and for its growing
social policy elements.

Transcending specific proportions in the various distributions, let us
consider possible explanations for the congruence of the preferences of
planning directors and chief executives. Explanations at three levels of

analysis are suggested: (1) community characteristics; (2) political structures; and (3) professionalization of the planning function.

The importance of the economic, social, demographic, and other city attributes may contribute in important ways to fostering common response patterns among these officials. In its crudest form this explanatory approach would reduce to a kind of ecological determinism. We avoid such extreme claims but do hypothesize that several community constraints contribute to narrowing the response limits of similarly situated officials. One example of such a community constraint may well be the size limits we originally imposed, perhaps inadvisedly, on the scope of our interest. Cities having between 25,000 and 250,000 people simply may not exhibit the variability we might expect. Recent findings on community success in securing poverty program funds show that city size, together with heterogeneity, age (of the city), and community need, are positively related to funds received.[30] It is entirely possible, if not highly probable, that the structures and functions of planning as well as the perspectives and preferences of local officials are affected by similar community environmental constraints.

Political structures are a second category of factors contributing to the nearly identical responses. This is a broad, inclusive category and is not restricted to formal political characteristics such as the form of city government or type of elections (partisan or non-partisan, at large or ward). It encompasses patterns of influence in the community, political party patterns, citizen participation, interest group activities, and associated characteristics. Much recent literature asserts that political factors explain only small variations in public policies (expenditures) in comparison with economic and social variables.[31] When the variables to be explained are attitudes and perceptions, however, there is evidence to suggest the importance of some political structure variables.[32]

What relevance do these findings have to the planner-executive responses? Superficially the convergence of response patterns appears to confirm the limited role of political structure variables, since there are presumably great variations politically among these cities. It is important to recall, however, that two contrasting types of variation are under discussion here. One is inter-unit variation; the other—the one central to this discussion—is inter-official variation in which the same units, essentially, are involved. It is the former rather than the latter type of variation where the explanatory power of political variables has been questioned.

[30] Michael Aiken and Robert R. Alford, *Community Structure and Mobilization: The Case of the War on Poverty* (Madison, Wisc., October, 1968).

[31] Thomas R. Dye, *Politics, Economics and the Public: Policy Outcomes in the American States* (Skokie, Ill., 1966).

[32] Deil S. Wright, "Executive Leadership in State Administration," *Midwest Journal of Political Science*, XI (February, 1967), 1–26.

But within a given city, where the political structures are identical for both executives and planners, we might anticipate relatively small variations in the perspectives of these two types of officials.

Political structures, however, may be only necessary, but not sufficient conditions to foster similar executive-planner perspectives and preferences. We suggest that this is probably the case and that the sufficient conditions are embedded in the third category of explanatory factors, planning professionalization. As employed here, this term does not refer to the personal attributes of individuals but to the common operations, norms, and expectations surrounding the planning function in local government. This accretion of activities and accumulation of outlooks has led to a broad based and common understanding about a wide range of planning-related matters. This "planning core" is sufficiently clear and concrete, we submit, that it transcends the boundaries of formal position in the municipal hierarchy and is reflected in the many parallel response patterns of the chief executives and the planners.

FORMAL STRUCTURE AND PLANNING DIMENSIONS

The perennial problem of structural arrangements for planning has usually been framed in a qualitative and categorical form. In a recent review of arguments about planning organization, it was observed that: "Even with little data on the planning organization question it is clear that the structural arrangements for the planning function are of significance."[33] Later in the discussion, however, the same author comes to a more cautious conclusion:

Too much emphasis must not be placed on the importance of planning institutions without considering other variables. We cannot conclude from this analysis, however, that the organization of the planning agency is an unimportant aspect of planning's governmental context.[34]

Rabinovitz and Pottinger suggested some of the "other variables" but they were necessarily imprecise as to what variables because of the heavy personal focus of their survey. They conclude with a statement and a criticism about structure.

Both those favoring independent commissions and those favoring staff departments may have overestimated the capacity of institutional form to assist the political effectiveness of city planning. And, both seem to have underestimated the complexity of the task of structural invention at a time when cities exhibit an enormous range of characteristics. Thus both promoters and critics have failed to allow for multiformity in devising new planning institutions.[35]

[33] Ranney, *Planning and Politics*, p. 46.
[34] Ranney, *Planning and Politics*, p. 60.
[35] Rabinovitz and Pottinger, "Organization," p. 31.

It is difficult to disagree with statements arguing that institutional arrangements do not affect the political effectiveness of planning in an invariant way. The argument parallels that of Herbert W. Starick who contends that the key to the planner's political effectiveness lies not with structural arrangements but with the exposure of the planner and the chief executive to each other's tasks.[36]

There has been an unfortunate tendency to couch debates on structure in terms of "significance," "importance," "effectiveness," and other categorical expressions. The latitude left for interpretations is great and the precision small. The definition and measurement of criterion variables such as effectiveness is usually so impressionistic that a high component of subjectivity is guaranteed. The purpose here is to reduce the tendency toward categorical conclusiveness. We pursue this aim in accordance with the previously specified objective of explanation. Our purpose is best served by considering the degree or extent of association between structural forms and the several planning dimensions.

The data analysis is chiefly in the form of bivariate contingency tables that have been condensed for presentation purposes. Two separate but interacting structural features are employed as independent and control variables: (1) type of planning organization (executive staff or independent commission), and (2) form of city government (council-manager or mayor-council). Table 7 presents percentages from cross-tabulations of planning organization and planning variables for both chief executives and planning directors. Table 8 provides a similar presentation for planning directors with the form of city government remaining constant.

Personal Variables

The individual attributes of both chief executives and planning directors differ with the planning organization. Cities with independent planning agencies tend to have older executives and directors who tend to reside in their respective communities longer than the executives or directors in staff-aide cities. In addition, chief executives in cities with executive-oriented planning agencies tend to be better educated. Obviously, the type of planning organization does not "cause" the age, education, or the mobility of a city's chief executive. What is reflected in these associations is the close connection between the executive type of planning organization and the form of city government, namely, the council-manager plan. For example, four-fifths of the council-manager cities have executive staff planning agencies whereas less than half of the mayor-council cities have this type of planning structure (see the number of cases at the top of Table 8). This strong association suggests the

[36] Herbert W. Starick, "Strive for Better Planner-Administrator Relations," *Public Management*, L, no. 6 (June, 1965), 139.

need to hold constant or control for the effect of form of government when considering the impact of planning organization.

The connection between personal attributes and planning directors holds greater interest and more probable interconnection. The direction of the associations suggest the presence of recruitment patterns that result in older and less mobile planning directors under the independent commission arrangement. This relationship holds for the two contrasting forms of city government (Table 8). But the most striking pattern emerges on the planning degree variable. A slight and non-significant relationship appears in Table 7 but Table 8 shows a higher proportion of directors with planning degrees in a staff capacity in manager cities and in independent commissions under mayor-council governments. It is still not certain that personal attributes can be utilized to measure differences in planning orientations such as the contrast between the "bureaucrat" and the "zealot" or the "local" and the "cosmopolitan."[37]

Performance Variables

A single strong association stands out in the performance sector. The duties and activities actually assigned to planning agencies in these cities show little variation by planning structure irrespective of official. The one performance exception involves Starick's "mutual exposure to each others' tasks," i.e., daily contact between the planner and the chief executive. The association, for planning directors at least, is stronger than any other relationship reported in Table 7. This is not the case for chief executives, where the difference runs in the expected direction but is modest and not significant. For directors, executive-planner interaction is strongly influenced by planning organization independent of the form of government. The executive staff arrangement produces higher interchange to about the same extent in both city-manager and mayor-council municipalities (Table 8).

Perceptual-Evaluative Variables

For chief executives three perceptual-evaluative variables have significant associations with planning organization. Executives with the staff pattern rank comprehensive planning higher and zoning lower than executives in cities with independent commissions. This finding is complemented by the direction but not the significance of the functions of the

---

[37] Downs, *Inside Bureaucracy*, esp. Chapter 9, 88–111, in which five types of officials are identified: climbers, conservers, advocates, zealots, and statesmen. Landmark articles on the distinction between cosmopolitans and locals are Alvin W. Gouldner, "Cosmopolitans and Locals: Toward an Analysis of Latent Social Roles, I, II," *Administrative Science Quarterly*, II (December, 1957 and March, 1958), 281–306 and 444–80. See also Norman Beckman, "The Planner as a Bureaucrat," *Journal of the American Institute of Planners*, XIX, no. 4 (November, 1964), 323–27.

Table 7: Planning-Related Variables by Type of Planning Organization
for Chief Executives and Planning Directors in
Cities of 25,000–250,000

PLANNING DIMENSIONS AND VARIABLES	CHIEF EXECUTIVES Type of Planning Organization			PLANNING DIRECTORS Type of Planning Organization		
	Executive	Independent	Tau[a]	Executive	Independent	Tau[a]
	(N=120)	(N=53)		(N=101)	(N=55)	
	(percentages)			(percentages)		
Personal						
Age: over 47 (under 37)[b]	46	53	−.12**	52	36	−.17**
Education:						
Graduate Degree	48	36	−.13**	39	40	
Planning Degree				40	47	
Residence:						
Ten or More Years	44	62	.20**	21	38	.19**
Performance						
Activities Performed:						
Zoning	97	94		97	93	
Urban Renewal	37	42		46	46	
Comprehensive Planning	95	100		98	100	
Capital Improvements	58	57		78	74	
Site Selection	54	62		69	71	
Surveys	86	87		92	96	
Street Location	58	64		65	58	
Public Housing	16	26	−.09*	17	16	
Traffic	43	38		9	16	
Contact With Planner (Chief Executive)[b]						
Daily	63	56		83	36	.44**
Planner Deviation from Prescribed Procedure:						
Often				24	30	
Perceptual-Evaluative						
Most Important Activity:						
Zoning	32	46		23	23	
Comprehensive Planning	58	46	−.12**	71	71	
Primary Function of Planning Commission:						
Zoning	41	50		39	26	.12*
Plan Formulation	50	69	−.16**	59	85	−.25**
Citizen Representation	26	13	.11*	41	22	.18**

Table 7 (*continued*)

PLANNING DIMENSIONS AND VARIABLES	CHIEF EXECUTIVES Type of Planning Organization			PLANNING DIRECTORS Type of Planning Organization		
	Executive	Independent	Tau[a]	Executive	Independent	Tau[a]
	(N=120)	(N=53)		(N=101)	(N=55)	
		(percentages)			(percentages)	
Evaluation of Planning Structure:						
Excellent or Very Good	56	59		42	41	
Plan Commission Accomplishment:						
High-Very High	52	72	−.17**	41	49	
Executive Support of Planning:						
Primary	57	58				
Influence on Planning:						
Strong	42	40		50	46	
Support for Planner on Controversial Proposals:						
Executive				61	27	.31**
Plan Commission				50	67	−.15**
Presentation of Planning Proposal to Council by:						
Executive	38	21	.14**			
Planner	70	71				
Preference						
Who Should Present Plan Proposals:						
Executive	39	21	.15**	27	20	
Planner	71	66		75	66	.09*
Change in Planning Responsibility:						
Yes, More	6	24	−.14**	20	15	
Policy Orientation of Planning:						
Strong	61	51		64	65	
Definition of Planning:						
Human Needs	21	27		36	24	.11*

[a] Kendall's Tau is a measure of the relationship between variables. See Sidney Siegal, *Nonparametric Statistics for the Behavioral Sciences* (New York, 1956), pp. 213–29.

[b] The portions of the Table stubs in parentheses refer to planning director variables.

* Indicates statistical significance at the .05 level of confidence.

** Indicates statistical significance at least at the .01 level of confidence.

Table 8: Planning-Related Variables by Type of Planning Organization
by Form of Municipal Government for Planning Directors in
U. S. Cities of 25,000 to 250,000

PLANNING DIMENSIONS AND VARIABLES	FORM OF MUNICIPAL GOVERNMENT					
	COUNCIL—MANAGER Type of Planning Organization			MAYOR—COUNCIL OR COMMISSION Type of Planning Organization		
	Execu-tive	Inde-pendent	Tau[a]	Execu-tive	Inde-pendent	Tau[a]
	(N=74)	(N=22) (percentages)		(N=27)	(N=33) (percentages)	
Personal						
Age: under 37	47	32	−.16**	63	39	−.21**
Education:						
Graduate Degree	35	36		50	42	
Planning Degree	44	36		30	54	−.23**
Residence:						
10 or more years	19	46	.18**	26	33	
Performance						
Activities Performed:						
Zoning	99	96		93	91	
Urban Renewal	46	36		44	52	
Comprehensive Planning	99	100		96	100	
Capital Improvements	76	64		85	82	
Site Selection	68	68		74	73	
Surveys	93	96		89	97	
Street Location	66	64		63	54	
Public Housing	15	14		22	18	
Traffic	8	5		11	24	
Contact with Chief Executive: Daily	83	36	.34**	82	36	.47**
Planner Deviation From Prescribed Procedures: Often	24	24		22	33	
Perceptual-Evaluation						
Most Important Activity:						
Zoning	20	24		33	23	
Comprehensive Plan	77	71		52	71	−.17*

Table 8 (*continued*)

PLANNING DIMENSIONS AND VARIABLES	FORM OF MUNICIPAL GOVERNMENT					
	COUNCIL—MANAGER			MAYOR—COUNCIL OR COMMISSION		
	Type of Planning Organization			Type of Planning Organization		
	Executive	Inde-pendent	Tau[a]	Executive	Inde-pendent	Tau[a]
	(N=74)	(N=22)		(N=27)	(N=33)	
	(percentages)			(percentages)		
Influence on Planning:						
Strong	51	36	.12*	46	52	
Primary Function of Plan Commission:						
Plan Formulation	57	76	−.14*	65	91	−.25**
Citizen Representation	51	29	.16**	13	18	
Zoning	39	10	.21**	39	36	
Evaluation of Planning Structure:						
Excellent or Very Good	40	43		50	39	
Plan Commission Accomplishment:						
High-Very High	44	40		32	54	−.24**
Support for Planner on Controversial Proposals:						
Executive	61	21	.28**	62	31	.30**
Plan Commission	53	53		42	76	−.33**
Preference						
Who Should Present Planning Proposals:						
Executive	32	14	.13*	15	24	
Planner	73	73		82	61	.21**
Change in Planning Responsibility:						
Yes, More	17	14		29	16	
Policy Orientation of Planning: Strong	67	64		58	67	
Definition of Planning:						
Human Needs	36	18	.12*	37	27	.15*

[a] Kendall's Tau is a measure of the relationship between variables.
* Indicates statistical significance at the .05 level of confidence.
** Indicates statistical significance at least at the .01 level of confidence.

planning commission. Executives with the staff arrangement perceive the commission less as a formulator of goals (plans) and more as a body to secure citizen representation. Among executives with independent commissions the reverse prevails.

There is practically no difference in the evaluations of the two executive groups concerning the existing organizational arrangements for planning. In both, the majority judges present performance as excellent or very good. When executives are queried specifically on the achievements of the planning commission a notable difference can be seen. A higher proportion of executives with an independent commission than with the staff organization rate commission achievement as high or very high. Executives with the staff organizational form harbor more doubts about the role and results of planning commissions in their cities. This is not too surprising and is in accordance with behavioral research findings that lesser significance (power, attention, prominence) contributes to greater role ambiguity.[38]

Some indication of executive prominence in the planning process is obtained from percentages of chief executives presenting planning proposals to the council. The staff form disposes the chief executive toward substantially greater involvement than does the independent commission arrangement. However, a majority of executives under both forms senses primary responsibility for supporting planning. In addition, there is no perceived difference in the influence of these executives on planning; about 40 percent of the executives under both organizational forms assess their influence as strong.

The findings on executives' perceptions and evaluations in relation to planning organization may be summarized in the form of a paradox. Process characteristics such as executive support, executive influence, evaluation of structure, and presentational roles are seldom related to the form of the organization. Differences dependent on planning organization are notable for variables relating to content or substantive features, e.g., important activities, plan commission function, and commission accomplishment. For executive perceptions, then, planning organization makes a difference in content or results.

When we look at planner perceptions the picture is clouded. There are significant relationships for only two variables: (1) the functions of the planning commission and (2) locus of support for controversial proposals. The former represents a content variable, the latter a process variable. The type of planning arrangement does make a difference for executives; it makes less of a difference in the perceptions of planning

---

[38] Robert L. Kahn et al., *Organizational Stress: Studies in Role Conflict and Ambiguity* (New York, 1964).

directors who, more than chief executives, are concerned with procedures and processes.

Like the chief executives, planning directors in staff agencies see a substantially lesser role for the plan commission in plan formulation. No direct measures are available to determine whether or not the executive-oriented plans are more policy oriented but the nature of the political backstopping perceived by the planner suggests that they might be. In controversial planning situations about three-fifths of the planning directors in staff settings would turn to the chief executive for support. In contrast, only about one-fourth of the directors functioning in an independent status would turn to executives for support; two-thirds would rely chiefly on the planning commission. These figures disclose in sharpest form the conflict between the doctrines of neutral competence and executive policy leadership.[39] The findings also dramatize the degree to which organizational structure can influence the perception of planners.[40]

A few further comments on planning director perceptions are appropriate. The tendency for staff planners to turn to chief executives for support, (especially when considered in conjunction with the contact variable), is one of reinforcing perceptions. Planning directors in staff agencies turn to chief executives for support because the latter are known and reasonably predictable actors. This is analogous to the concept of reciprocities multiplier, that is, behavior in mutually expected beneficial directions increases the probability of further positive interaction.[41]

Preference Variables

We had originally posited that preference variables would reveal several strong associations with planning organization. The results fell far short of expectation and to the extent that there were significant associations (four of ten instances in Table 7) they were different for the two types of officials. Chief executives preferred their actual reported involvement in presenting planning proposals. There is, in short, little discrepancy between wish and reality.

Desire for change in planning responsibility is partially explicable by planning structure. Executives with planning staffs are not interested in securing more responsibility for planning; only six percent voice such a desire. Of executives with independent commissions, however, about

[39] Herbert Kaufman, "Emerging Conflicts."
[40] Conventional wisdom and administrative practice have generated a semi-serious "law" to describe the situational character of personal views: "Where you stand depends on where you sit!"
[41] Parsons, *The Social System*, esp. p. 205. It is Alvin Gouldner who coined the term "reciprocities multiplier" in his article "Organizational Analysis" in R. K. Merton, L. Broom, and L. S. Cottrell, Jr., eds. *Sociology Today* (New York, 1959), p. 423.

one-fourth express the desire for executive aggrandizement. This sentiment for greater executive prerogative is expressed despite previous acknowledgment of an independent commission of high accomplishment. For the executive, the independent commission is evidently a fly in the ointment of municipal policy, one that a moderate proportion of executives could do without. Perhaps the desire for greater executive control is either in spite of or designed to spite the independent commission. The chief executive may view these high accomplishments as the "wrong" results.

Preferences of planning directors are inconsistent. Planners under staff arrangements desire more executive and planner involvement in the presentation process, but the latter is barely significant. The tendency for directors in staff situations to opt for greater personal and executive involvement is representative of a more general phenomenon. Anthony Downs describes it as the desire of all staff officers to enhance the role and influence of the executive because they know in advance that a part of the increased authority will come to them.[42] In this sense, then, current preferences are the children of possessed prerogatives and the parents of promised power.

Two additional themes can be detected in these results. First, Downs's principle of rational self-interest can be found in planner responses. That principle asserts that "every official is significantly motivated by his own self-interest even when acting in a purely official capacity."[43] Second, there is no zero-sum game relationship between the planning director and the chief executive. The power relationship between these two actors is not viewed by the planning director as categorical and substitutive. Note that the planning director in the staff context can visualize both the executive and himself playing a stronger role in the presentation of planning proposals.

The other significant difference in directors concerns the definition of planning. Proportionately more of the executive staff define planning in terms of human needs than do independent commission directors. We may be observing here an emphasis on a "people program" in the content of planning. It stands to reason that this substantive component would be channeled through institutional structures that best facilitate its transmission, i.e., policy-oriented chief executives.

GOVERNMENTAL FORM, PLANNING STRUCTURE, AND PLANNERS' PERCEPTIONS AND PREFERENCES

Additional observations on planners' perceptions and preferences in relation to planning organization may be made if we control for the

---

[42] Downs, *Inside Bureaucracy*, p. 154.
[43] Downs, *Inside Bureaucracy*, p. 2.

effects of governmental form. This is accomplished in the third and fourth segments of Table 8.

Originally (in Table 7), executive estimates of the importance of zoning and comprehensive planning were linked to planning organization but directors' perceptions were not. With governmental form held constant, a relationship between directors' perceptions and planning type does appear, but only in mayor-council cities. Directors of independent commissions emphasize comprehensive planning more than staff directors do in mayor-council cities. This result is consistent with figures noted earlier in Table 8 showing the highest concentration of directors with planning degrees (54 percent) located in mayor-council cities under the commission arrangement.

An added datum should be noted. The proportion of commission directors in mayor-council cities who rank comprehensive planning important is the same as similar directors in council-manager cities and slightly lower than the proportion of staff directors under the manager form of government. Council-manager government evidently enhances the emphasis on comprehensive planning and overrides the effect of planning organization. Among the weaker executive (mayor-council) cities the effects of planning structure are discernible.

The contingent character of planning form is demonstrated further by perceived influence on planning. No significant difference exists at the zero-order level (Table 7). Introduction of governmental form as a control reveals a significant difference in council-manager cities where more staff directors than commission directors estimate their influence as strong. In addition, the difference runs in the *opposite* direction among planning directors in mayor-council cities.

Other examples of the effect of governmental form are seen in Table 8 in tabulations on the three functions of the planning commission. The proportions indicate that planning organization is associated only with plan formulation in both council-manager and mayor-council cities. Greater emphasis on goal-setting is significantly linked to the independent commission under both forms of government. But the representation and implementation functions are associated with planning organization only in council-manager cities. The contingent nature of the impact of planning structure is again evident and especially its dependence on the council-manager form.

Some intuitive but untested explanations for the above relationships can be posited. One is that the "strong" executive features of the manager plan tends toward objective-setting in quarters considerably removed from the planning commission, namely, in manager-council interactions. A second connects community characteristics and the administrative emphasis in council-manager cities with the role of the planning commission on zoning. Its rationale is as follows: council-manager cities are the fastest growing communities in the nation; growth precipitates intense zoning controversy; the instrumental character of this function combines with the administrative orientation of planning staff directors in council-manager cities to emphasize zoning. The commission status of the planning director in council-manager cities insulates him from executive pressures to emphasize zoning. A third explanation involves the notion of compensatory adjustment. This refers to a perennial problem posed for the council-manager form of government, i.e., representation. The manager form has long been criticized as inadequately representative. While firm and faultless data have seldom documented the charge, the greater representation emphasis on the plan commission in manager cities, and especially by staff directors, may reflect an underlying effort to build greater citizen representation. These three possible explanations offer some rationale for the importance of governmental form as a factor that requires recognition in understanding the impact of planning structure on officials' perceptions.

The two explicitly evaluative variables contained in this dimension offer an interesting contrast to the results reported thus far and at the same time confirm our contention about the governmental form factor. Planning directors were asked to evaluate both the existing planning structure (form) and planning commission accomplishment (substance). In neither case did planning organization alone reveal sharply divergent attitudes among directors (Table 7). When form of government was introduced notable differences appear among staff and commission directors in mayor-council cities. When considering planning organization the staff directors are more favorable than commission directors, although the difference, fifty to thirty-nine, is not statistically significant. When commission accomplishment is evaluated, commission directors are much more favorable than staff directors in mayor-council cities. It is possible that the latter figures mirror some effects of the goal or results emphasis noted earlier in the chief executive perceptual data. Should this emphasis be evident in mayor-council cities and not council-manager cities? Yes, if we grant the tentative conclusions pointing to the prominence of structural, procedural, and process considerations in council-manager government.[44]

Executive support for the planner remains strongly related to planning form regardless of form of government. But the original association between planning organization and plan commission support (− .15 in

[44] Evidence supporting an emphasis on administration, structure, and process factors in large council-manager cities in the U.S. is offered in Deil S. Wright, "The City Manager as a Development Administrator" in Robert T. Daland, ed. *Comparative Urban Research: The Administration and Politics of Cities* (Beverly Hills, Calif., 1969), pp. 203–48.

Table 7) is substantially altered by controlling the form of government. No association can be seen for council-manager cities, a strong relationship ($-$ .33) found for mayor-council cities. These results show that staff and commission directors in council-manager cities are equally likely to secure support from planning commissions. In mayor-council cities, the mayor-appointed planning director is likely to discount the support of his plan commission whereas the commission director finds the commission, not the mayor, his main bulwark in the political storms. Stated somewhat differently, directors of planning commissions in council-manager cities rely less on support from the planning commission than do directors in mayor-council cities. The locus of political support for planning appears to be clearer and also more polarized in mayor-council than council-manager cities.

At this point a logical question should be posed: Do executive perceptions of support for planning proposals correspond to those of planning directors? That is, are executives' views related to the form of their government and planning organization in the same way as our planners' views? The earlier thesis of the similar outlooks of executives and planners spurred us on to search for relationships similar to those described above for planners. The search was fruitless and, contrary to expectations, neither similar nor consistent relationships appeared in the data analysis of executive perceptions and evaluations. In fact, very few statistically significant relationships were uncovered, e.g., using controls for form of government, only two of the eighteen contingency relationships for perceptual-evaluative variables were significantly associated with planning organization. While executives and planners have, as earlier data show, similar outlooks in the sense of marginal distributions, one cannot expect that the operation of similar forces will produce the same results. Differences in position, education, career patterns, as well as organizational and community roles, would have to be studied. Most of these data are beyond the reach of this study. One possible variable worth exploration is executive-planner contact. The extent of "mutual exposure" might be one important avenue toward identifying the conditions under which executives and planners arrive at common conceptions of their planning and political milieu.

What happens to the tenuous relationships between planning organization and planning directors' preferences when governmental form is introduced? Table 8 shows that the two original significant zero-order associations in Table 7 are altered (planner presentation and definition of planning), and a new contingent relationship appears.

Staff directors, more than commission directors in council-manager cities, feel that the executive should be involved in the presentation of planning proposals. The relationship is just the opposite for directors in mayor-council cities. The existence and direction of the first relationship confirms the importance of planning organization in council-manager cities, especially when roles or functions of the executive and plan commission are involved. The relationship in mayor-council organizations, while suggesting the pertinence of planning structure, shows lesser centrality of the chief executive. The greater readiness of staff directors in mayor-council cities to assume power supports the idea of a more loose and open system for planning in mayor-council cities.

It is possible, however, to reverse the interpretation of these data. The mayoral system might be more "closed" or executive-dominated than the manager framework. Staff directors in mayor-council cities may be more self-assertive than their commission brethren because they enjoy a clear charter, and firm support from the mayor. Because they enjoy the mayor's confidence, these staff directors see no compelling need for executive involvement. They do, of course, perceive the need for executive support but they, more than the other three planner groups, can afford to discount support from the planning commission. These planners, who might be called policy entrepreneurs, are the group with the lowest proportion of planning degrees and they exhibit the greatest desire to increase their planning responsibilities.

In contrast to the policy entrepreneurs are the executive supporters, the planners who operate in a staff role under the city manager. These planners score highest on desire for executive involvement in the presentation of planning proposals. They may opt for executive involvement because they think the decision system for planning is too open and they want to tighten it up and focus more sharply on planning policies. This group is also to be contrasted with commission directors in council-manager cities who are least sympathetic to greater executive leadership.

Let us briefly summarize the findings from Table 8 concerning the effects of planning organization on personal, performance, perceptual, and preference variables. The type of planning structure employed, executive staff or independent commission, has significant bearing, regardless of governmental form, upon five variables:

1. age of the planner
2. planner contact with the chief executive
3. the plan formulation function of the planning commission
4. executive support on controversial planning proposals and
5. a definition of planning centering on human needs.

Planning organization *does* make a difference! More precisely, the organizational mode for planning is associated with some important and consequential features of planning programs and the organizational variable overrides the effect of governmental form in the above instances.

For several planning variables, however, the role of planning structure was significantly modified and qualified by the type of city government in which the planning process operated. Planning organization was associated with the following variables only in council-manager cities:

1. length of residence of the planner
2. planner influence on planning
3. representational function of the planning commission
4. zoning function of the planning commission, and
5. chief executive involvement in the presentation of planning proposals.

Organizational arrangement for planning was associated with the following variables only in mayor-council and commission cities:

1. planner with a planning degree
2. comprehensive planning as the most important planning activity
3. evaluation of planning commission accomplishment
4. planning commission support on controversial proposals, and
5. planner role in presentation of planning proposals.

The conclusion drawn from all of the above is, chiefly, that organizational structure is both directly and conditionally linked to the perceptions, preferences, and personal characteristics of planning directors. In one sense, we might conclude that these results vindicate Walker's general thesis: the location of the planning function has identifiable behavioral consequences. It is also necessary to add, however, that a larger contextual structural feature needs to be considered, namely, the form of city government. This latter variable both conditions and interacts with planning structure in influencing city planning directors.

CONCLUDING OBSERVATIONS

To sum up the impact of planning structure on various dimensions of planning, the following observations would seem to apply:

1. the consequences of planning structure are neither uniform nor do they extend across all the dimensions: personal, performance, perceptual, and preference

2. there is a high degree of congruence among the responses of chief executives and planning directors, except for personal attributes; but planning structure affects executive and planner perspectives in distinctly different ways

3. if structural conditions fail to explain inter-official differences, is there any sense in which they order explanations between dimensions for each type of official? Some rough ordering does exist as a basis for identifying the relative explanatory power of planning structure. The ranking

of the four dimensions are: (a) personal; (b) preference; (c) perceptual; and (d) performance. This ordering suggests that structure is more important in explaining individually based variables and least powerful in accounting for variations in more objective performance-based activities. Planning structure is related to and presumably conditions the people chosen (or choosing) to enter and remain as actors in the planning process. On a highly selective basis, structure affects the preferences and the perceptions of key actors. With one prominent exception, planner-executive contacts, the activities and behavioral performance of municipal planning are unrelated to the type of planning organization

4. the foregoing suggests a converse and more general conclusion. The nature of city planning, as defined by activities performed and functional roles, is the result of forces quite disparate from types of planning organization. We posit a secular trend in the clarification, confirmation, and consensus on the components and roles of planning as the chief contributors to commonalities in planning performance. This trend, enhanced by a substantial degree of professionalization, tends to reduce the variance explained by structural features to relatively small proportions.

New departures along two routes may substantially alter the "corporate" character of planning and with it perhaps breathe new life into the semi-dormant debate on planning structure. One avenue involves content, reflecting an emphasis on "people" programs. A second and closely allied movement is the participation discussed above in connection with the potential shift in the functional role of the planning commission. One or both of these developments may become linked with a new structural form for planning and start a new clash of interests over the location of the planning function in urban government

5. most importantly, however, we have observed that the single structural feature of planning organization shows greater explanatory power when considered in conjunction with a second structural variable, the form of municipal government. The strength of several relationships increased when form of government was held constant. Of special note were the combined effects of the council-manager form of government and the executive staff form of planning organization.

But the presence and significance of relationships under the mayor-council form also suggest the prescience of Frederic N. Cleaveland ten years ago when he observed that the municipal chief executive was becoming the "chief planner" in municipal affairs.[45] Both the marginal distributions and the cross-tabulations presented and discussed in this paper confirm the arrival of the then discernible trend.

Executive leadership and a staff role are the dominant forms for

---

[45] Cleaveland, "Organization," p. 69.

planning today. A detectable ambiguity and a clear shift are in the process for planning commissions, from an emphasis on outputs and goals to one focusing on inputs and process. The entrenchment of the former leaves the planner locked in the vise-like grip of competing institutional actors and planning ideologies for which there is no easy way out. The congruence of views between executives and planning directors on performance, perceptual, and preference dimensions is important and provides an operating base for the planner. The substantially non-routinized nature of planners' behavior indicates his possible adeptness at defense from flank attacks.

From a positive or offensive standpoint, however, the planner will have to guard against the three elements jeopardizing his hard-won and well-deserved status: (1) the insensitivity and "trained incapacity" that professionalization instills; (2) the temptations and pressures of immediacy or short-term results; and (3) identification with "the establishment" in times of turmoil when existing values as well as traditional structures of decision-making are severely challenged. But if challenge is not a standard component of the planner's job, then someone should rewrite the position specifications.

III: DOES TECHNIQUE HAVE A ROLE?

INTRODUCTION

Rein's taxonomy of the planner's search for legitimacy (see p. 5 above) includes as a major category the rationalization of process and technique to accomplish one or both of two ends: to find a solution which is convincing at face value because of its quality or to convince a client or client group of quality by reference to the process and technique incorporated in reaching the solution.

Planners have adopted and adapted technique and process from a wide number of the social, natural, and physical sciences. The four selections that follow describe technique and process, in the main, with strong normative allusions to their appropriateness to the work of planning, the ways in which they can be, should be, and are being used, and the issues involved in their current use.

In the first selection of this section, Norman Beckman discusses the role of the professional bureaucrat, with specifics drawn from his extensive experience in the Department of Housing and Urban Development. As is emphasized in the introductory chapter, it is the bureaucrats who do most of the actual work of planning, and many planners are bureaucrats, whether they like the term or reject it in favor of less pejorative nouns. Beckman asserts that there is much which can and should be done with the existing framework before what is valuable is discarded with what is not. Emphasizing a traditional model of bureaucratic behavior, he argues for new attitudes on the part of "bureaucrats," so that they may effectively deal with problems which are only beginning to be recognized. Beckman's message is to recognize the liabilities and assets of the bureaucratic role and to infuse that role with new attitudes and concerns.

Lathrop and Hemmens have attempted to throw the rational planning model with its attendant systems analysis–systems engineering–operations research technique into perspective. The faults of its usual cost-benefit basis have earned this conceptual model a considerable amount of criticism during the past few years. Lathrop and Hemmens, as well as Beckman, re-consider the question of proper role and use of an approach with emphasis upon relevance to decision-making and communication between the systems analyst-planner and the decision-maker.

The third selection in Section II, by Kenneth Howard, treats yet another conflict in the legitimacy and communication area: that between the budgeteer and the planner, with the focus falling on the much-maligned Planning, Programming, and Budgeting System. One view holds that PPBS is an administrative manifestation of the urge to rationalize and improve governmental process and decision-making. The correspondence to the rational model is obvious, but Howard has chosen to discuss conflicts in role definition and formalization, not unlike those examined empirically by Wright. Another part of the problem hinges on the hoary thesis that he who holds the purse-strings eventually holds the power.

Robert Chartrand has been involved in serving the information needs of the legislative branch of the Federal Government. Information is the foundation of decision-making, and power derives from the possession of superior information. Chartrand's subject in the final piece in this section is the introduction and use of modern data-processing techniques and computers in the Congress and the subsequent changes wrought in the traditional distribution of power between the legislative and executive branches. From a political point of view there are anticipated, actual, and most interesting perhaps, suspected benefits of modern data processing.

This small sample of the rich technique "bag" available to the planner and politician, while taking normative positions, offers no clear-cut solutions to the fundamental question of the relationship between planner and politician. Technique offers no panaceas. Neither do organization or administrative procedure. They do open up alternatives. The four pieces that follow offer some insight into the potential of technique, organization, and technology as well as views of the appropriate application of that potential.

The New PPBS:
Planning, Politics, Bureaucracy, and Salvation*
NORMAN BECKMAN

Scratch a profession and you will find problems. There are ample problems to choose from in the planning profession. This paper addresses itself to the role of the planner in a democracy and a responsible bureaucracy.

Planning literature is introspective, self-critical, and articulate, all at the same time, and it is deeply concerned with the subject of role. The literature suggests that planners distrust and dislike politics and politi-

* The views presented here are solely those of the author and do not necessarily reflect the outlook or position of the Library of Congress.

cians; devote only limited attention to implementing the planning process; resist dealing with the major domestic problems of our time—race, poverty, and housing; and are willing to tolerate the dichotomy that exists between planners and public generalists—the budget, managerial, and other technical administrative staffs—whose amorphous profession is public administration.

The problems of planning must be viewed in terms of certain fundamentals: (1) the unique capability of planning to identify the public interest; (2) the inevitable involvement of planners in the political process and the dominant role of the elected official in that process; (3) the necessity for planning to function responsively and responsibly in the public service; and (4) increased federal efforts to make planning relevant to major national domestic goals as well as an intrinsic part of effective and capable state and local government.

THE PLANNER AND THE PUBLIC INTEREST

In an age of increasing fragmentation and disenchantment, the quest for the holy grail of "the public interest" becomes all the more elusive. Like the man who discovered that he has been speaking prose all his life, it may come as a surprise to the planning profession that it is making a unique contribution to the reconciliation of separate interests resulting in a new and binding sense of community.

The logic for this role is rooted in political theory that predates America as a nation. In Number 10 of the Federalist Papers, a defense of the proposed Constitution, James Madison develops a theory of public interest that has significance for planners today. Madison first defends the elaborate system of separation of powers by showing that majorities could become authoritarian or tyrannical, and then argues in defense of "large republics."

Madison's thesis was essentially thus:

1. In any society there are a number of conflicting interests which will seek expression in politics;
2. Political divisions are therefore inevitable;
3. However, the larger the community, the greater will be the variety and number of interests included, and the less likely will it be that any one interest will constitute a majority of the citizenry.

The size of the community is therefore a measure of safety against domination by any particular group. It follows from Madison's thesis that in a large community—for Madison, the nation—the general or public interest is more likely to be achieved than in a community where any one group or interest can play a dominant role. In the large community, majorities can be produced only by compromise and accommodation among a variety of groups.[1]

---

[1] See E. E. Schattschneider, *Party Government* (New York, 1942), pp. 8–9. Chapter I, "In Defense of Political Parties," pp. 1–16, develops this thesis more fully.

Who at the metropolitan level is concerned with the general interest? A shifting coalition of politicians, editors, businessmen, and labor leaders often takes the lead in tackling areawide problems—usually on an ad hoc, piecemeal basis. But they serve voluntarily from an institutional base which has no authority to resolve regional issues, no power to tax or spend, and their interests may not be representative of the metropolitan constituency.

Today's urban areas magnify the multiplicity of interests. The pattern of local government in metropolitan areas is complex. There are increasing economic, social, and racial disparities between the central cities and suburbia. The new urban melting pot bubbles with new professions; federal aid increases in amounts and variety; and parts of the population feel increasingly alienated from the political process.

Now, enter the planner. Melvin M. Webber eloquently describes the planner's skill and role in relating or integrating divergent interests in urban regions—the task of identifying the general or public interest which Madison assigns to the larger community:

> The city planner's idealism, his orientation to the whole city, and his focus upon future conditions have placed him in a position of intellectual leadership. With increasing numbers and varieties of skilled specialists now entering the city's employ, the city planner's outlook will become increasingly vital, and his educational mission more difficult. But simultaneously, as the state of our knowledge improves with respect to relationships among aspects, rational integration will become increasingly possible.[2]

This is the ideal. Even the planning profession does not expect that planning will fully integrate federal, state, and local development decisions or by itself solve domestic problems. The public official's duties—once described by Andrew Jackson as "plain and simple"—are today about as plain and simple as solutions are quick and easy. Contemporary proponents of plain and simple solutions use the tactics of the cosmetics industry which administers to our wan unconscious hope of reincarnation. It is obviously cheering to be told that it takes only moisture balm, grease strained through silk, or essence of royal ant gland to be reborn with another face. Similarly, if we could only clean up the mess in Washington, create shiny new metropolitan-wide governments (with instant cost-benefit analyses), remove planning and zoning from politics, add a dash of space technology spinoff—presto!—you would have a whole new look on the face of the nation.

Planning and urban development are recognized as complex, and, interdependent systems. Government has a stake in planning because in

---

[2] Melvin M. Webber, "Comprehensive Planning and Social Responsibility: Toward an AIP Consensus on the Profession's Roles and Purposes," *Journal of the American Institute of Planners*, XXIX (November, 1963), 238.

an urban society urban and community interests become the public interest. At the heart of the planning process are the earliest principles of the American federal system: to mobilize the nation's resources to support programs of nationwide interest, and, in turn, to administer those programs at the state and local levels. The carrot of planning grants and the stick of federal program planning requirements have made every local government conscious of the need to look ahead and to think in terms of "the public interest."

As a result, planning programs are becoming increasingly oriented toward human concerns, local political leadership, an areawide approach, and service to other governmental planning and implementation efforts. The planning process is expected to identify alternatives and determine the means of achieving them. Planning must use the country's resources for her physical, economic, and social well-being. Never before have planners been in such a strong position to influence the quality of life in America. And they are expected to do just that.

THE CASE OF CONFLICTING IDENTITIES

Those who seek elected office, especially local office, are frequently regarded with suspicion of venality, hypocrisy, or outright dishonesty. This is not an encouraging or healthy situation at a time when the government is being called upon to expand public services and when governmental power is being given to the state and local levels. One can only speculate as to whether the average planner shares this attitude. At the same time, the public may identify the planner as a politically controversial figure. The "politically expendable planner," who so often vanishes in a change of administration, can be as damaging to the cause he serves as the "planning technician" who forgets nothing and learns nothing as he pursues his value-free sterile planning exercises.

The identity of the planner must then be examined in light of the similarity of the roles of the politician and the planner and the conflict this engenders; the vulnerability of the planner in challenging the elected official for community leadership; the unique capability of the planner to serve the chief executive (governor, county board, mayor, or manager); the special character of government employment and the place of the public servant in a responsible bureaucracy. Expert advice must be given on how to survive and be effective in the public sector. Now as never before, established political processes at the local government level are being criticized or challenged as an elaborate put-on at best, or as not meeting the needs of the people at worst. Buckminster Fuller may articulate an extreme view of this position:

Take away the energy distributing networks and the industrial machinery from America, Russia and all the world's industrialized countries, and within six months 2 billion swiftly and painfully deteriorating people will starve to death.

Take away the politicians, all the ideologies and their professional protagonists from those same countries and leave them their present energy networks, industrial machinery, routine productions and distribution personnel and no more humans will starve or be afflicted in health than at present.[3]

But government is crucial to urban development, not because it supplies the shelter, the food, or the clothing needed by urban populations—it doesn't. Government is important because it is the major mechanism for protecting the public interest, refereeing or resolving conflicting interests, achieving greater equity in social and economic opportunity, and doing, in Lincoln's words, "for a community of people whatever they need to have done, but cannot do at all, or cannot so well do for themselves, in their separate and individual capacities."[4]

Daniel P. Moynihan's *Maximum Feasible Misunderstanding* states the case for exercising great caution before meddling in the fundamentals of our governmental system by :

denying the legitimacy of those institutions of electoral representation that had developed over the years—indeed, the centuries—and which nominally did provide community control.

All of a sudden the city councilman was not enough, the State assemblyman not enough, the Congressman not enough, the mayor and the governor and the President but tools of the power structure. Plebiscitory democracy, the people-in-council, became the seeming nonnegotiable demand of many.

The institutions of representative government, imperfect as they may be, have the singular virtue of defining who speaks for the community in certain set circumstances.[5]

One useful working definition of politics describes the politician as a "broker-mediator." His role is to coordinate, adjust, and reconcile views into sufficient harmony for action. His job is to unite the judgment of the expert and the "will of the people." Of course, he must win elections to remain in office, but reelection is dependent upon how successfully he meets the competing demands of citizens and interest groups. One of the rapidly growing industries in the national capital area has been the opening of offices representing special interest groups and asso-

---

[3] R. Buckminster Fuller, "Planners May be Left Behind by Technological Revolution," *The Planner in Emerging Urban Society—A Confrontation* (Proceedings of the Annual Governmental Conference of the American Institute of Planners in St. Louis, Missouri, 1965), p. 22.

[4] Fragment on Government [July 1, 1854], *Complete Works of Abraham Lincoln*, ed. John S. Nicolay and John Hay (New York, 1905), II, 186–87.

[5] Daniel P. Moynihan, *Maximum Feasible Misunderstanding: Community Action in the War on Poverty* (New York, 1969), p. 182.

ciations. Our governmental system has been durable because of its capacity to meet the demands of any one group in a manner consistent with the public interest. Successful politicians must understand and adjust to these constant and ever changing demands. The competition for political jobs is keen and the turnover rate high.

Descriptions of the politician as a broker-mediator are strongly related to Webber's definition of the role and function of the planner:

As men who have specialized in the general, the truly effective city planners have functioned as catalysts for the developmental plans of the more specialized groups in government. By bringing representatives of public and private agencies together, they have helped to synthesize new amalgams that better reflect both the separate and the mutual goals of the various participants. Individual plans for components have been reframed to accord with criteria established by the plans for the next-larger systems of components that, in turn, conform to more comprehensive overviews of the future and of the community's objectives.[6]

Examine the similarity of themes: "coordinate," "harmony," "reconcile," "public interest," "adjust," "synthesize," "next-larger systems," "comprehensive overviews." Note that both politician and planner are assigned responsibility for integrating the independent development decisions and their attendant social and economic effects into the community, and for providing leadership in achieving the good life. Each may argue that he is best fit—through training, experience, and institutional expectations—to serve the public as broker-mediator, coordinator, and goalmaker. There is clearly a problem of conflicting identities.

This conflict of identity can best be resolved, and the planners effectiveness enhanced, if he is willing to accept the vital but more limited role that our system assigns to the public employee.

The tools of the planner's trade and his comprehensive view give him a special competence, perhaps above all other public service professions, to assist and serve the elected policy-maker. Indeed, the *sine qua non* of the planner's profession—the land use map and the master plan —is really an attempt to interpret and guide a multitude of public and private decisions affecting a given political jurisdiction.

It may be argued that the planner's bias toward the long-range and the politican's bias toward the immediate open the door for continuing conflict. The politician faces frequent elections before a specific constituency which demands short-range performance, while the planner may be more concerned about broad geographic areas, the interdependence of decisions, or the future population. But are long-range interests really inconsistent with immediate issues? Until all the basic questions concerning

[6] Webber, "Comprehensive Planning," pp. 236–37.

long-term development and goals—such as patterns of growth, the characteristics of the population, the economic base of the community, and the needs and resources of its people—are answered, it is difficult to determine the most effective means of providing any given service. Surely the alternative—uncoordinated development, conflicting land uses, depreciation of city property values, exclusionary zoning, housing shortages, and uneconomical public facilities—is not good politics.

The planner is vulnerable in any competition with the politician. His job demands that he become deeply and inevitably involved in politics and the political process. Every administrative action in government, from the surly behavior of a licensing clerk to a health department decision to prohibit individual wells and septic tanks in an urban area, is weighed on a political scale. Actions which benefit or hurt individuals produce a reading on that scale and it is difficult to anticipate which ones will be elevated to public attention. For example, in my own community, a single zoning decision to permit construction of an apartment house along the Potomac resulted in the unseating of several members of the county board of supervisors. Planning helps determine "who gets what, when, and how," and to do that is to function politically.

The commission form of organization and the professionalization of the occupation were presumably designed to "remove planning from politics," the operating relationships of planning agencies with other local, state, and federal agencies and their effect upon and exposure to large numbers of citizens subject planners to political attack. Because planning agencies are concerned with the "obstetrics of public policy" and must operate on the cutting edge of politics and administration, they are especially vulnerable to such attack.

The planner uses his professional skills, meritorious ideas, and ability and willingness to promote the exchange of information with other governments and agencies. Despite the facade of autonomy and independence behind which planning has sought to bring about the heavenly city of the twentieth century, it must constantly be remembered that planning agencies have almost no levers, no gifts, no grants, no weapons, no operating programs, no strong base of independent political support. It is, therefore, imperative that planners be closely allied as key management staff to responsible officials possessing executive powers—the governor, mayor, county council, or city manager.

Lay citizen boards that insulate local planning staffs from the responsible public officials who desperately need facts, alternatives, and recommendations, are being discarded rapidly. At the metropolitan level, elected officials supervise the regional planning staff, participating in the selection of plans and studies, injecting community values, and judging priorities, budgets, and projects. At the state level, planning agencies focus upon servicing the governor and the chief elected state officials, and resource allocation is being increasingly geared into the budget process.

Today's planners work for chief executives and elected officials whose time is short, and who want answers to real questions now. In order to assume the central role they should play, planners must become far more a part of the workaday world of decision-making. They must grapple with such questions as where the money is to come from, what kinds of people are needed to do the job, what legal changes are necessary, and what interest group conflicts must be resolved.

Politicians, even lay planning commission members, often welcome the opportunity to let planning staffs advocate new development proposals. If the interest groups howl, plans can always go back to the drafting board for new formulas to be devised, perhaps, by a new planning director. Getting very far ahead of commission members and elected officials is a dangerous game for any bureaucrat.

It is an occupational hazard of the professional public employee (and planners perhaps are especially susceptible on this score) to become convinced not only that his "plan" is right but that the plan, the zoning ordinance, and the zoning decision are ends in themselves. For a public servant to have that kind of faith is disastrous. Much of the sense of frustration from which all too many planners suffer springs from expecting immediate, measurable, and conclusive influence, and finding it hard to understand why responsible officials do not do what he believes is the best thing to do. Planners tend to forget that their function must be limited to blending, synthesizing, and adjusting programs to the hopes and fears, likes and dislikes, of the politicians they serve.

SURVIVAL IN A BUREAUCRACY

It is fundamental to our system of government that public employment "does not require partisans of a particular general outlook, whether Republican or Democrat, conservative, progressive, or socialist, but it does require specialists who know their job and will, therefore, effectively execute the general rules decided upon by executive or legislative leadership in accordance with popular preferences."[7]

Max Weber's idealized construct of bureaucratic organization still has validity: (1) the head of the organization owes his authority and position to election; (2) the remaining staff are organized in a defined heirarchy of office; (3) they are selected on the basis of technical qualifications; (4) an appointment constitutes a career, including promotion based on seniority and achievement as judged by superiors; (5) the person filling the office works entirely separately from ownership or the

[7] Carl J. Friedrich, *Constitutional Government and Democracy* (Boston, 1950), p. 409.

means of administration; (6) he is subject to strict and systematic discipline and control in the conduct of the office.[8]

The character of government employment for the planner is difficult because of the scope, impact, and ramifications of his assignment; the public accountability to which he is held; and the political character of his work which requires him to ask before making any decision: Who is going to be mad? How mad? Who is going to be glad? How glad?

Because the planner serves in an official rather than in a personal capacity, he is going to be frustrated or disheartened by decisions made by his superiors—elected or otherwise. General Dawes, first director of the United States Bureau of the Budget, explained how the system works: "If the President wants us to spread garbage around the White House, it is our job to figure out how to pile it deeply and uniformly and at the least possible cost."

Not every one is built for the bureaucratic life. If "idealism" and "professionalism" make life in an institutional setting intolerable, perhaps the planner can contribute as an academic, researcher, or a methodological specialist far removed from the action. Whether or not planners participate, the government bureaucracy will continue, and in the long run, the planners' contribution to administration is best achieved by formal participation in the governmental hierarchy.

An Illustration: The Bureau of the Budget

The experience of a staff agency generally considered successful in serving a chief executive is instructive. The Bureau of the Budget has responsibility for developing the president's budget, coordinating his legislative program, and serving as an extension of his office in seeing that administration programs are supported by often decentralized departments, agencies, and bureaus. The charge is clearly a political one. But how many budget personnel were replaced when Mr. Nixon took over from President Johnson? Perhaps five. A similar number were changed when President Kennedy took over after eight years of Republican administration. A former deputy director (now comptroller general) served at the directorate level under four presidents. Several years ago he was given a present by Budget Bureau staff—a large seat cushion with a donkey on one side and an elephant on the other.

Orientation literature presented new Bureau of the Budget employees contains some clues to why the bureau has had success in serving elected officials and in indirectly affecting public policies. The bureau's advice is paraphrased here and applicable elsewhere:

The employee has a difficult role to play. He must be humble, self-effacing,

---

[8] Max Weber, *The Theory of Social and Economic Organization,* trans. A. M. Henderson and Talcott Parsons, ed. Talcott Parsons (London, 1947), pp. 329–40.

and quietly loyal. He will have little or no opportunity to use pronouns in the first person singular. He must be self-effacing because his role is institutional. He is a team player. His loyalty to the politician must be that of the disciplined soldier in combat who has been trained to know that while his commanding officer will protect him to the extent possible, he is nevertheless expendable, both as an individual and as part of a unit. This means that the staff member must develop his instinct for self-preservation to the highest possible point. He cannot afford to make many mistakes. The consequences to himself, his agency, and the elected official may be much too serious.[9]

An administration represents a point of view on public policy. The staff member's job is to understand that point of view and to assist the public officials to achieve certain objectives. He cannot raise obstacles for the public official. So, every professional must strive to keep his personal notions about public policy in check, and must resist revealing strong attitudes which might raise doubts in others about his objectivity and, therefore, about his agency's goals. Proposals are most usefully presented in the form of a range of alternatives, identifying the strengths and weaknesses of each, their probable political ramifications, and a staff preference.

Is this intellectually dishonest? The planner serves all the people. Planners do not have to compete for jobs on a political basis. This does not mean avoiding controversy within an agency or the government generally, or finding out what the boss thinks before voicing an opinion:

The decisions that "work" are not produced by the pliant collaboration of yes-men, but by loud and cheerful argument among colleagues who know they are all trying to catch a glimpse of the same moon from different parts of the forest.

The job of the top administrator is not primarily to make peace within his own organization. It is to tighten the web of tensions he deliberately creates, weighing the options revealed by the arguments among his staff, and then to elicit the loyalty of these same people to the wider public interest as expressed in his decisions.[10]

Planning agencies, like other institutional staff—in the Bureau of the Budget, the city manager, the school superintendent—must be sensitive to shifts in public policy. A professional should be able to weather any political transition. Once the staff advisor loses the confidence of his political superior his usefulness is finished. Those too closely identified with the ideals and aims of the previous administration must be expected to depart quietly, or not so quietly. This kind of adaptability is the hall-

[9] William D. Carey, "The Bureau Staff Member," remarks at the Staff Orientation Conference, Bureau of the Budget, September 17, 1954, pp. 3–14.
[10] Harlan Cleveland, "The Case for Bureaucracy," *New York Times Magazine,* October 27, 1963, p. 114.

mark of the professional bureaucrat at any level of government. And the track record for planners could be better.

Even if not subject to changes in administration, planner-bureaucrats must be able to revoke or modify decisions on important issues. This is an important criterion of the successful administrator. It requires planners to abandon the irrevocability, infallibility, and inviolateness of a "land use map approach" and they are now increasingly and properly emphasizing "the planning process" rather than "the plan."

Planning is the Art of the Possible

Constant attention must be paid to the problems and implications of implementation. No "unseen hand" will bring about orderly urban development. Planners today must not only be sewer, water, air pollution, highway, housing, community relations, anti-poverty, and recreation experts, they must have legal, organizational, and economic competence, and they must be political pragmatists with a sense of good public relations.

Chester Barnard, a long-time practitioner in public and private administration, has stated four conditions that must be met before a proposal is accepted. These conditions may serve as a guide to the planning profession in its work. The politician or public will accept a proposal as authoritative if: "(a) He can and does understand the communication; (b) He believes that it is not inconsistent with the purpose of the organization; (c) He believes it to be compatible with his personal interest as a whole; and (d) He is able mentally and physically to comply with it."[11]

Planners, above all others, cannot afford to be called dreamers who live in ivory towers. To distribute proposals that have little chance of acceptance and accomplishment inevitably reduces the planner's always limited supply of public confidence and makes acceptance of subsequent proposals less likely, regardless of their merit.

Richard Neustadt's book, *Presidential Power,* makes two observations of direct relevance to planners: The fact that the president issues an order does not necessarily mean that it will be carried out; resistance all along the line can frustrate the president's wishes. Every defeat a president suffers reduces his prestige and effectiveness in subsequent efforts, even in unrelated fields. If this is true for the presidency, it is also true for lesser executive and staff whose plans are not accepted, or, are accepted and not implemented.[12]

The high rate of turnover of elected officials makes continuity and accumulated experience valuable assets to the bureaucracy. A number of

[11] Chester Barnard, *The Functions of the Executive* (Cambridge, Mass., 1938), p. 165.
[12] Richard Neustadt, *Presidential Power* (New York, 1960).

small victories can be as important as a major victory: "As trifles make the sum of human things, so details make the substance of public affairs." Toward the end of his life, William James commented that he was "against bigness and greatness in all their forms." This philosophy is appropriate to those discouraged by a lack of bold planning goals or prompt, resolute actions to achieve them. Like James, they perhaps should be for "the invisible molecular moral forces that work from individual to individual, stealing in through the crannies of the world like so many soft rootlets, or like the capillary oozing of water, and yet, rending the hardest monuments of men's pride if you give them time."[13]

What federal incentives are there to support the planner in his bureaucratic travail? What is the federal role in making planning relevant and supportive of the political decision-making process at the state and local level? How can federal planning assistance bring about a linkage between strong, capable governments on the one hand, and equity, opportunity, choice, and the public interest on the other? To answer these questions, it is necessary to move on from the subject of role of the planner in government to the role of the federal government in planning.

FEDERAL EFFORTS TO ACHIEVE MAXIMUM FEASIBLE RELEVANCE

There has been a major shift in federal programs designed to help the city and its poor, especially in the areas of housing, health, education, food distribution, job training, and crime control. New programs have been established and existing programs, with no explicit social purpose, are being reoriented to meet the pressing priorities of the urban poor. As federal programs move more clearly in this direction, the states are assuming increased urban roles and responsibilities. This pervasive trend in public policy has fundamental implications for the fields of planning and administration.

These new directions are rapidly changing the field of urban planning. Professional planners are now directly involved in the execution of major federal social programs—including model cities, law enforcement assistance, and community action—and in the planning aspects of labor and manpower programs, health and hospital activities, and economic development programs. Federal support for planning of all kinds is beginning to require planners to concern themselves not only with economy and orderly development, but with advancing fundamental civil and social values—reducing poverty and unemployment, increasing opportunity and choice, and providing public services on an equitable basis.

Federal planning assistance to the state, areawide, and local plan-

[13] James to Mrs. Henry Whitman, June 7, 1899, in *The Letters of William James,* ed. Henry James (Boston, 1920), II, 90.

ning levels of the public sector has evolved outside of any master strategy or administrative framework. In the decade and particularly during the last few years of the sixties, the number of federal planning assistance programs has steadily grown. Only nine such programs existed in 1964. Nine new programs were established in 1965 to provide state and local governments with the capacity to plan higher education, health, transportation, outdoor recreation, and other facilities. Seventeen programs have been added since 1965, and congress is considering new programs for primary and secondary education, airport development, and governmental management and coordination.

Currently there are more than thirty-six federal programs providing grants to state and local governments and combinations of these governments in metropolitan and rural areas. Some are designed to assist chief executives and/or combinations of elected officials to make informed and prudent decisions concerning the overall development of the area. Other programs support specific functional areas, such as air pollution or outdoor recreation.

The fiscal ramifications are impressive. Federal planning assistance to state, areawide, and local agencies totaled approximately $300 million in the fiscal year of 1969. Even more important is the fact that many of the activities that these programs support help satisfy a vast array of federal planning requirements. So these programs annually trigger the release of billions of dollars to state and local governments through federal "hardware" grants. Eligible recipients of these federal grants now include practically every city, state, and duly constituted regional agency in virtually every area of the nation.

But is there a cultural lag in the profession at a time when the resources and levers are at hand? A recent thoughtful appraisal of the planning profession by Brooks and Stegman concludes that "Poverty and racial conflict are the paramount problems afflicting our cities today. The profession has shied away from a direct confrontation with its responsibility in this area for a number of years. If it would remain dynamic and relevant to America's future, it can no longer afford to do so."[14]

Two new dimensions in planning are emerging. First, federally supported comprehensive planning programs are being redirected in order to make them more relevant to the housing, human resources, minorities, low-income, and citizen participation elements of the planning process. Second, greater support is being given to the implementation dimension of planning to strengthen the management capability of chief executives in states and communities.

[14] Michael P. Brooks and Michael A. Stegman, "Urban Social Policy, Race, and the Education of Planners," *Journal of the American Institute of Planners,* XXXIV (September, 1968), 275.

What follows is essentially a case study of the Department of Housing and Urban Development's Comprehensive Planning Assistance program. It serves as a major example of how federal planning programs can and do increasingly focus on social concerns, political accountability, and improved government performance.

These new dimensions of the comprehensive planning assistance program are a response to the implicit reality that a plan for orderly growth cannot be isolated from a broader concern with the needs of the community and its people. They are based on the assumption that social concerns and effective government are inextricably linked.

Similar changes in direction must also occur for the public administration profession. Planning and management make up the major staff resources available to the chief executive. The professions closest to decision-makers, planners, and public administrators are equally responsible for seeing that land is allocated to meet total community needs and that one economic class does not control its environment at the expense of another.

Both groups consider themselves concerned with the general welfare and the public good. There is increasing recognition of the inextricable linkage and interdependence of the two professions. Planning is, as the old acronym PODSCORB recognizes, a first and necessary part of management.

A symbiotic relationship must be established by the two professions. Planners' past reluctance to giving in-depth attention to what is good for the community and also what is needed to achieve that good has drained the reservoir of goodwill previously enjoyed by the profession. Public administrators have been criticized for tunnel vision, an excess of caution, and the eighth deadly sin—dullness.

SOCIAL CONCERNS OF LOW INCOME AND MINORITY GROUPS

Among the instruments available to the federal government in reallocating resources to meet priority issues are legislation, administrative regulations (now more benignly called guidelines), funding priorities, and special demonstration efforts. All sorts of devices are being used to bring planning to the social concerns that dominate the domestic political scene.

Work programs which ignore high national priorities can make only a dubious claim on national funds. For example, HUD planning assistance constituents working with the poor and minority groups—whether in transportation, planning, housing, employment, or whatever—receive high priority in funding.

During the past several years, the "701" program has played a major role in the development of planning institutions at the state, areawide, and local levels. Continued support for these agencies now increasingly depends upon the degree to which they are effective. The amount of funds earmarked for an agency is based, therefore, on a careful evaluation of the effectiveness of the agency in critical areas of endeavor.

Evaluation of agency effectiveness includes an analysis of how planing has resulted in an allocation of resources on the basis of socially responsive priorities, has led to a better environment for all persons, and has saved dollars. It determines (1) what progress has been made in implementing housing plans and programs; (2) how planning has led to the improvement of neighborhood facilities and services; and (3) whether or not citizens involved in the planning process have an opportunity to create an impact on policy development and implementation. An evaluation establishes the extent of minority representation on agency staffs as well as the agency's personnel practices of recruitment and training for such minorities.

Required Housing Element

Traditionally, comprehensive planning agencies have not been specifically concerned with one major departmental effort—providing housing. The 1968 Housing Act, which strengthens and broadens the arsenal of federal aids for housing, states that the nation's housing goal was 26 million new units by 1978. In marshalling efforts to this task, the legislation brings the "701" program to bear by requiring every comprehensive planning program to include a housing element.

In one sense, this requirement is an extension of planning's traditional concern for the quality of the physical environment. It adds a housing dimension to highways, sewage treatment facilities, schools, and other physical features of the urban environment. But the housing component has a much more apparent and compelling social dimension—the problems of black and white, income levels, costs and codes, equal access and discrimination, taxation and exclusionary zoning.

Planning for housing received high priority in awarding comprehensive planning assistance grants in the fiscal year of 1970. The department sought planning to increase the supply, quality, and choice of housing for all individuals and families, particularly those with low and moderate incomes and those minorities whose choices are constrained by discriminatory practices. Support was available for the preparation of plans and programs and delivery of technical services to implement Operation Breakthrough, a new program to pave the way for volume housing production through innovative techniques and new materials by aggregating sites and the demand for housing. Priority activities supporting Breakthrough include:

revision of state or regional initial housing elements (work programs) to include a Breakthrough Operation Plan

preparation of estimates of potential housing in metropolitan areas and regions

establishment of housing production targets

analysis of existing geographic distribution of housing by type and cost and families by income, size, and ethnic character

identification of housing sites

review of development plans and zoning

modernization of building codes

provision of technical assistance to sponsor and developer

preparation of administrative, legislative, and financial programs to reduce obstacles and/or promote the construction of Breakthrough or traditional housing.

Model Cities Support

The department's model cities programming focuses upon social problems and how to cope with them in neighborhoods and communities. States have indicated that they want to establish more effective working relationships with the cities and to share in local model cities neighborhood efforts. Governors of all forty-five states having model cities have designated representatives to coordinate supporting activities at the state level.

Maintained by federal planning assistance grants, these state staffs will seek to have state funds earmarked for and technical assistance provided to model neighborhoods. Statutes and administrative regulations which inhibit implementation at the local level will be revised and information systems will advise municipalities of the availability of state resources for planning and implementation.

Citizen Participation

One of the most significant social changes in HUD programs has resulted from legislative and administrative support of poor and minority group participation in the decisions which affect their lives. All too often, citizen participation does not occur until a final publicized "plan" is presented for public hearing. Comprehensive planning agencies are just beginning to learn to work with disadvantaged citizens in developing meaningful avenues of participation which do not undermine political accountability or raise barriers to effective action.

The comprehensive planning assistance program is attempting to assure flexibility in the forms of citizen participation employed. To this end the program requires that there be a designated mechanism which recognizes low income and minority groups and directly involves residents of the planning area in the planning process.

IMPROVING MANAGEMENT CAPABILITY

Well-managed governments are increasingly bringing planning into the central role it should play. The full range of management activities stemming from the planning process are now recognized as legitimate concerns of HUD's comprehensive planning assistance program. Through "701" and related programs, HUD is now the largest federal sponsor of improved state and local administration and management reform. During 1969 the program supported the administrative reorganization of state government in five states, major planning-programming-budgeting projects in seven states and three counties, reform in the relationships between the state and its local government in seven states, and the first comprehensive examination of governmental personnel and methods of improving existing staff capacity in six states.

For the first time, program policy and priority explicitly and formally support as eligible "701" activities such traditional public administration concerns as : (1) reform of local and state government organization processes and procedures; (2) analysis of the local government's legal and financial resources and capabilities; (3) evaluation of the adequacy of state and local legislation; (4) identification and evaluation of available state and federal financial and technical assistance programs; and (5) analysis of needed personnel, skills, training, and salary structures for the local government in efficiently managing its programs and meeting development objectives.

Departmental instructions to field offices administering the comprehensive planning assistance program clearly state that a major objective in the fiscal year of 1970 is the support of elected officials or appropriate executive authorities of state, areawide, and local jurisdictions through activities designed to improve the allocation of resources and the delivery of services. These activities include the development of basic planning information systems, planning, programming and budgeting systems, and coordination of federal, state, and local programs and projects. Applicants are encouraged to strengthen planning staffs through training and improved personnel practices, and by increasing the number of minority members on professional staffs, to increase citizen participation activities in order to make policy development and management in local government responsive, and to utilize volunteer resources in the preparation and implementation of plans.

State Organization

Although many states have made significant gains toward modernization, a cumbersome and fragmented organizational structure frequently typifies the executive branch of most state governments. In general, executive authority in most states continues to be diffused among a number of elected officials with governmental activities dispersed among a variety of separate agencies. Grants recently made in this subject area include:

support for a citizen task force effort aimed at improved organization and management of the entire New Hampshire state government

funds to implement the proposal consolidation of some 140 existing Minnesota departments, boards, and commissions into ten major departments.

Much recent state administrative reform has been the result of the states' realization of their growing responsibilities in the field of urban development and community affairs. This is particularly true in such areas as planning, coordination of federal-state programs, manpower development and training, urban information, and technical assistance. The growing interest of states in local affairs has led to various administrative arrangements to meet the needs of community and urban development. Approximately half the states have now established some form of state-local affairs agency, most of which receive their basic support from the comprehensive planning assistance program. Many other states are contemplating similar action.

Related efforts under way include support for state-local relations studies examining the vertical relationships, functions, and responsibilities for providing urban services, statewide and metropolitan urban development manpower surveys to identify manpower shortages, future skill requirements, and training facilities and programs required to meet public manpower needs.

PPBS

Planning, programming, and budgeting attempt to strengthen the governmental decision-making process by integrating the planning and budgeting functions and including systematic program design and analysis.

Although PPBS has been adopted by the federal government and by several state and local jurisdictions, there has not been enough careful and deliberate study and testing to judge its usefulness in state government. HUD, therefore, is encouraging several states to include PPBS in "701" supported innovative studies.

The purpose of these efforts is to determine the most effective way of adapting the systematic methods of PPBS to a state's long-term planning process, annual or biannual executive budget, and appropriation request. The goal is to provide the governor and his top agency executives with information and analytic tools for the planning, coordination, direction, and evaluation of state programs to attain state objectives.

Toward these ends, the department made grants to a number of states. In Pennsylvania, HUD funding helped to prepare the executive budget for the fiscal year of 1970 in a program format, develop quantified output measures for various state programs, devise a new accounting approach which relates expenses to programs rather than line item expenditures, and support issue analysis in selected health and welfare programs, training courses in quantitative analysis, economic analysis, and computer technology.

PLANNING—MAKING IT OR JUST FAKING IT

Most of these new policies and programs linking planning, politics, social concerns, and the governmental process are relatively new:

in implementing the new housing element, only a few earlier housing studies worthy of the name made by state or regional planning agencies could be found

planners, as a profession, continue to be characterized by high mobility, thus reducing the opportunity to meaningfully assist communities in follow through efforts

disproportionately few black and other minority persons are entering the profession despite the fact that their skills are increasingly needed in dealing with the urban crisis. Most planning school curriculums need updating to reflect social concerns

comprehensive planning at the local, regional, and state level is weakened by the plethora of separate functionally oriented and sponsored planning agencies

inconsistencies in the multiplicity of federal funding sources for planning assistance and federal planning requirements have only begun to become unravelled

the state role in model cities is just beginning as the first group of model cities complete the one-year planning stage, which must precede project-to-project decisions

"701" citizen participation guidelines were issued in July, 1968, and the assessment process has just begun

statewide and regional public sector manpower studies, state reorganization programs, and state PPBS projects each set precedents in the use of federal funds to support improved general government capability.

Virtually every social and governmental problem in our urban and rural communities will require the concerted use of federal, state, and local resources. The advice given by Brooks and Stegman to students of planning is valid for everyone concerned with the future of planning, public administration, and social change:

While the planner cannot eliminate racial discrimination from our society, he can nevertheless encourage local efforts to provide minority housing outside of the ghetto; while he cannot alter the distribution of national wealth between blacks and whites, he can act to encourage a more just distribution of local resources; while he cannot give the nation's black minority a greater voice in the formulation of national policy, he can act positively to increase their role in local planning activities.[15]

Planners and administrators are faced with still another new challenge—the ability to establish linkages which reinforce work undertaken in the vast range of functional fields. Planning funds for education, employment, welfare, health, and air pollution are threatening to make the comprehensive planner and the public administrator technologically unemployed. Yet few social problems today are solved with one grant program and one kind of planning. The planner and public administrator face a challenge and an opportunity in relating the functionally specific planning and management processes to the social goals of our communities.

Both professions, like Thursday's child, have far to go if they are to meet the challenge and negate the criticism that established political processes are not meeting the needs of the people.

Planners in government are involved in the political process. If this conclusion appears to exalt planning, it is chastening to remember that, in our system of government, politics subordinates the public employee, grants responsibility and power to the politician, and gives ultimate authority to the voter.

[15] Brooks and Stegman, "Urban Social Policy," p. 275.

Systems Analysis, Politics, and Planning: A Brief Discussion

GEORGE C. HEMMENS and GEORGE T. LATHROP

Our first responsibility is to make some specific comments about what is and is not discussed here under the topic of systems analysis. The two words are taken in a general and perhaps unusually inclusive sense. Yet, much is connoted by "systems analysis" which is excluded. What *is* included is the rational decision-making or rational planning model.

The decision-maker considers all of the alternatives (courses of action) open to him, i.e., he considers what courses of action are possible within 1. the conditions of the situation and in the light of the ends which he seeks to attain; 2. he identifies and evaluates all of the consequences which would follow from the adoption of each alternative, i.e., he predicts how the total situation would be changed by each course of action he might adopt; and 3. he selects that alternative the probable consequences of which would be preferable in terms of his most valued ends.[1]

This model has reached a high stage of development in several parallel fields over the past twenty to twenty-five years. It is perhaps not fair to characterize all of these parallel developments as variants on the statement quoted above, but it is certainly reasonable to point out the similarities in operations research, systems engineering, and management science, as well as specific administrative schemes such as planning, programming, and budgeting, cost-utility analysis and cost effectiveness analysis. There are also strong ties of kinship to the "scientific method."

Here the intent is to discuss the application of systems analysis, the rational planning model, as its counterpart has come to be called in long-range planning, to large-scale long-term problems.

Perhaps the term "systems analysis" is used most frequently to describe the design of a specific physical system, a water system, a fire protection system, or, a weapons system. Most traditional applications (if a technique of fairly recent formalization can be said to have developed a tradition) have been characterized by a short time scale and a fairly well-defined system boundary and, most importantly, a well-defined objective growing out of a straight-forward goal for the system, usually an economic one. In this instance, however, we speak of public "systems" with long time horizons (frequently up to twenty years, occasionally thirty or forty years) and shifting or evolving objectives or goal structures.

This seems almost self-evident when the nature of the application of systems analysis to problems of urban or regional physical and social change is considered. These certainly have time and scale complexities in direct contrast to the comparatively self-contained physical systems mentioned above. And their goal structures, and hence their objectives, have the scope, level, and scale of politics and political decision-making. One of the major complications of applying systems analysis techniques to public planning obviously is the changing nature of public *political* goals *over the time periods necessarily involved.* (Contrary to the inference in some quarters, it is obvious that systems analysis, if it is to be successfully applied to urban and regional systems, must be adapted to the new context, not the context to the requirements of systems analysis.)

---

[1] Martin Meyerson and E. C. Banfield, *Politics, Planning and the Public Interest*, (New York, 1955), p. 314.

THE RATIONAL PLANNING MODEL

In theory the requirements of the model are as strict in our context as they might be in a systems engineering context in which an optimum solution is to be obtained or in any of the other more rigorous areas cited above. The objectives or goals of the system must be clearly and unambiguously stated, and they must be so well inter-related as to form, in essence, a single objective. The measurement of the objective must be in such terms that its achievement can be clearly determined in at least ordinal comparisons and perhaps in intervals.

The decision-maker must have a wealth of knowledge; he must consider all alternatives, else he will be unable to assure himself that he has found the best. He must have a sufficient understanding of the process by which the desired change will take place to identify the outcome of every alternative strategy, program or action. These results must be measured in the terms referred to above which will permit comparison.

Unfortunately, the more abstract and long-range the particular goal or objective becomes, the less likely it is that these requirements will be fulfilled. The requirements are particularly onerous when the objective involves some public welfare goal and the frequently conflicting objectives of a broad spectrum of the public must be resolved. It has been demonstrated, using the framework of logic, that the requirements imposed by the strict model are impossible to fulfill in the public welfare situation which is, almost by definition, that case involved in politics, public decision-making.[2]

The implication in the rational model, and in the general practice in the various fields pursuing a similar rationale, is that of optimization. The above suggestion of a "best" solution is a less specific way of saying essentially the same thing, and it is this process goal which has received the majority of comment and criticism. Current solution techniques, particularly mathematical programming, are limited to a small subset of the total spectrum of problems to which the process of systems analysis or rational planning might be applied, and in most cases operate under such restrictive assumptions and oversimplifications as to make the solution obtained only of general relevance to the problem.

No less demanding than the requirements for clarity and specificity of objectives and for a solution technique of sufficient power and generality is the requirement for "perfect" information, both in devising alternatives and in predicting the outcomes of the alternatives proposed as solutions. To state unequivocally that all alternatives have been considered is an outright impossibility: there is *always* another just outside the experience of the analyst or decision-maker. The recourse has usually

[2] Kenneth J. Arrow, *Social Choice and Individual Values*, (New York, 1951).

been to attempt to bound the solution set in some manner deemed satisfactory (for example, by establishing extrema ranging from "do nothing" to an investment of resources clearly beyond the possible scale) and to limit analysis to those alternatives falling between the extrema.

The second aspect, knowledge of all outcomes, is not impossible but obviously presents much the same sort of problems that fortune-tellers have tried to overcome since time immemorial: a good guess *may* predict the outcome of action or policy equally as well as all the available wisdom. Of course, it is possible to reduce this uncertainty, to include it in analysis and to quantify it in weighing various proposals. Yet uncertainty remains a major difficulty, for which one of several more or less uncomfortable accommodations must be made.

Reactions to the demands of the rational model have appeared, stemming either from an attempt to more closely parallel human behavior and thought processes in decision-making or from an attempt to formalize a model which deals with the situations arising in the absence of perfect knowledge.

The incremental model suggests that the decision-maker does not in fact take the long-range all-inclusive view, but instead makes decisions which deal with immediate or near-immediate situations incrementally. "Incrementalism is a method of social action that takes existing reality as one alternative and compares the probable gains and losses of closely related alternatives by making relatively small adjustments about whose consequences approximately as much is known as about the consequences of existing reality, or both. . . . [Incrementalism] is the system of change practiced in all the durable polyarchies of the West."[3] Dahl and Lindblom divide the continuum of rational calculation processes into "science, incrementalism, calculated risks, and utopianism."[4] The rational model outlined earlier is an example of the first category of their typology.

A calculated risk is an action the consequences of which no one can predict with much certainty, but, for which "on balance, the risk [seems] to policy-makers to entail no consequences worse than those of existing reality."[5] The implication here is a lack of information (about (1) the outcome of continuing a present course or (2) taking some other action) so severe as to make some change from the present course as attractive, or more attractive, than continuing on the same course.

Utopianism differs from the other three suggested in assuming that the desired end-state will result from the recommended course(s) of ac-

³ Robert A. Dahl and Charles E. Lindblom, *Politics, Economics and Welfare* (New York, 1953), p. 82.
⁴ Dahl and Lindblom, p. 78 ff.
⁵ Dahl and Lindblom, p. 85.

tion.[6] The other three represent (in comparison to Utopianism) decreasing faith in the efficacy of prediction: the model of the outcome of some action.

Contending that the rationality of "economic man" must be viewed with some skepticism, Simon suggests that in a situation involving multiple persons—"the rationality of more than one"[7]—*a unique* solution may not be available at all, and that, in any event, the assumption of omniscience necessary to support a completely rational choice is far from realistic. In propounding the *principle of bounded rationality,* he says:

The capacity of the human mind for formulating and solving complex problems is very small compared with the size of the problems whose solution is required for objective rational behavior in the real world—or even for a reasonable approximation to such objective reality.[8]

The uncertainty involved in most choice or decision problems is, as suggested above, more difficult to contend with than the assumption that all alternatives are being considered. In modeling the behavior of individuals confronted with choices, Simon suggests that reality more nearly resembles a thermostat: that small changes in strategy, policy, or action direction are made in response to changes in knowledge (or information, more specifically). In short, man behaves like a system governed, in its behavior, by a feedback mechanism. The term coined by Simon to describe this behavior, and now commonly used to differentiate it from maximizing, is *satisficing.*[9]

Perhaps the most significant difference between satisficing and maximizing, however, is not so much the difference in philosophy as the difference in perspective or orientation. Maximizing is essentially an ideal, a goal of action. Satisficing, on the other hand, is a *model* of observed behavior. "If the proximate goal of economic and administrative theory is to describe and explain actual human behavior—'intendedly rational' or not, as the case may be—a theory that leaves out the 'relative, human difficulty' and consequently finds itself unable to account for 'struggle' and 'surprise' cannot be of much help."[10] But Simon's statement emphasizes the point: satisficing is a model *of* behavior, maximizing or rationality are models *for* behavior.

MODELS OF OUTCOMES

The model of the outcome is a central element of systems analysis and of every rational decision-making process or technique. As with the

[6] Dahl and Lindblom, p. 86.
[7] Herbert A. Simon, *Models of Man* (New York, 1957), p. 197.
[8] Simon, *Models,* p. 198.
[9] Simon, *Models,* p. 204.
[10] Simon, *Models,* p. 203.

words systems analysis, the word "model" has come to mean many things to many people, but here, at least initially, it too is intended in a general sense.[11]

The simplest and most unsophisticated (at least in mathematical or computational terms) model might be the plainest sort of verbal statement: If I drop a rock, it will fall to the ground (given certain conditions); if I hit Johnny, he will hit me back. A model, therefore, is a statement which indicates what will happen if a certain action is taken. As with the two statements or models above, there are elements of uncertainty in almost any model. If you are in orbit, the rock will not fall; it will float near at hand. If Johnny is smaller than you are, he may run and cry. (Not coincidentally, the involvement of human behavior in the second example suggests some of the greater complexities in "modeling" human behavior and has something to do with the comparative success of physical and social science in the application of strict modelling techniques.)

In the laboratory, rocks may be dropped under varying conditions until the outcome, under those conditions, can be predicted with considerable accuracy. Not only is it possible to repeat the experiment, it is only because of the scale of the action being examined that it is possible to experiment at all. There is really little concern about the fate of the rock and the supply of rocks is large.

The consequences of experimenting with large-scale public decisions are quite different, and here the model is seldom able to be subjected to empirical testing and verification at full scale. It is not even feasible to engage in large public work projects to "see if they work." While that may be the effect under some circumstances, the initial decision to act is usually accompanied by confidence (or reassurances) that the action will have the desired outcome.

Simulation is used as an alternative to full-scale testing of many systems, providing a method for *predicting* outcome for various alternative courses without the accuracy about outcome or the breadth of sensitivity that full-scale testing of alternatives might provide. In most instances it offers a greatly shortened time-scale and a markedly reduced investment of resources in comparison to trying out alternatives at full-scale. To illustrate this, physical simulation models come immediately to mind. Perhaps one of the most prominent is the Corps of Engineers' model of the Mississippi River located at Vicksburg, used to evaluate the conse-

[11] Model has been used, now, for two apparently different meanings. The rational planning "model," a "model" for behavior, and other references above refer to its use to describe *either* a desired behavior or sequence of actions *or* one observed. In the following paragraphs it takes on the aspects of a *theory*, an if-then statement. In the most general sense the two meanings are not different, but the second is specifically closer to classic experimental models.

quences of various flood control works on the river. Falling into the classification of analog models, such physical models have been used since antiquity and are still in active use today, incorporating modern innovations such as the use of electrical circuits to study the behavior of building frames and the familiar wind-tunnel tests of aircraft.

Abstract models, verbal or mathematical, also have a long and honorable history. The falling rock (more specifically, an apple) inspired Newton to formalize the law of gravity as a "model" mathematical formula. In many instances physical analogs have been used until relationships were well enough understood to permit mathematical formulation. In these instances for which precise mathematical relationships cannot be stated, theories or models nevertheless are described which indicate outcomes of an action or actions. All of these techniques might be lumped under this same term—simulation.

Simulation has become a particularly popular word and technique since the advent of the digital computer, a device which has been made widely available only since World War II. The digital computer has permitted the computation of outcomes of mathematical relationships once impossible to cope with because of their difficulty or of the scale of the system being described. While not changing the fundamentals of modeling or, really, of simulation, it has given rise to a new spectrum of techniques which reflect the level of involvement of the machine and the tightness of the structure of the model. At one extreme, the purely mathematical and theoretically precise model may, quite likely, be solved directly on a computer: the outcomes of various inputs reflecting public policies are calculated. Less well-structured models may require human interference in adjusting outcomes from computer runs, and successive approximations may be necessary to iterate to a solution which satisfies all the conditions of the policies. At the other extreme, gaming has gained popularity, and again, it may or may not involve computers. In this case, a situation is established, various human "players" assume roles, and the rules of behavior are specified. Policies are tried in a microcosm, with the explicit assumption tha the outcomes in the game simulate those that would occur in real life.

COMMUNICATION: VOCABULARY OF ANALYSIS

It was noted earlier that the outcomes must be stated in terms which permit comparisons to each other and to the goals of the decision-maker (or of the public). The most popular single indicator or term for outputs has been dollars or economic value. Many items of interest to the decision-maker are directly measured in dollars, many more can be related to some economic value or surrogate, and, in most cases of private investment, economic consequences are of central importance.

Since profit, or more specifically, efficiency of operation in economic terms (defined by the point at which a unit of input fails to yield at least an additional equally valued unit of output), has become the most popular mode of expression, a major concern in the application of systems analysis techniques has been the use of money alone to express outputs which have values defying economic description.

One method of circumventing the difficulty of non-monetary outputs is to restate the problem slightly. The familiar process of setting standards and meeting these at the "least cost" provides a method of expressing different alternatives in common terms, provided that the standards are uniform. Another method is to hold to a budget restriction and evaluate alternatives in terms of the amount of output which each yields. So long as the outputs remain comparable, the ranking is clear and unambiguous, the most desirable alternative will be apparent. Both of these techniques escape the requirement that all inputs and outputs be expressed in the same terms. Rarely, however, do these alternatives solve the problem. Frequently one output will produce six of A and four of B while the other produces five of each. The decision as to which is best rests again with the question of a common denominator describing the relative value of A and B.

In a more pragmatic vein, the use of economic indicators has for years guided decision-makers in the public and private economic sector. Gross national product, per capita income, and disposable income are examples. While in all instances there may not be a clear relationship between the value of a given increase in GNP and an increase in per capita disposable income, the numbers do provide a strong basis for evaluating the efficiency of various policies and plans.

More recently it has been suggested that a set of "social indicators" might be evolved using data commonly available to government agencies (or obtained through special surveys) which would reflect in a meaningful way the *social* condition of some part of the population. More importantly, according to Olson, they might do what is suggested here: measure performance of various programs, policies, or actions rather than using dollar or manpower *inputs* as the only barometer of activity or success. Organized production of social indicators is, in many ways, still an infant science. On the other hand, many statistics commonly available today give an indication of *social* condition: infant mortality, crime statistics and so forth.[12]

This emphasis on the statement of output of the model suggests one

[12] Daniel Bell and Mancur Olson, "Toward a Social Report," *The Public Interest,* no. 15, National Affairs, Inc. (Spring, 1969), pp. 72–105. This article, describing in general the contents and intent of the recent government report of the same name, is an excellent review and reference describing current activity and thought on the subject of social indicators.

other important criterion for a useful model and analysis: the variables which are *input* to the model to reflect different policies, programs, or actions *must* do so. This seems obvious, but all too frequently during the course of putting together a model, concern for outputs, algorithms, and techniques leads farther and farther away from the original notion of input, until input variables become completely irrelevant to the problem. Perhaps even more seductive is the urge to introduce more and more input variables until the model becomes self-fulfilling: what goes in comes out. While this too may have its value as a learning or research procedure, it changes the emphasis of the "model" considerably. (It may also add another stage to the process: a new model will be needed to create the inputs.)

ROLES AND RESPONSIBILITIES

Now we turn to the question of who does what in applying the systems analysis approach to public or political decisions. The principal actors are, of course, the public decision-maker, and, let us assume he is an elected rather than an appointed official, and the systems analyst, who is presumably a staff member of the government unit which the decision-maker serves and leads. Our point will be to show that each is dependent upon the other for successful application of systems analysis techniques. Although responsibility for some of the tasks in the analysis and evaluation of alternatives clearly falls to one or the other of the actors, the process requires considerable interaction and mutual understanding.

In the classic situation described here the decision-maker initiates the activity. He has a problem which he must resolve because of external pressure to make a decision. But he lacks full knowledge of the situation, or of the alternative decisions he could take, or of the effects of his decisions, or of all of these. So he turns to an analyst for assistance. We are assuming that the problem is well defined, the need for a decision is strong, technical assistance is available, and there is time to utilize it. We will consider the functions of decision-maker and analyst in this ideal case.

THE DECISION-MAKER

The decision-maker has the major responsibility for setting the objectives to be achieved, for determining the criteria to be used in selecting actions to be taken, and for establishing the context within which the problem is to be analyzed. These three things: objectives, criteria, and context are all part of the definition of the problem and must be supplied to the analyst, at least in skeletal form, before he can proceed.

The setting of objectives is simply the specification of what is to be accomplished—in response to the problem. The scope of objectives can range from elimination of the immediate problem to a much broader view in which the decision-maker sees the problem as symptomatic of a more fundamental difficulty and asks the analyst to examine the means of achieving some positive objective which will resolve the basic problems. However the objectives are stated, they are a necessary input to the analyst because they provide not only a technical guide to what should be accomplished by any actions taken in response to a problem, but also a political understanding of what the feasible objectives are in response to a *particular* problem. Thus the statement of objectives serves in part to further define the problem for the analyst and also serves in part to establish the boundaries within which the "acceptable" solutions may be found.

The selection criteria are used to evaluate the various alternative ways of dealing with the problem. In essence this involves adding to the statement of objectives those constraints which the decision-maker considers of sufficient importance to affect his decision. A constraint is typically a "but don't" statement. The objectives are "do" statements. For example, "Do improve the condition of the streets, but don't put us in a position where we will have to raise taxes." Such constraints are essentially an elaboration or refinement of the objectives. They may also show the analyst the way in which the decision-maker understands the problem.

The problem context involves further definition of the problem and further constraints on the solution. The problem context includes the decision-maker's understanding of what the problem situation actually is and how it is related (or not related) to other situations or events. The analyst, if he is to fulfill his role, in effect needs to know what the decision-maker's "model" of the world is. The analyst needs to know how, when, and under what circumstances the decision is to be made. Finally, the analyst needs to know the kind of quality of implementation capability available for dealing with problems of this type. All of these things help the analyst to understand what the decision-maker thinks the problem is, and they provide him with additional, if less precise, constraints for determining the range of feasible solutions.

In summary, the decison-maker's prime role, in the application of a systems analytic approach to a public decision, is to define the problem. In a formal sense this can be viewed as the setting up of objectives, establishing selection criteria, and establishing the problem context. These useful distinctions highlight the different kinds of information the decision-maker is giving to the analyst. In actuality this part of the process is likely to be characterized by the decision-maker's lack of precision, ambiguity, and perhaps even reluctance to commit himself to objectives, criteria, or context except in a very general way.

THE ANALYST

His prime role is modeling. He must develop, validate, and exercise a model of the problem situation. The analyst has, then, the responsibility for providing the decision-maker with estimates of what the effects will be of the various actions the decision-maker can take (including inaction).

The analyst builds a model of the real situation in which the problem is found. This might be called the problem context, but then the words would mean something quite different from what they did previously. Here the context is the empirical substance of the problem situation. The factors are variables that are actually involved and the relationships between them.

The analyst's task is an extremely difficult one. He is being called upon to represent the way some tiny part of the world works now, and *how it will work when some of the existing conditions are changed*. He must formulate the model so that variables over which the decision-maker has influence and which affect the problem are included and correctly represented. And of course he should formulate the model so that the objectives sought by the decision-maker can be evaluated.

Validating the model involves demonstrating its reliability for making if-then statements about future changes in the problem situation resulting from actions of the decision-maker and other factors. This is a major technical problem. And it is uniquely the analyst's responsibility. Exercising the model is simply using the model to test the effectiveness of various actions available to the decision-maker. Again this is largely a technical task and falls to the analyst.

JOINT ROLES AND INTERACTION

It should be obvious from the above discussion that the roles and responsibilities of the decision-maker and the analyst cannot be neatly divided into separate compartments between which interchange occurs but interaction does not. Successful use of the systems approach is very likely to involve significant interaction involving changes in the thinking of both decision-maker and analyst as a result of information exchanged in the process of going from the problem statement to selection of a course of action to deal with the problem.

Consider problem definition. The decision-maker states the problem, from the viewpoint of his position. In attempting to model the problem situation, the analyst takes an objective, empirical viewpoint which attempts to operationally define the problem in terms of observed or observable real relationships. These two statements of the problem are very likely to overlap to a considerable degree, but they are unlikely to coincide. To make them coincide the two must exchange information and approach a common definition in which the political realities seen by the decision-maker and the empirical relationships observed by the analyst are both represented.

Similarly the bounding of the problem by selection criteria and context, and model development and validation require considerable interaction. For example, the analyst may find that the decision-maker has set the criteria and context too loosely so that the area is ambiguous. Or the analyst may find that the context has been described too narrowly and a part of the problem situation is being excluded. On the other hand, the decision-maker viewing model results may find that the analyst, in concentrating on measureable variables and relationships, has failed to capture some important dimension of the problem. Inevitably a successful application of systems analysis will involve considerable learning by both the analyst and the decision-maker. Such learning primarily involves bringing together information about the problem situation which comes from the different perspectives of the participants in both the analysis and decision processes.

Thus far we have discussed the joint responsibilities of decision-maker and analyst. All of the previously discussed elements of the systems approach for both the decision-maker and the analyst involve summarization and extrapolation from experiences and rational calculation. Both the analyst and the decision-maker are involved in trying to order and relate all the information they have about a problem situation—its content and context. The attentive reader will note, however, that we have not mentioned one of the principal components of the systems analysis approach—the design of alternatives. The responsibility for this function is not well-defined. The reason for this ambiguity lies in the special nature of the task.

When we turn to design of alternative actions to achieve objectives we are, except in one special case, reaching beyond the realm of experience and attempting to find some new reality. Quite simply, developing alternatives is in large measure an act of the imagination. The process, successful or not, cannot be repeated with a guarantee that by following the same steps you will come out with the same results. This is not to imply that something magical occurs. We are simply recognizing that the method of finding a solution to a problem situation is not as well understood as that of defining the problem. And we should emphasize that the whole systems approach is oriented toward first establishing an information environment in which the probability of discovering all useful actions for dealing with a problem is maximized, and then second, establishing an information environment which will make possible an objective evaluation of all alternatives considered.

Perhaps the best way to illustrate the nature of the design problem is to consider the special case in which the design of alternatives does not reach beyond experience. Consider a situation in which you know exactly what you wish to achieve, you know all the factors that can contribute to the achievement of your objectives, and you know how these factors interact with the problem situation and with each other. Then the problem of designing alternatives involves only the relatively simple task of considering all the different ways in which these relevant factors may be combined and selecting that combination which rates best according to your selection criteria. This, of course, is the classic optimization problem. If certain limiting assumptions are accepted the problem can be readily solved by available techniques of mathematical programming.

The important thing about this special case is that no "new" information is gleaned from any of the possible solutions to the problem. All of the possible solutions are contained in the description of the problem situation. It is exactly this kind of problem situation that many people expect when they discuss systems analysis. But decision-makers or analysts do not often face this situation in dealing with public policy problems. Instead, existing knowledge does not permit a definition of the problem situation so that "the solution space" is known. Both the analyst and the decision-maker are faced with the task of combining past experience, insight, and intuition to develop a set of alternatives which will include at least some representation of all possible solutions to the problem.

Clearly neither the analyst nor the decision-maker can claim unique authority and responsibility for the design of alternatives. In practice the task often falls primarily to the analyst. His job, as defined, includes the design of alternatives as well as their testing. The special skill he brings to the task is probably his sense of a variety of useful actions. The reverse of this is also likely to be true. The analyst's preoccupation with particular variables and relationships in the modeling process may lead him to ignore certain types of alternatives—particularly those whose first effects fall outside the domain of the evaluation model. When confronted with the task of designing alternatives the sensible analyst will seek the advice of the decision-maker along with others involved with the actions to be taken, if for no other reason than to discover their "pet projects" so that these may be evaluated with all other proposals.

In summary, the successful use of systems analysis in public policy decisions requires continuing interaction between decision-maker and analyst. The interaction takes the form of information exchanged on the objectives, the selection criteria, the problem context, and the model to be used. The result of this exchange is that, while the functional activity of analyst and decision-maker remains clear, their roles and responsibilities in the process become less distinct.

LIMITATIONS OF SYSTEMS ANALYSIS

We need to consider carefully the limitations of systems analysis in local public decision processes, because both the critics and supporters of these ideas are inclined to overstate their cases. The supporters, attracted by the logic and simplicity of the ideas involved, are inclined to sweep away all cautions and trust that sweet reason will win out in the end. The opponents often seem to be equally blinded to the merits of the systems approach by, in their case, an almost philosophical objection which denies the possibility of objective analysis and, in extreme cases, the possibility of rational behavior.

The real limitation of systems analysis is that, contrary to both the vigorous supporters and violent critics, it contains no magic. In the words of a worn but appropriate phrase, it is no substitute for thinking. True, it provides a framework in which thinking can be organized and hopefully enhanced. But it is not a method like a mathematical formula for which, if you proceed according to the rules and plug in the appropriate values, you are guaranteed the solution to the problem.

This point should be stressed. Systems analysis is characterized more by "looseness" than by "tightness." While the elements of a systems analysis must be worked through with all the care and scientific rigor the analyst can muster if it is to be valid, a systems analysis as such is not a prescribed set of procedures. Methodology used in modeling may change drastically from one application to another. And of course the kind and quality of data will change. Obviously then, a systems analysis is not a procedure that *does* thinking, it is a procedure *for doing* thinking.

There are many conceptual and practical limitations of which the public decision-maker must be aware once any misconception about the basic capabilities of the approach is cleared up. Let us first look at some conceptual problems. The most difficult task in a systems analysis is to build a "model" which will simulate the real world problem situation and permit the meaningful evaluation of possible solutions to the problem. The fundamental source of the difficulty is theory. Simply put, we have a very limited understanding of the way the world works. And the depth of understanding required for a useful model is intimidating. Recall that the model must provide useful conditional predictions, if-then statements about the effects of changes made by public policy decisions in the situation being modeled. Note that in the social sciences, the substance of which is often the subject for such a model, our scholarship has been oriented more towards explanation of what has happened (usually from a cross-sectional view) than towards prediction.

The difficulty the analyst faces is plain. He is not a theoretician and all too often he cannot find an adequate theoretical base on which to model his problem situation. Since the model is the crucial central element to systems analysis, this is a less than happy state of affairs. The analyst *and* the decision-maker must both understand the model well enough to know its limitations. The decision-maker who accepts the analyst's model unquestioningly may be accidentally misled, but more important he will not get any of the value which can be obtained from even a weak model by appropriate, cautious use.

A related difficulty in applying systems analysis to public decisions is often called the "measurement problem." As discussed earlier, it is often quite difficult to find suitable, comparable measures to describe the many variables that ought to be represented in the analysis. Again this limitation presents severe difficulty only in those few instances in which the analyst, the decision-maker, or both, are insensitive to the techniques they are using.

In addition, there are a number of practical problems facing the public official at the state and local level who wants to implement systems analysis. We will discuss these briefly in two groups: production problems and communication problems.

There are four common difficulties likely to arise in producing a systems analysis in such settings.[13] The analysis, primarily model development and validation, inevitably takes much longer than anticipated. There are many reasons for this to occur. The two fundamental reasons are that the process is fairly unfamiliar to its users and that there is little past material on which to draw. So there is usually a great deal of exploratory work with consequent difficulty in maintaining schedules. The highly variable problem situations which may be presented add to the difficulty of maintaining adequate stand-by capacity. The result is likely to be frustration for both the decision-maker, because he can not get a good answer to his question when he needs or wants it, and for the analyst, because he must give an answer before he is ready.

Systems analysis in general and models in particular require a very great amount of information. The lack of adequate data resources at the local and state levels is often a difficulty. A rather highly trained cadre of professional people is needed for any substantial analysis. Finally, a fairly large sum of money is required to do decent analysis. The requirements of time, data, staff, and money pose fairly serious practical difficulties for a policy maker who wishes to use a systems analysis approach. But then, time, data, staff, and money problems impinge on everything

---

[13] These difficulties as experienced in the process of building urban land use models are discussed in detail in George C. Hemmens, "Survey of Planning Agency Experience with Urban Development Models, Data Processing and Computers" in Hemmens, ed. *Urban Development Models* (Washington, D.C., 1969).

else a public official may wish to do. So he should not be unduly alarmed.

The second type of practical difficulty to arise in implementing a systems approach is communication. Two communication problems are particularly relevant to the decision-maker. First is communication with the analyst. As discussed above, close interaction between decision-maker and analyst is the desirable mode of operation. If this does not occur, the decision-maker has trouble. And usually the analysis is less than useful to him. Secondly, the decision-maker must communicate with his public. When he uses a model for analysis of the problem and for potential solutions, he may find himself tempted to communicate on the issue with the public through the model. This is natural because he has to some extent come to communicate with the analyst through the model. But this has occurred over a period of time with gradually increasing shared understanding of the relation of the real situation to the model with its high level of abstraction and restrictive assumptions. This is more a potential than a real problem, since there is little evidence, except for a few isolated cases, of decision-makers with this new malady which we might label "model in the mouth" disease.

We can sum up this discussion of the limitations and difficulties involved in applying systems analysis to state and local public decision-making thusly. We are not well-equipped in public policy making at the sub-national level in terms of people, data, models, and understanding of the way the world works. Because of the central role of the model in systems analysis, the embarrassment of not knowing enough comes quickly to the surface and provides a handy target for critics. But this embarrassment is not properly laid at the feet of systems analysis. If anything it ought to serve as an indictment of other approaches to solving the same problems which would permit the decision-maker to function *in ignorance* of his own ignorance.

TOWARDS AN INTEGRATION OF THE ANALYSIS AND DECISION-MAKING PROCESSES

As we have discussed above, the application of the systems analysis approach to public decisions is not accomplished simply by hiring a person or staff labeled "systems analyst" and telling them to go to work. Success in such a venture is likely to be directly related to the extent of participation in the analysis process by all those concerned with the issues—politicians, public administrators, technical personnel, and analysts.

Further, to be really useful the systems approach, like any other planning or problem solving process, must have some follow-through. Someone must monitor the issue which was the subject of the analysis and see what effect the action taken has on the situation. This is extremely difficult because many other factors relevant to the problem situation may change simultaneously with the public action. Ideally, a monitoring process should accomplish two things. First, it should provide information to evaluate the "model" that was used in the analysis by comparing real world events against those expected from use of the simulation model. By discovering errors in the modeled relationships in this way, subsequent analysis can hopefully be improved by developing a more refined model. The monitoring process thus provides feedback to the analyst about the adequacy of his past technical decisions in model design and analysis.

Second, the monitoring process is essential to inform the decision-maker of the results of his action. If there are indications that the action is not likely to solve the problem, if the problem situation should actually worsen, or if some problem related in some way either to the original problem or to the remedial action taken should arise, the decision-maker will need to know as soon as possible. Similarly if the action taken was directed towards some long range target the decision-maker needs to know if the expected progress is being attained. This statement implies the need for an information system and continuing analysis. An information system is simply a set of procedures for collecting, retrieving, and analyzing data. The key point here is that the analyst and the decision-maker need an information system that is directly relevant to the problem situation and the model. That is, the information system must produce the output measures used in the analysis. Continuing analysis is called for simply because the analyst and/or decision-maker do not want too much delay between their first hint that things may not be going as they thought they would, and confirmation of their suspicions. It could be too late. So they repeat the analysis, perhaps with an improved model of the situation and with other changes to reflect the current status of the situation, and attempt to estimate the likely outcome of current trends. The next step, of course, is for additional remedial action—a new decision.

We have discussed a negative situation—failure of the original decision to solve the problem. The opposite is equally possible. The monitoring process may show that more improvement than expected is occurring in the problem situation. This may lead the decision-maker to re-examine the objectives and perhaps attempt to achieve a higher level for this objective or a new objective.

To reemphasize, systems analysis is not a one shot process. Its real value comes in the continuing application of analysis and the constant reexamination of objectives and criteria. Viewed in the most general way, systems analysis can be considered a part of an information system.[14] The

[14] Raymond A. Bauer, "Societal Feedback," *The Annals*, CCCLXXIII (September, 1967).

importance of feedback and continuity in this process has led to suggestions that the model of planning inherent in such a process is strongly analogous to the cybernetic model.[15]

It should be clear first that the *use* of systems analysis in public decision-making is not a cure-all for the *difficulties* of public decision-making. It does not replace intuition, experience, or judgement. To the contrary, it highlights these and hopefully permits their fullest possible utilization in problem solving. Secondly, systems analysis is not something that is done to handle a problem in the mechanical or rigidly structured sense of "handle." Rather it is a way of organizing for decision-making which calls for the rigorous use of scientific tools. Finally, systems analysis is not done *for* a decision-maker. It is done *with* a decision-maker.

In summary, systems analysis provides one method for utilizing the scientific method and objective analysis in public decisions. It is only one variant of a number of ways by which we might approach problem solving from a rational perspective. A major feature of this approach to public decisions, if it is correctly used, is that the analysis and decision processes are essentially one. There are several actors and many roles. But the roles are not fully separable. In this age of increasingly sophisticated techniques, this central thrust—in systems analysis—for the integration of decision and analysis processes may be the strongest point in favor of the approach.

[15] Bauer, "Feedback."

Planning and Budgeting: Marriage Whose Style?

S. KENNETH HOWARD

A budget is a plan, but not all plans are budgets. All administrators should plan—that is, utilize a planning process—but some professional staff personnel specifically identify themselves as "planners." Professional planners and public administrators are wary of "politics," but they increasingly recognize that public policy decisions lie at the heart of politics and that the effectiveness of truly professional staff work is demonstrated by the impact that work has upon policy decisions.

These statements summarize a series of dilemmas and ambiguities that currently confound the fields of planning and budgeting. The advent of planning-programming-budgeting systems has re-emphasized certain underlying truths about both planning and budgeting and the necessary relationships between these two activities, but it has also exacerbated the ambiguities, insecurities, and the not totally compatible movements and changes that have been taking place in the planning and finance fields.

This selection will focus upon the changes that are taking place in both planning and budgeting, as efforts are made to respond appropriately to an ever more rapidly changing society. This analysis will be placed in the context of planning-programming-budgeting systems on the assumption that such systems will, for the foreseeable future, be a major part of the framework within which planning and budgeting activities will be carried on at all levels of American government.

A SUMMARY OF PLANNING-PROGRAMMING-BUDGETING[1]

The scope, content, and procedural methods employed in PPB systems will have an impact upon the kind of policy decisions that result. Here lies the basis for a straightforward political struggle with many interests and forces seeking to shape this new process through which public policy issues will be filtered.

For the purposes of this analysis, the more important characteristics of PPBS are these:

1. PPB focuses on identifying the fundamental objectives of the government and then relating all activities, regardless of organizational placement, to these objectives. It emphasizes the outputs, or results of governmental action, rather than the means, or inputs, used to accomplish the results obtained

2. future-year (that is, beyond the next budget year or biennium) implications of program objectives, outputs, and costs are explicitly considered

3. all pertinent costs are recognized—capital as well as operating or other noncapital costs, and supporting as well as direct costs

4. alternative actions are analyzed in a systematic manner. Systematic analysis is the crux of PPB.[2] For this analysis to be most helpful in evaluating alternative actions, the generalized goals or statements of objectives must be "operationalized" by making them ever more specific, concrete, and quantifiable

---

[1] These ideas have been developed in this format in the publications of the State-Local Finances Project. See particularly, *What is PPB?* (Washington, D.C., January, 1967), pp. 2–7, and Selma Mushkin and Marjorie C. Willcox, *An Operative PPB System: A Collaborative Undertaking in the States* (Washington, D.C., 1968), pp. 19–21.

[2] *What is PPB?*, p. 2. This point is also made continually throughout the "Bible" in this field. See David Novick, ed., *Program Budgeting: Program Analysis and the Federal Government* (Cambridge, Mass., 1965).

5. a mechanism is established for monitoring what actually occurs as programs are implemented and for obtaining feedback information so that programs can be adjusted as necessary.

In accordance with these characteristics, an operational PPB system should produce at least three types of documents. The first is an across-the-board governmental program structure that identifies basic governmental objectives and categorizes activities and expenditures accordingly. The second is a multi-year program and financial plan that displays, in accordance with the program structure, all pertinent program costs, associated revenues, and program outputs or measures that will indicate the scope and magnitude of the contemplated programs. Typically these projections extend five years beyond the current fiscal year. A third set of documents is in-depth program analyses. These studies can be undertaken only after the organization has developed a capacity for systematic analysis. Emphasis in these analyses is placed upon the effectiveness with which a particular course of action achieves a goal rather than upon the efficiency with which that action or program is carried out.

With effectiveness stress is placed upon attaining the desired result or goal, while efficiency connotes producing something without wasting resources. The two concepts are not unrelated, since the failure of certain actions to obtain a desired result means that the resources used in those activities have to some extent been wasted. Effectiveness does require that resources be consumed at some level of efficiency greater than zero, and efficiency cannot be measured without some concern for goals. However, a useful distinction between them can be made by recognizing that an operation can produce a given result efficiently (such as meeting certain cost and other engineering specifications in building a highway) but not produce the result desired (linking certain population centers or reducing highway deaths). Thus a program can be operated very efficiently and be ineffective while another activity may be rather inefficient but nonetheless very effective. Such alternatives will differ in their costs as well as in their levels of effectiveness. Analytical studies are used to evaluate both sets of differences.

Analyses will vary in the extent of their coverage, from entire programs to special problems or issues within particular programs, but they should include:

1. a clear definition of the problem(s)

2. identification of the basic governmental goals or objectives involved

3. selection of "criteria" or "measures of effectiveness" that will permit evaluation of progress toward the stated objectives and aid in differentiating a good decision from a poor one. Both quantifiable and nonquantifiable or intangible criteria should be included

4. identification and description of the alternative courses of action that will meet the problem(s). These alternatives may include different programs, different levels of activity in a given program, or both of these possibilities and may even in a few cases lead to consideration of alternative objectives or basic policy goals

5. estimates of the total costs of each alternative, showing both long-range and immediate cost implications. The time period covered should be adapted to the specific characteristics of the options under consideration; thus different analyses might have different timetables while a common summarizing five-year program and financial plan could be retained

6. presentation of the cost-and-effect "trade-offs" that exist among the alternatives. What costs and effects would be gained (or lost) if one alternative were selected rather than another?

7. identification of the major uncertainties. Uncertainty is inevitable and should probably be quantified. Whether quantified or not, the uncertainties and their possible impact upon various alternatives should be made explicit

8. explication of the major assumptions that underlie the analysis with an indication of the extent to which the results of the analysis are sensitive to changes in those assumptions

9. sufficient documentation so that others can understand and evaluate what has been done and judge how accurate the assumptions, findings, and conclusions are likely to be.

PPB can be summarized as involving:

1. Appraisals and comparisons of various governmental activities in terms of their contributions to . . . objectives. 2. Determination of how given objectives can be attained with minimum expenditure of resources. 3. Projection of government activities over an adequate time horizon. 4. Comparison of the relative contribution of . . . activities to . . . objectives. 5. Revisions of objectives, programs and budgets in the light of experience and changing circumstances.[3]

SOME ASSERTIONS

The balance of this discussion will be built around the following assertions:

Planning is a responsibility of all administrators.

Planners are now openly engaged in politics.

The emphasis in government budgeting is changing and is generating conflicts between planners and budgeteers.

A budget is more than a plan.

[3] Arthur Smithies, "Conceptual Framework for the Program Budget," in Novick, *Program Budgeting,* pp. 26–27.

THE PLANNING PROCESS

Planning is a key responsibility of all executives, and not inappropriately does the first letter in the acronym POSDCORB stand for planning.[4] Since planning is something that is expected of all administrators, it is not surprising that there are many kinds of planning. Even a cursory look at writing in this field will reveal references to long-range, short-range, futuristic, policy, advocacy, operational, organizational, functional, program, departmental, economic, fiscal, strategic, tactical, regional, comprehensive, and contingency planning. This listing scarcely exhausts the possibilities, but it does highlight the degree of semantic confusion that abounds under the general rubric of "planning." Few words are less sharply defined or more widely employed today in the field of public administration.

In its simplest form, planning may be defined as rational forethought,[5] and, as with the flag and motherhood, few can oppose it. But if generalizations are to be helpful, they must certainly get beyond this level. Since planning comes in such varied forms, it must be the underlying process rather than specific plans that is common to this wide spectrum of purposes and planners. This, then, is the first important point: planning is a process used by all kinds of officials for varying purposes; it is not the unique province of a few who call themselves "planners."

Differences in viewpoint do exist, however, between professional planners and operating administrators, as the following exchange between the planning director of a large Midwestern state and the former finance director of a border state indicates:

PLANNER: I view state planning as a process in which the whole social, economic, and physical system of the state is analyzed and the options are developed as to the optimum development of the state as people (with development occurring) through the state's and executive's intervention into those social, physical, and economic systems. This occurs and is implemented by virtue of the budget in resource allocations, through legislative programs, through changing the rules of the game—the basic law and structure of charters—through executive leadership in leading the private sector, through incentives to the private sector, through local government—both mandating local governments to do certain things and through other instruments of getting incentives—through

---

[4] It was Luther Gulick who suggested that management consists of planning, organizing, staffing, directing, coordinating, reporting, and budgeting. See Luther Gulick and Lyndall Urwick, eds. *Papers on the Science of Administration* (New York, 1937).

[5] For a more systematic definition of planning and its components, see Yehezkel Dror, "The Planning Process: A Facet Design," *International Review of Administrative Sciences*, xxix, no. 1 (1963), 44–58.

channeling of federal money. What I am trying to say is that there are many ways state plans are implemented and budgets are only one of them.

FINANCE
DIRECTOR: I cannot distinguish between your description of planning and what I would regard as a description of administrative government. As far as I am concerned, you have described what government is.[6]

Perhaps some other recent definitions of the planning process will shed some light on this matter:

State comprehensive planning is most effectively employed as an element of the executive function of State government. The Governor, therefore, is the official primarily responsible for its conduct and execution. The State comprehensive planning program should be conceived as a continuing process to provide central policy formulation for the inter-related social, economic and physical aspects of State development, to give direction to the various governmental programs involved, and to effect coordination of departmental or functional agency activities and programs.

The primary tasks of State comprehensive planning are: (1) to articulate goals and objectives for the development of the State; (2) to identify and analyze significant development problems and opportunities facing the State; and (3) to propose alternative courses of action to be taken by the State to solve the problems or realize the opportunities. The consequences of each alternative course of action should be presented in terms of its relation to the goals and objective for State development, to the efficient allocation of resources for State development, and to specific programs activities and proposals.[7]

Slightly less sure of its footing and admitting that "there presently is no single universal definition of state planning on any but the most general level," the Committee on State Planning of the American Institute of Planners stated:

The state planning process is often seen as either all, or any combination of: the identification and formulation of state objectives; the provision of information to facilitate decision-making, coordination and the production of a comprehensive framework for social, economic and physical development efforts in local government, state government, federal assistance programs, and the private sector. It also is frequently viewed as providing the policy basis for gubernatorial action in the development of a legislative program and as an aid for the legislature in policy determination....

---

[6] These quotations come from an unpublished transcript of "Symposium on the Link Between Budgeting and Planning," Institute on State Programming for the 70's, Chapel Hill, N.C., April 25, 1968.

[7] U.S., Department of Housing and Urban Development, Office of the Assistant Secretary, "State Comprehensive Planning," Chapter 5 in *Urban Planning Program Guide*, (December 12, 1966).

Assuming that a basic purpose of state planning is to introduce more systematic thought into the decision-making process of state government, then state objectives become a primary framework in providing direction for the state planning process.[8]

These two definitions can now be compared with one from the budgeting field:

The crux of a PPB system is program analysis. The term "program analysis" as used in a PPB system essentially consists of the process of determining the relevant objectives, synthesizing alternative means toward these objectives, and identifying the costs and effectiveness (i.e., the "benefits" or "returns") of each alternative. Estimation of the costs for alternatives and the estimation of how the costs are likely to vary with changes in significant program characteristics are major parts of the analysis.[9]

If these quotations can be accepted as representative, they lead to several observations. First, PPB, at least in its key element of program analysis, is a prime example of the planning process at work. Bereft of verbiage, these statements seem to indicate that the planning process consists of defining the goal, finding alternative ways to achieve that goal, evaluating those alternatives, and selecting the most appropriate one. These ideas are scarcely new; they are the major components in the long-standing model of "rational" or "economic" man. Thus, what is new about PPB and the new style of "planning" is not any unique underlying ideas, but rather the combination of these two with other ideas and technologies in a single conceptual scheme and operational system along with an emphasis upon quantification. The rational approach to problem-solving undergirds the planning process and one of its latest offspring—planning-programming-budgeting.

It is also clear that planners are increasingly concerned about having an impact upon the decision-making process in government. To do this the planners must demonstrate their usefulness to chief executives and other key decision-makers. Yet, if the underlying rationalistic ideas of planning should be common to all administrators, what role is the planner supposed to play? This question leads to the second assertion—that today planners are overtly engaged in political struggles.

THE PLANNER MEETS POLITICS

Planning, per se, is ineffective unless the actions taken are affected by the information and analysis produced by the planning process. To have relevance, planners must work on problems that are important to

---

[8] The Committee on State Planning, American Institute of Planners, *State Planning in the Sixties,* (December, 1968), p. II-1.
[9] State-Local Finances Project, George Washington University, "The Role and Nature of Cost Analysis in a PPB System," *PPB Note 6* (April, 1967), p. 1.

key decision-makers and present ideas or proposals in a way that indicates understanding of the viewpoint of the executives concerned.

The suggestion that planners should be concerned about policy matters and the political efficacy of their work is scarcely new:[10]

Our planning programs may be ineffective if we do not understand that the essence of planning is policy and the essence of democratic planning is choice.[11]

In practice, however, policy is only a polite word for politics—that struggle over whose will shall prevail in the distribution of the rewards and deprivations available through the workings of the political system. Policies determine gains and losses as social directions and actions are set or changed. To suggest to the planner that he concern himself with policies is to throw him immediately into the crucible of politics. He is often ill-prepared for this role, and for too long the mythology of the planning profession eschewed such a role entirely.

The state planner, with little or no physical planning base to rely upon, is virtually forced to enter this political thicket if he intends to prove that his talents can contribute to the general improvement of society. Many urban planners have reached the same conclusion, but professional mores have not yet fully accepted this viewpoint. To be sure, state planners do grasp the more traditional physical planning base when they can find one, particularly in the form of state capital programming and budgeting.[12]

Perhaps state planners move toward this role faster than their local counterparts because the need for staff help in policy formulation has been more apparent in gubernatorial than in city mayors' or city managers' officers. Whether that bit of whimsy is accurate or not, executives at all levels of government have increasingly sensed their need for help in formulating their programs and policies. However, this need gives rise to a kind of planning that is far removed from the comprehensive physical master plan document syndrome of earlier times. Modern planning has a decision and action orientation that is almost antithetical to the contemplative, inventory-taking, long-range goal-setting and projection processes associated with traditional city planning. In making their staff available to executives, planners have found themselves closer to the key deci-

[10] To select only one of many possible sources making this same point, and to show that this kind of thinking is going on among practitioners as well as academicians, see Frederick T. Aschman, "The 'Policy Plan' in the Planning Program," *Planning 1963* (Chicago, 1963), pp. 105–11.
[11] Aschman, "Policy Plan," p. 105.
[12] Statements encouraging planners to involve themselves actively in capital budgeting can be found in the following: Alan Walter Steiss, *A Framework for Planning in State Government* (Chicago, 1968), p. 54; *State Planning in the Sixties*, p. II–7; and *A Strategy for Planning* (Report of the Committee on State Planning, The National Governors' Conference, October 18, 1967), p. 10.

sion-maker—nearer the real action and excitement—than they ever were in planning organizations more isolated from the chief executive. In this setting, planners' work must be evaluated from the point of view of the chief executive as to its relevance, reliability, and realism.[13]

The dilemma is clear. To the extent that the planner enters into struggles over policies he becomes embroiled in politics and his professional objectivity becomes questionable. He quickly realizes that support-building, compromise, and coalition in-fighting are skills of the politician. These skills are learned only in part, and the techniques are hardly the property of only one profession. "To ask the planner to seek political effectiveness is to ask his profession to require proficiency in skills which it cannot monopolize."[14]

To the extent that value struggles enter into the decision-making process, a different kind of rationality may come into play from that which traditionally undergirds the planning process. In fact, the more the planner pursues the goal of traditional rationality in finding all alternatives and projecting their consequences, the more he brings up for consideration those possibilities about which he is less and less able to provide complete and reliable sets of predictions.[15]

There are, of course, good reasons why the norms of the planning profession have generally discouraged planners who adopted more politicized roles. At the same time, it becomes ever more apparent that "although the myth of a political action remains, the success of planning is tied to the operation of the political system."[16]

Despite the pitfalls inherent in responding to it, the planner harkens to the following challenge:

The message is clear. State planning must focus on the issues and problems confronting the state leadership, and must work to aid that leadership more directly.[17]

Unable to define their role precisely but eager to demonstrate that they can contribute significantly to public policy formulation, planners, not surprisingly, have grasped planning-programming-budgeting proposals with alacrity. After all, PPB contains the magic word "planning" within it, its analytical procedures advocate the rationalistic approaches that are at the heart of the planning process, its implementation would provide access to key decision-makers, and its operation should make

---

[13] See *Relevance, Reliance and Realism* (Report of the Committee on State Planning, The National Governors' Conference, July 22, 1968).

[14] Francine F. Rabinovitz, "Politics, Personality and Planning," *Public Administration Review*, XXVIII, no. 1 (March, 1967), 19.

[15] For a fuller exploration of this point, see Yehezkel Dror, *Public Policy-making Reexamined* (San Francisco, 1968), pp. 129–53.

[16] Rabinovitz, "Politics," p. 21. This article provides excellent references to the extensive literature that generally supports the position taken here.

[17] *Relevance, Reliance and Realism*, p. 4.

planning more relevant and plans more effective. Unfortunately for the planners who try to use PPB to carve out a role in the administrative process, the field of budgeting has been going through its own metamorphosis that has contributed to direct conflicts between planners and budgeteers over the new system. Thus we come to the third assertion.

THE CHANGING NATURE OF PUBLIC BUDGETING: CONFLICT GENERATED

Modern budgeting in this country began at the local level before it was undertaken by the national government.[18] Its establishment coincided with the rise of scientific management, and great emphasis was placed upon achieving economy and efficiency in governmental affairs by means of tighter fiscal management, including budgeting. Its inauguration came during the nadir of morality among state and local officials when citizens wanted to demonstrate their revulsion at the boss rule and corruption then so prevalent in our city halls, county courthouses, and state capitols. The financial systems that were devised stressed accountability, control over spending, and doing the public business efficiently.

The budget and accounting systems stressed means rather than ends and used resource inputs and organizational structures as their basic criteria for categorizing financial activities and for reporting. Budgets listed line items or objects of expenditure such as personnel salaries, travel, heat, office supplies, and the multitude of other resource inputs that are used to produce various governmental services. These inputs were normally listed by organizational unit, so that the executive, the legislator, and the general citizen knew precisely how much was being spent for travel in the fire prevention bureau in the fire department. In terms of what it set out to do—namely, to focus attention upon doing things efficiently and to assure control and accountability—the line-item budget succeeded and continues to succeed admirably.[19]

While this watch-dog and control system of budgeting worked well, the problems of greatest interest and concern to elected officials and the public became less and less those matters of honesty and efficiency. While honesty and efficiency continued to be desired, they came to be expected rather than goals sufficient in themselves. Increasingly responsible officials and concerned citizens wanted to know what was being done with those inputs and what was being accomplished. They sought actions that were wise and effective, not just efficient.

[18] Jesse Burkhead, *Government Budgeting* (New York, 1956), p. 13.
[19] The kind of thinking produced by a control orientation to budgeting is roundly criticized in Allen Schick, "Control Patterns in State Budget Execution," *Public Administration Review*, XXIV, no. 2 (June, 1964), 97–106. This critique was not greeted with ready acceptance by state budget officials. See "Budgetary Controversy," *Public Administration Review*, XXIV, no. 3 (September, 1964), 202–7.

The next step in this progression was "performance budgeting" in which organizational units were expected to demonstrate, preferably through some quantifiable measure, what they were doing with the various resource inputs given to them, or what they would do with the various resources they were requesting. Efficiency concerns still remained important during this phase: thus one need know not only how many miles of street were paved, how many gallons of water were pumped or how many fires were fought, but also how much was spent per mile, per gallon, or per fire. With this information departmental administrators could see what was happening to their costs and were able to make comparisons from year to year, to take corrective administrative action where necessary, and to project future costs.

But finding meaningful quantitative performance indicators and installing and maintaining the requisite record system was difficult and expensive, and this type of budgeting declined. Nevertheless, the need to give policy-makers information better suited to their requirements remained.

Efforts were next made at national, state, and local levels to undertake what was then called "program budgeting." Under this system, organizational units were asked to identify their major programs and budget totals were accumulated on this basis, although budget and accounting control systems could, and usually did, remain on a line-item basis. Thus a fire department might show that it had fire-fighting, fire-prevention, training, communication, and equipment-maintenance programs. A police department might show general patrol, traffic control, vice control, detective, laboratory, training, and communication programs. Costs within each of these programs could still be broken down and presented in the traditional input line-item basis. By the time PPB came upon the scene, many governmental units had passed well beyond the line-item control stage in their budgeting. In these units, decision-makers were given information about, and, when appropriate, some quantified measures of the programs being conducted by the government's various organizational components.

The usefulness of the budget as a management tool for establishing and controlling policy and programs has long been recognized. POSDCORB may begin with planning, but it ends with budgeting. Throughout the history of budgetary changes given here, and especially since World War II, the planning and policy aspects of budgeting have received increasing attention and consideration in budget offices, as concentration upon the managerial control and accounting aspects of the budget diminished.[20]

---

[20] For a more thorough history of the evolution summarized here, see Allen Schick, "The Road to PPB: The Stages of Budget Reform," *Public Administration Review,* XXVI, no. 4 (December, 1966), 243–58.

It is not surprising that when PPB came upon the scene, career budget personnel and others knowledgeable in the field saw the new system as a logical extension of trends already under way. Nor is it surprising that budgeteers who were seeking to make the budget more useful to key executives ran into planners who were trying to demonstrate that their skills could be useful in policy formulation and decision-making. Awareness of differences in the approaches of budget and planning staffs became more widespread, and in many jurisdictions relations between the two staffs deteriorated as each sought to gain control over the movement and shape it to its own particular concepts and goals. In reviewing his problems with his budget and planning staffs, a former governor of a Western state said:

> I don't really know what the problems were. I don't know how much of it was a personality difficulty or how much of it was pride of position or professional pride. I do know that despite strenuous efforts on my part to knock heads together I was quite unsuccessful in my opinion in the four years I served as governor in obtaining the kind of relationships that I think are essential between these two very important officers.[21]

What emerges is a clear battle in systems politics—that is, a struggle over the process (system) by which decisions or policies will be made rather than over the substance of those decisions. The stakes are high in such a struggle. The positions or roles to be played in the new process need to be settled. At stake here is the distribution of the power necessary to shape the decisions that result from the application of the new process. Differences also arise over the measures that ought to be used in determining which policy alternative is more desirable. There may be disagreement over the continuing validity of the measures employed. The measures themselves may change, like an elastic yardstick, or they may simply become inappropriate under changed circumstances. Even if there is agreement over the measures and their validity, there may not be agreement over the weight in decision-making that ought to be assigned certain measures.

The potential issues in this political struggle could be spun out much further, but the point should be clear. It is noteworthy, however, that the participants in this struggle accept a basic premise: *how* decisions are made affects *what* decisions are made.

In this struggle the budget staffs have held most of the trump cards, both organizationally and conceptually. Money is a resource common to virtually all public programs; budget staffs have long been at the center of public policy decision-making operations. They are usually close, organizationally, to chief executives. Their usefulness to the key decision-

[21] Transcript of "Symposium on the Link Between Budgeting and Planning."

makers over a long period of time has given them the access to these
power-holders that planners now seek and that is the envy of nearly every other governmental agency. Budget staffs are more action oriented
than planners and much more sensitive to the political implications of the
alternatives being evaluated at any given time. Budgeteers are naturally
reluctant to allow others to share the power base that has been so carefully nurtured over the years, and because of their position, they can
make it extremely difficult for other groups to obtain access to key decision makers.

Budget staffs have been more able than planners to accommodate
themselves to the time perspectives of politicians—perspectives that usually have difficulty getting much beyond the next election. Budgeteers are
unburdened by any notion that their actions should be divorced from
politics. Although budget staffs include many trained in the traditional
professions (lawyers, engineers, accountants, economists, and the like),
budgeteers as such have not sought recognition as a professional group in
the customary sense. No advanced degrees are conferred in budgeting.
No large national association is trying to establish even slightly rigorous
criteria for memberhsip other than position in or association with the
budgeting function in governmental organizations.

In trying to shape the emerging PPB system, the planners have operated at a disadvantage in many jurisdictions. They have not had much
access to key decision-makers, they have not always proved their usefulness and relevance to such officials, they have had to contend frontally
with one of the most entrenched and powerful bureaucracies in any government on an issue that strikes directly at the heart of that bureaucracy;
and they have not been convinced intellectually that they should even be
in the midst of such a political thicket, or that it is truly professional for
them to advocate a stronger position for themselves in policy formulation.

A genuine managerial problem arises because the budgeting process is rather
well institutionalized. Over a long period of time procedures, practices, and
roles have been established. This is not true with a central planning unit.
These groups are new and their roles and functions are not well established.[22]

The reason for their disadvantage is not that planners have been
politically unaware or insensitive in their struggles. They quickly recognized "grantsmanship" as a potent weapon in political frays and have
guarded it accordingly. Nor has their key difficulty been their inability to
provide a cohesive identity for planning and planners. This particular
shortcoming may actually have given planners the flexibility needed for

---

[22] George A. Steiner, "Problems in Implementing Program Budgeting," in Novick,
Program Budgeting, p. 346.

responding to new demands or opportunities, such as advocacy planning. Rather, planners have simply lacked the constituency, informational technology, and organizational base so vital in political combat.

Under these circumstances, the planners must have something going for them or they would have been wiped off the field of combat long ago. They have drawn their strength from deficiencies in existing budget practices. Annual or biennial time perspectives have proved too short. Budget requests have become routine actions rather than opportunities for creative review and analysis within requesting agencies. Mired in concerns about controlling expenditures, budget staffs have failed to provide executives with timely and relevant information, evaluations, and analyses. The planners have offered an approach to policy decision-making that is less encumbered by hoary bureaucratization.

The advent of PPB accelerated two different movements—broadening the application of the planning process to more and more public activities, and making the budgeting process more helpful to decision-makers. The two movements are scarcely incompatible in all respects, but their undulations have reminded all participants of an important factor common to both approaches: a budget is more than a plan.

THE BUDGET IS MORE THAN A PLAN

This analysis began by stating that "a budget is a plan, but not all plans are budgets." More precisely, the budget presents for a given future period the financial implications of a whole range of decisions to be made currently. Thus a budget can be viewed as one item in the series of products that should be produced by a variety of planning activities taking place simultaneously within a government. All too often, the budget process is the only effective systematic means employed for looking to the future at all.

Although not all vital decisions made in a government concern resource allocation, year in and year out the budget is probably the most important policy statement a given administration makes. Efforts to provide public services and to meet public needs almost always require money in amounts roughly proportional to the size of the need and to the intensity of the desire to do something about that need. The budget, more than any other institutionalized administrative process, raises key issues and brings into sharpest relief for the political decision-makers the hard priority choices they must make in allocating limited resources. The budget confronts those decision-makers with the gambler's adage "Put your money where your mouth is!" The budget reveals for all to see whether efforts to do something about improving police protection, reducing slum housing conditions, increasing welfare benefits, or improving educational opportunities are in fact to be substantial ones. The budget brings all these hard choices into focus—it is a final decision document.

Budget decisions require a high degree of political sensitivity because conflicting values are often at stake. "If politics is regarded in part as conflict over whose preferences shall prevail in the determination of policy, then the budget records the outcome of this struggle."[23] It is misguided to view the budget solely as a mechanism for "costing out" selected alternatives.

As with plans and planning, it is more appropriate to talk about budgeting as a process than about budgets as literal documents. Like planners, budgeteers are eclectics drawing insights, techniques, and help from wherever they can. Although budget personnel have historically come from the discipline of accounting, they have probably left this particular phase of their work far more rapidly than planners have left physical planning.

Yet important differences between planning and budgeting must also be noted. First, planning is concerned with a wider variety of activities, including both public and private actions, whereas budgeting predominantly focuses upon public actions, particularly spending programs. Second, budgets retain their traditional legal, political, and managerial control functions, despite their usefulness in program formulation and appraisal. The budget process can be extremely important in fostering planning within a given government, but the budget system still must fulfill operational requirements that do not similarly constrain the planning process. It is therefore not surprising that the classifications and measurements needed for planning are frequently different from those needed for the control function of budgeting. The same accounting system may be able to produce figures that are useful for both planning and control purposes, but it is apparent that the informational demands of the two activities are not the same. Furthermore the time spans of budgeting and planning are usually different, and the kinds of filters through which men experienced in each of these fields view problems vary similarly.[24]

Planning must start with a broad vision, and only secondarily are the immediate steps considered which lead in the direction of the plan. In contrast, the emphasis in budget making has been on the ensuing year for operations reasons, and only as a supplement have longer-term budget outlooks been adopted or recommended.[25]

Although both processes require feedback about past accomplishments, budgeting tends to be a more retrospective and planning a more prospec-

[23] Aaron Wildavsky, *The Politics of the Budgetary Process* (Boston, 1964), p. 4.
[24] These suggestions are taken from Gerhard Colm, *Integration of National Planning and Budgeting*, National Planning Association, Center for Development Planning, Planning Methods Series, no. 5 (March, 1968), pp. 18–25.
[25] Colm, *Integration*, p. 23.

tive process. Planners tend to think of spending money to meet needs, while budgeteers tend to think of cutting expenditures to meet available resources. Planning tries to be comprehensive while budgetary decisions tend to be incremental and marginal.[26]

Besides differences in concepts, planning and budget agencies have assumed rather different kinds of operating responsibilities. Budgeteers have central review, analysis, coordination, control, and management-improvement responsibilities. They tend to respond to ideas initiated by others rather than themselves. Budget staffs look to others—planners of all sorts—to make physical, economic, and social studies and to formulate alternative plans, projects, or programs. Budgeteers obviously do some initiating, but, in most governments, planners are more responsible administratively for seeing that such activity occurs. On the other hand, planners have many central coordinative responsibilities, especially in a wide variety of intergovernmental programs and grants, but the effective coordinating that comes with control over the purse strings is lacking.

The characteristics and importance of the budgeting process, as well as its similarities to and differences from the planning process, are well summarized in the following:

In the operating life of organizations the budgetary process is a unique activity. It is related to the complete administrative range from analysis through planning to management and control. In its end product, the budget, it summarizes (1) the problems to which analysis has been applied, (2) the analytic concepts and techniques brought to bear on these problems, (3) the information relevant to their solution, (4) the proposed (ultimately, the determined) decisions, and (5) the administrative structure through which performance of the approved budget will be executed, controlled, and appraised. If, as many students of the managerial process assert, what management is all about is making and implementing decisions, then the budget is perhaps the most essential management tool. It organizes, influences, facilitates, and expresses management thought and management action. It must, therefore, be related to organizational objectives, policies, practices, and structure. Rationally designed, it contributes powerfully to the effective and efficient accomplishment of managerial tasks.[27]

The discipline of an annual budget can be a very sobering and beneficial one for planning, and budgets will continue to be important management tools. Nonetheless, budgets can be seen as components of a more comprehensive planning process, a process that considers long-range goals and raises choices about how best to use resources to achieve

---

[26] This generalization appears to be true of state as well as federal budgeting. See Wildavsky, *Politics,* and Thomas J. Anton, *The Politics of State Expenditure in Illinois* (Urbana, Ill., 1966), pp. 248–55.

[27] Melvin Anshen, "The Federal Budget as an Instrument for Management and Analysis," in Novick, *Program Budgeting,* p. 3.

those goals. Goals and strategies should provide the framework within which more specific budgetary choices can be made; the compilation of budgetary matters should not be allowed to determine effectively what the goals and strategies will be. It is probably easier but not wiser to decide to cross a bridge when it is reached than to decide in advance what bridge to reach and what new bridges to build and how.[28]

Both planning and budgeting are government-wide in scope, but budgeting appears to be more derivative, resulting from a more general and inclusive planning process that recognizes events and actions well beyond the usual jurisdictional bounds of governments. This idea is not alien to budgeteers. As one Southeastern state budget director noted:

We have come to this view that planning is the more important of the aspects and that budgeting should be one of the tools of planning and not relate solely to money. I think that both functions should be under the same head and I would suggest that they both be under a planning department.[29]

The ideas presented here are neither new nor unique, as the following summarizing quotation indicates.

The problem of giving intelligent direction to the administration of public programs through adequate planning cannot be divorced from the budgeting function. The linking of the two in practice has proved the sterility of the theory, widely held among the professional planners, that planning must be divorced from administration and "political" influence in order to preserve its purity. Fortunately, a substantial and growing number of planners have recognized the futility of attempting to detach planning from administration. To them it will come as no great shock to think of budgeting as a form of planning and of planning as the basis of progressive budgeting. If the planners will accept the accomplished fact that planning, as a function of government, is as broad in scope as governmental activity itself—and hence is coextensive with the budgeting function—the organized planning movement will have taken an important step toward restoring its lost vitality. Otherwise, budget agencies may be expected to assume an even greater responsibility for encouraging and coordinating program planning, for good planning is the base upon which good budgeting must stand.[30]

JOBS TO BE DONE

Although at their base planning and budgeting are inextricably linked, it is still possible to separate at least analytically a variety of activities that need to be performed in aiding key public officials as they seek to make effective use of the modern tools and aids available to

[28] This language and the idea are paraphrased from Dror, *Public Policy-making Reexamined*, p. 136.
[29] Transcript of "Symposium on the Link Between Budgeting and Planning."
[30] Robert A. Walker, "The Relation of Budgeting to Program Planning," *Public Administration Review*, IV, no. 2 (Spring, 1944), 107.

them. In the broadest sense, the problem is to bring together the operating, analytical, control, coordination, and decision-making operations that exist within every government.

All planning should be comprehensive. Every level of government, and each section, bureau, division, commission or department should plan. The central planning office should have the capacity to require that all agencies use the same information base, relate all planning activities to the governor's program, and insure that broad goals result in specific action in the shortest possible time.[31]

The most acceptable approach is for state planning agencies to assist other state agencies develop better departmental or functional plans by insuring that overall state goals which have been formulated by the chief executive are infused into such plans, and by providing basic information, technical assistance, and other necessary coordinative activities.[32]

Goal-Setting and Long-Range Projections

Any attempt at rational forethought requires appraisal initially of what is expected and what is sought. Some unit of a government, other than the chief executive and the legislature, that is removed from the crisis orientation of operating programs needs to explicate goals, explore the interrelationships among goals, and develop techniques for making projections. Such a unit should be placed organizationally so that it has an overview of the entire range of problems confronting a particular government. Although the responsibilities borne by this unit will be great, the staff itself need not necessarily be very large. Quantification techniques and model-building of all kinds may be of great use in this field.

Goal-setting is hardly an easy task. It raises crucial questions about participation in the process and about the representative nature of existing political institutions such as legislatures. Goal-setting requires much more than simply aggregating goal statements proposed by governmental agencies or gathered from other sources. Ideally it would entail reviewing the purposes of government, compiling information about the present status or condition of the jurisdiction, enumerating existing problems, forecasting probable developments, developing alternative goals, and trying to establish priorities among goals.

The goal statements derived by this process will probably be much broader and encompass more value conflicts than the operational goals essential in PPB. The planner should soar in this endeavor. The primacy of the basic planning process over budgeting is clear at this point. Weaknesses and lack of sophistication in establishing goals will threaten the

[31] *A Strategy for Planning*, p. 9.
[32] *State Planning in the Sixties*, p. III–4.

effectiveness of the entire system of planning, programming, and budgeting.

Planning implies choice; where there is no choice, there is little need to plan. For this reason, broad amorphous goals are of little aid to planning or PPB. To be useful in PPB, proposed goals should not reach beyond that point at which some limited selections or division among alternatives for reaching a more general objective are still available.

Program-Planning

While it is not clear where goal-setting ends and programming begins, objectives must be made specific if they are to provide any real guidance to operating officials in making decisions and evaluating results. PPB emphasizes making goals operational and developing measures of effectiveness. This emphasis suggests that these activities will be less participatory and collaborative, and more technical and professional, than broader goal-planning. It is generally assumed in PPB proposals that programming and budgeting activities will take place within a framework of previously established goals.

Although long-range planning and goal analysis may be done on a more centralized basis by some central staff, programming will require the intimate and detailed program knowledge of the relevant individual agencies and cannot be done as well by some isolated central staff acting alone. Acquaintance with the program operations will be of inestimable help in devising alternative ways of getting away from the present situation to a more desirable state of affairs. To the extent, probably very considerable, that program plans cut across departmental and agency lines, some means of central co-ordination will be required to assure that all actions are headed in the same direction and in proper sequence. Programs are undertaken to achieve goals, and it is those programs that give rise to all the various expenditures, both operating and capital, included in the budget. PPB has brought to the forefront of management thinking a very old truism: programs underlie budgets and sound planning for all aspects of operating programs, not just the financial aspects, is necessary for truly effective budgeting.

Analysis

Systematic analyses should be made of all the relevant alternatives that are available to a decision-maker. Economic, social, and political implications of policy choices should be evaluated. This analysis obviously cannot be made with complete accuracy or comprehensiveness, but analytical efforts have borne fruit in the past and will do so in the future. PPB stresses analysis in quantified terms, but quantification may, in many instances, be irrelevant to the problem for which a solution is sought or beyond the capacity, fiscal and otherwise, of the governmental jurisdiction. The higher the relevant decision-maker is in the organization and the broader his concerns, the more his ability to quantify and be specific is probably diminished. The more complex the issues involved, the less mathematically rigorous analyses can be relied upon for guidance to the best choice.

PPB seeks to have administrators of all types and at all organizational levels asking the right questions; it is not dependent upon having available expertise in all the latest high-powered techniques for answering questions, whether or not the questions (or even the techniques) are right. The important point is that the planning-analytical process can and should be institutionalized so that this kind of thinking prevails among all officials. Analysis is not the magical property of some super whiz-kid group in a central staff agency.

Analysis will require give-and-take among a variety of personnel, but particularly between line-agency program planners and central staff program coordinator-planners. It will continue to be important that those who make analyses and present recommendations based upon them do not themselves criticize their own work and proposals. Among other things, this fact suggests that legislatures should have their own analytical units to review the proposals prepared by the executive's planning-budgeting apparatus.

Provision of Data

All decisions are based on some kind of information, on a data base. Much has been said and written about management information systems, but the hardware capacity for data-handling has far outstripped our conceptions of the kind of information that executives in fact need. In making most choices, administrators will want information from a variety of sources, but great coordination will be required to present timely and accurate data in a form that is useful to them. Some kind of central staff participation in the development and operation of an information system is necessary, but so also is line-agency participation if the information system is to be a total one. Decisions of all kinds can rarely be any better than the information on which they are based, and deficiencies in existing information systems have been exposed quickly where PPB efforts have been undertaken. It is not surprising that in practical situations, concern for the data processing capabilities of an organization have become an integral part of the efforts to improve planning and budgeting arrangements.

Coordination and Control

Most public officials accept the need for coordination in our highly complex society, but this intellectual acceptance usually diminishes rapidly when coordinative controls affect some specific operational activity of concern to a particular official. Admonitions for coordination, like admonitions against sin, are far more acceptable in general than in specific. Nevertheless, the need for coordination grows apace as programs broaden and proliferate so that overlapping becomes more likely and the plethora of uncoordinated federal grants continues unabated.

As there can be plans of differing scope and purpose, so can there probably also be different types of coordination and control. For example, plans for operations may be coordinated but actual operations may be left uncoordinated. On the other hand, both operations and planning may be coordinated, most typically by making a single administrator responsible for all the activities to be coordinated. Obviously there are differences between long-range strategic planning or goal-setting on the one hand and operational control on the other, where the purpose is to assure that specific tasks are carried out effectively and efficiently.[33] The type of planning that is desired will probably vary with the type of coordination and control sought with the nature of the decisions to be made. In structuring the PPB system, it will probably be useful operationally to make distinctions among various types of plans and methods of coordination.

Budgeting

All governments will continue to require budgets as an operating necessity no matter how sophisticated their planning operations. Some agency will have to be responsible for seeing that the detailed budgeting process proceeds in an orderly fashion and that the managerial benefits achieved by pursuing this institutionalized procedure are realized and maximized. The unit that is responsible for operating the budgeting system per se may be separate and distinct from the unit that prepares and reviews analyses.[34]

SUMMARY

There can be no doubt that today top governmental policy-makers, elected officials, and career public servants alike need a great deal of "staff" help. In reaching decisions, responsible officials have to understand first the choices before them, and second, that they in fact have a choice to make.

To be effective, planning activities must be linked to some such implementing mechanism as the budget. Planning and budgeting are both concerned with decision-making. However, execution is as much a part

---

[33] These conceptualizations are fully developed by Robert Anthony, *Planning and Control Systems: A Framework for Analysis* (Boston, 1965).

[34] Such a distinction was suggested to New York State officials. See "Allocating PPBS Responsibilities Between the Division of the Budget and the Office of Planning Coordination," (Unpublished memorandum, McKinsey and Company, September 29, 1967).

of decision-making as planning, but execution and planning for execution are two quite different things. Although both may be part of a larger process, they can be separated both in concept and operation.

The process of planning, which should be practiced by all administrators, needs to be separated from the creation of an organizational unit that is specially assigned to do this kind of work. Workable distinctions among the various parts of the administrative process are clearly needed.

If everybody doing any kind of planning is going to be labeled "a PPB-er," obviously the ship could soon sink from its own weight.[35]

At least six functions or jobs need to be done in any planning-budgeting system that has significant utility to key decision-makers: goal-setting, programming, analysis, provision of data, coordination and control, and budgeting. The exact allocation of responsibilities in a structural sense will appropriately vary from one jurisdiction to another. To make these conceptual distinctions will help in devising a workable organizational arrangement that provides for all these essential activities. In terms of effectiveness, it would appear most desirable to locate as many of these activities as possible in an executive-concerned policy agency.

Planning may perhaps best be viewed today as a series of continuous staff functions or responsibilities that need to be performed *somewhere* in all governments. This kind of help and thinking is needed in *all* agencies within a political jurisdiction, not just in the staff offices around chief executives.

Socially useful and beneficial public careers (even if not "professional" ones in the most stringent meanings of that term) can be devoted to preparing and analyzing information on which decisions can be based so long as the individuals doing this work understand the advisory nature of their role.

Budgeteers are not and should not be in the seat of decision-making power. Nor should planning staffs. Decision-making is reserved for line managers. But the line between recommendation and decision-making is often hard to find.[36]

Planning and budgeting processes are in a sensitive and ill-defined area precisely because they do provide a link between the political and professional aspects of government decision-making. As institutionalized processes, planning and budgeting probably have too many functions that are distinctly their own and not totally compatible with each other to suggest some simple or mystical integration of the two activities into a

---

[35] John Haldi, "Promises and Problems of PPB" in *Analysis for Planning-Programming-Budgeting* (Washington, D.C., 1968), p. 55.
[36] Steiner, "Problems in Implementing Program Budgeting," in Novick, *Program Budgeting,* p. 346.

cohesive whole. Nevertheless the feeling persists that these activities are really parts of a seamless web that has been rather arbitrarily rent in the past. Governments seek to meet social problems through programs, and program choices have impact over a period of time. In order to provide these programs, governments become involved with planning and budgeting processes because the processes arise from a common necessity and relate to the same programs and so they are parts of a single fabric.

For too long, planning as a vital responsibility of all administrators has been overlooked, POSDCORB not withstanding. Although the budgeting process, properly conceived, could have been utilized as a planning mechanism, it became a routine matter to most officials, and its powers of innovation were lost in the drive for control and accountability. At the same time, professional planners preached a myth, suggesting that planning was a separate kind of responsibility that could be exercised only by certified and qualified "planners"; it was not something generalist administrators could be expected to assume or have the ability to pursue.

While organizational distinctions undoubtedly should be made between different types of planning, budgeting, and control, it may be useful to think in terms of the policy formulation process and the role of policy analysts.[37] As with all planning, policy can be effective only if it is tied to action, but the budget is only one vehicle that might be employed. Unfortunately the operational requirements and procedures of budgeting may drive out the creativity required for good analysis. Indeed, some observers contend that policy analysis should be saved by cutting it free from the rest of the PPBS trappings.[38]

Staff agencies responsible for analysis work should be marked by the diverse nature of their personnel and of the skills they possess. The skills most useful in such work may turn out to be more general and personal than specific, technical, and trainable. There is something inherently incompatible between innovation and the casting of systems and bureaucracies. Yet a satisfactory level of innovation may be possible if there is sufficient diversity and interchange within the policy-advising staff so that responsible officials in fact are offered choices. The administrative arrangements divined for accomplishing these tasks will need to be adapted to the locale.

Perhaps the suggestion of marriage—whose style?—between planning and budgeting is off-base. Perhaps a better analogy to express the need is a reconciliation among marital partners who should not have been separated in the first place and whose continued separation would

[37] For some suggestive insight along these lines, see Yehezkel Dror, "Policy Analysts: A New Professional Role in Government Service," *Public Administration Review*, XXVIII, no. 3 (September, 1967), 197–203.
[38] See Aaron Wildavsky, "Rescuing Policy Analysis from PPBS," *Public Administration Review*, XXIX, no. 2 (March-April, 1969), 189–202.

be detrimental to both, the terms of the reconciliation being set by the specific conditions and circumstances in which the partners find themselves, but each partner retaining his own distinct identity and responsibilities.

Congress, Computers, and the Cognitive Process
ROBERT L. CHARTRAND

In considering the kaleidoscopic responsibilities and activities of the contemporary Congress, it is imperative that a historical perspective be achieved. The pastoral simplicity of revolutionary America, with its opportunities for a more measured evaluation of the problems of government, has been replaced by almost incomprehensible complexity. The burden of governing exceeds anything ever experienced, and this burden is sure to increase as the population grows and the process of urbanization continues.

A matter of high concern, both to those who govern and to those who study the democratic form of government, is whether Congress as it is now constituted and oriented can perform its constitutional functions. The myriad tasks, the unprecedented demands on time and energy, the necessity of making decisions on dozens of diverse issues—it would seem that the member of Congress must be a veritable Everyman. In his classic work on the Congress, Ernest S. Griffith poses the question in this way:

How can a group of non-specialists, elected as representatives of the electorate, really function in a specialized and technological age? For surely no one will deny that the overwhelming majority of the great problems facing the government are complex to such a degree that the most skilled specialization and the most profound wisdom are none too great to deal with them.[1]

A search is underway, then, in an often informal and subliminal way, to discover and develop those decision aids, procedures, and techniques which will enable the congressman to perform his job.

THE ROLE OF THE CONGRESSMAN

The essential elements of the congressman's job have varied little since the convening of the First Congress. A member is required to function in three discreet roles:

[1] Ernest S. Griffith, *Congress: Its Contemporary Role* (New York, 1961), p. 74.

1. as a legislator, responsible for exploring and rendering decisions on issues of national and international significance;

2. as the representative of his district or state, charged with the responsibility for its welfare and all requisite legislative actions related thereto; and

3. as an unofficial *ombudsman,* accessible to each constituent and responsible for attempting to provide assistance on any problem, whether serious or trivial.

The enormity of these responsibilities is often unappreciated by outsiders, but to the member it is very real. Not only must he be prepared to answer hundreds of quorum calls, yea and nay calls, teller, division and voice votes, but he must serve on numerous committees and subcommittees. This latter function may require heading an investigatory effort, cajoling and convincing colleagues of a certain course of action, or obtaining (and examining) witness testimony on a matter of public concern.

In addition to legislative demands upon his time, the member is the recipient of countless letters, telephone calls, and visitors. A typical list might include:

> How much Social Security will my wife get?
> Can you speak to my civic organization?
> Would you check my Veterans' benefits?
> Why didn't our city get a Demonstration Cities' grant?
> Could you find my daughter a job on Capitol Hill?

As one might imagine, these types of appeals are infinite in variety and often require considerable staff time. The individual American, in an age of increasing impersonality, wants to feel that he can turn to "someone who cares," in this case the congressman. Perhaps what confronts the citizenry in our time is the lack of viable communication.

Dr. John S. Saloma, in his book entitled *Congress and the New Politics,* identifies two functions performed by Congress which enable it to communicate with its constituents:

In performing the *informative* function, Congress informs and educates the public on matters of public policy and communicates information to constituents. In performing its *service* function, it answers constituent requests and assists specific constituent interests, especially through casework.[2]

As the harassed congressman and his staff labor to do a passable job—and simultaneously to keep the political fences mended so that re-election is ensured—they continue to search for ways to "work smart." Above all, there is the need for *information*—facts, quotations, statistics, guidelines, citations, research summaries—information that is timely, ac-

---

[2] John S. Saloma III, *Congress and the New Politics* (Boston, 1969), p. 170.

curate, as comprehensive as possible, and relevant. There is a long-standing cliché that "information is power," and this has proven to be a durable byword. The committee chairman controls certain key information, and its dispensation is his prerogative. The individual member has numerous opportunities to acquire, hold, and disseminate valuable data, whether it be to colleagues, constituents, or the public at large.

Each decision is arrived at by a process which involves logic, hard facts, expert interpretation, a comparison of alternatives, political acumen, a "gut reaction," and consideration of the real world situation as the member sees it. How much can improved information availability help in this process? A glance at a typical calendar maintained by a congressman may serve as a point of departure for further discussion of possible support:

7:30 a.m.	Breakfast with constituent group
8:45 a.m.	Review speech draft with Administrative Assistant
9:00 a.m.	Discussion with two colleagues of terminology in a bill up for debate
9:30 a.m.	Telephone conversation with staff member in district office about pressing local problem
9:50 a.m.	Meet with visiting constituent who has a distressing problem involving an executive branch agency
10:15 a.m.	Go over background material on upcoming subcommittee session with Legislative Assistant
10:30 a.m.	Subcommittee meeting, including appearance of witnesses requiring member questioning
12:15 p.m.	Luncheon with lobbyist group representatives seeking support on nearing vote

Even the most cursory examination of this truncated schedule reveals the variety of research, staff interaction, and decision-making which must take place. And all the while, the cacophony of ringing telephones, visitor inquiries, and cascading correspondence serves as an abrasive to the nerves and a deterrent to the sensitivities of personal interactions.

INFORMATION REQUIREMENTS AND RESOURCES

The inadequacy of the information available for decision-making has been noted and discussed in surveys of congressional offices, but the desired antidotal action has never been agreed upon. Some congressmen see the "information problem" in terms of furthering the imbalance of power between the executive and legislative branches. The delays, compromises, and necessity of convincing many persons—and not a single monolithic arbiter—led former Representative Donald Rumsfeld to comment that "it is easier to stare at a mountain than to study the shadows and slopes across a rolling terrain."[3]

There is, of course, *nothing new* in Congress' information-decision dilemma. However, the scope and diversity have increased enormously. The horns of this dilemma are seen by many to be enlightened foresight and comprehending hindsight. The public coffers are not bottomless, and the demands upon them must be made today with a degree of understanding the problems and commitment of resources never before required. The Arthur D. Little "Management Study of Congress" recommended that:

Congress should develop an improved ability to test in advance the *relative* effectiveness of alternative courses of action. Cost-effectiveness analysis has become a standard tool of American management. Because effectiveness must be measured in tangible results affecting people, it cannot be measured solely in accounting terms. What is needed is operations analysis, disclosing what people get from alternative expenditures of time, effort and money.[4]

If one accepts Thomas B. Curtis's premise that Congress "is a mechanism for gathering together the knowledge and wisdom existing with the society to make judgments to solve the problems facing society," then it logically follows that there must be a set of actions encompassing information acquisition, indexing, storage, retrieval, and use. Former Representative Curtis identifies three processes by which this information is assembled for use by the Congress:

First, the distilled wisdom (i.e., that which has been reduced to books and other units of storage) contained in the Library of Congress is further refined for Members of Congress by the Legislative Reference Service of the Library.

Second, the current wisdom of the society is collected through the standing committees of Congress with the help of professional staff employed by the committees. It is in these forums that the knowledge of experts in the executive branch and in the private sector is brought to bear on public problems and national goals. The testimony is received in public hearings with the witnesses under cross-examination and their statements subject to rebuttal.

Third, from the letters and conversations of constituents and self-interest groups in the society, Members of Congress gather knowledge of the subject upon which the individual citizens are uniquely expert: how the laws as written and administered affect them.[5]

[3] Donald Rumsfeld, "The Operation of the Congressional Office," in *We Propose: A Modern Congress,* ed. Mary McInnis (New York, 1966), p. 281.
[4] A. D. Little Company, Inc., "Management Study of the U.S. Congress." Report to NBC News (November 24, 1965), p. 31.
[5] Thomas B. Curtis, "Foreword" to Mary McInnis, *We Propose: A Modern Congress,* p. vii.

The potential resources for information useful to the Congress include the federal executive agencies and departments, the Legislative Reference Service of the Library of Congress, lobbyist organizations, universities and foundations, and other private sector groups (e.g., industrial firms). Patterns of reference have developed over the years which cause the majority of members to turn—for purposes of convenience, confidence in the researchers, or time considerations—to supporting services in the Washington, D.C., area. Executive branch elements have hundreds of congressional liaison personnel available to expedite the treatment of congressional requests for data. The Legislative Reference Service, over a period of twenty years, has had to cope with an increase from 29,000 requests from congressional offices in 1949 to 140,000 in 1969. The role of automatic data processing in responding to congressional information needs was a subject for member comment as early as 1964. In addressing the Eastern Spring Computer Conference, the then Senator Hubert H. Humphrey told the assembled technologists:

Just think how a U.S. Senator—"fresh"—or weary from the 39th day of debate on the civil rights bill—views your world—a contrasting world—with pushbutton, command controls, automatic programming and snappy pert scheduling. Ah, how I long for such conveniences in the Senate.[6]

Steps to match the congressional requirements for better information with up-to-date capabilities took the form of legislation to create a congressional computer facility in 1966. Representative Robert McClory introduced the first bill, and on this and other occasions set forth some of the congressional information needs which might be fulfilled by the use of computers:

(1) Daily printouts summarizing the previous day's congressional action;
(2) An automated index of congressional documents and legal periodicals;
(3) Up-to-the-minute information on legislative issues scheduled for debate;
(4) Vote summaries on bills already passed;
(5) The status of legislation pending in committee;
(6) Description of information stored in computer files in the executive departments.[7]

While the Congress has moved slowly to establish a formal com-

[6] Hubert H. Humphrey, "The Computer Revolution—Address by Senator Humphrey before the Eastern Spring Computer Conference, Senate," *Congressional Record*, CX (April 25, 1964), 9075.
[7] Robert McClory, "Congressman McClory Suggests Computer Uses for Congress, Extension of Remarks of Honorable Tom Railsback, *Congressional Record*, CXIV (January 29, 1968), E276.

puter center it has come to recognize the critical need for applying systems tools and techniques in various aspects of legislative functioning.

POTENTIAL APPLICATIONS OF COMPUTERS IN CONGRESS

Concurrent advances in computer technology and in the level of understanding of the role of automatic data processing by legislators have made possible the identification of a spectrum of applications for computers and systems technology. The exercise of discovering and discussing these applications has not been limited to the Congress. State legislatures have initiated a number of improvements. New York, Pennsylvania, Florida, Iowa, Wisconsin, Hawaii, and North Carolina have used the computer to index, store, and retrieve statutory information, draft bills, maintain key data on the status and content of pending legislation, trace appropriations activity, and record committee schedules of hearings.

A thorough review of candidate applications for congressional use of automatic data processing and systems techniques was conducted during the hearings held by the Joint Committee on the Organization of the Congress. Students of the legislative process such as the late Dr. George B. Galloway[8] have offered suggestions as to which tasks and procedures might benefit from technological support. Dr. Charles R. Dechert enunciates several questions which may arise when the desirability of furnishing computer-stored data to the Congress is considered:

The problem of congressional access to information might be better defined as a problem of information management. What specific elements of information are needed to make what judgments? Where are these elements located? How are they to be retrieved? And how should they be presented in order to be meaningful?[9]

There are certain legislative and administrative functions of the Congress which might be improved by a modification of traditional procedures, the establishment of an on-line capability for immediate access to information files, or provision for automatic data processing services performed on a less accelerated basis (e.g., the grouping or "batching" of requests to be handled by the system).

The advantages of maintaining a centralized computer-oriented store of information have been proven in countless government and business environments. In the case of the Congress, there is a recurring need

[8] George B. Galloway, "Congressional Reform: Agenda and Prospects" (Address before the Tenth Southern Assembly, Biloxi, Miss., January 28–31, 1965).

[9] Charles R. Dechert, "Availability of Information for Congressional Operations," in *Congress: The First Branch of Government* (Washington, D.C., 1966), pp. 172–73.

for such information as that on the *contents and status of bills*. With more than 29,000 bills and resolutions introduced during the 90th Congress, the problem of knowing even the most rudimentary facts about a given piece of legislation is significant.

Another type of information of recurring utility is that on *committee activity*. Not only are the time and place of committee and subcommittee sessions sometimes difficult to determine, but related information such as the names of witnesses to appear and the topics to be discussed may not be available.

The handling of other sorts of committee information, such as *legislative calendar material* and historical documentation on committee and subcommittee legislation, meetings, memoranda, and other memorabilia continues to be the subject of study for possible automatic data processing support. With the development of reliable computer terminals committee staffs may now maintain up-to-the-minute status information on information ranging from bills before the committee to related bibliographic items of value to members.

Congressional needs for *topical research information* are endless and highly varied. Since the establishment of the Congress, complaints have arisen concerning the availability of subject-oriented information, both narrative and statistical. The usefulness of a "Selective Dissemination of Information" (SDI) system has received much favorable comment. The concept of creating an "interest profile" for each individual congressman or committee, and placing that profile in computerized form, first was developed in industry.[10] The system features the matching of profile keyword descriptors against a set of keyword descriptors which reflects the contents of books, articles, and other types of documents. Each recipient is informed of new acquisitions which match his interest criteria; then he may indicate his desire to acquire the document for review.

The difficulty of obtaining access to certain categories of *federal fiscal and budgetary data* long has bothered many congressmen with responsibilities in the authorization-appropriations cycle. With the advent of PPBS, the outlook is for additional confusion as program versus agency activities are presented for review. Appropriations subcommittees often have had to make their decisions on the basis of sampling information. Dr. Richard F. Fenno categorizes this as (1) program information; (2) confidence information; and (3) support information.[11] At the present

[10] International Business Machines Corp., "Selective Dissemination of Information: IBM Data Processing Application." (White Plains, N.Y., 1962), p. 7.
[11] Richard F. Fenno, "The Impact of PPBS on the Congressional Appropriations Process," in *Information Support, Program Budgeting, and the Congress*, ed. Robert L. Chartrand et al. (New York, 1968), p. 181.

time, the Bureau of the Budget prepares certain selected aggregate budget data in automatic data processing form, but there are indications that heavier use of computer analysis will be made in the future. As the executive branch use of automatic data processing in handling these data increases, it will become imperative that Congress have timely access to comparable information. The importance attached to enhancing congressional knowledge about budgetary proposals and the status of program funding is indicated both in the Brooks Bill for a computer facility for Congress and in the Reorganization Act of 1969.[12]

Information about *federal assistance programs* often is not readily available. Representative William V. Roth has introduced legislation providing for the issuance of a catalog on federal assistance programs and has been joined by a large number of House members. Concern over the absence of assertive control of federal programs, and in particular a lack of measurement of program performance, has led to a number of bills being introduced in the 90th and 91st Congresses calling for the use of "objective, scientific, and empirical analysis" in evaluating all federal programs and activities. This would be achieved through the establishment of an Office of Program Analysis and Evaluation and its legislative counter-mechanism, a Joint Committee of Congress on Program Analysis and Evaluation.

Information on *federal contract awards* (by subject, contract recipient, and congressional district) often is requested, and, if maintained in automatic data processing formats, could be used for periodical listings and to respond to special inquiries. Also, these data could allow an examination of industrial resources applied to government projects.

Repeated criticism of the *indexing of key congressional documents* —the *Congressional Record,* for example—has focused on the limited and often arbitrary retrieval word list available to the users. In many instances, hearings are not indexed at all, or only in such general terms as to be almost useless. Members and other interested parties have pleaded for the improvement of such indexing, pointing out that the utility of the document should dictate how the costs are to be allocated: in data collection, conversion, indexing, processing or retrieval.[13]

A related area allowing for improvement is that of creating *a master listing of all congressional documents.* Incomplete listings are prepared by the Government Printing Office, the Library of Congress, and other establishments, but the importance of developing such an information

[12] U.S., Congress, Senate, Committee on Government Operations, *Legislative Reorganization Act of 1969,* 91st Cong., 1st sess., 1969, H. Rept. 91–202, p. 58.
[13] Congressional Information Service Index to Publications of the United States Congress now offers a monthly, ADP-generated publication.

base cannot be denied. Here again, it is critical to devise and publicize a listing (i.e., thesaurus) of retrieval terms which will allow public and private users to find that which they seek.

Information on the *status of activities in each chamber* of the Congress would be of value. Congressmen often are summoned to the floor to vote with virtually no information on the legislation under consideration. (A service provided members of the House allows them to dial a special number and be given the number and title of a bill next to be voted upon or related information on current legislation. This system was established by the Office of the Clerk of the House, and recently has been adopted by the Senate.)

Registration data on lobbyist groups and individuals, described as "one of the most valuable sources of independent information available to Congress,"[14] would lend itself to computerization. Such a file might contain the name of the individual (or group), the name and address of his employer, the area of his special concern, the amount of contributions made during the calendar year, and any papers, periodicals, or publications in which he has caused editorials or articles to be published.

Legal information of several types is much used by the Congress. Available today in machine readable form are numerous sets of data and information in full text or abstract form. For example, the Department of Defense maintains the Project LITE (Legal Information Through Electronics) file of more than 60 million words, including the contents of:

United States Code (1964 ed.)
Unpublished Comptroller General decisions (from June 1955 to January 1967)
Published Comptroller General decisions (vols. 1–45)
Armed Services Procurement Regulations (through revision 22)
Appropriation acts of 1966 and 1967
DOD international law material (treaties and agreements of interest to DOD)[15]

Other types of legal information are obtainable through the services of the ASPEN Systems Corporation, an outgrowth of the University of Pittsburgh Health Law Center group which pioneered full text retrieval using computers. This capability makes available the Internal Revenue Code and Regulations, decisions of the United States Supreme Court and

[14] Kenneth Janda, "Information Systems for Congress," in *Congress: The First Branch of Government* (Washington, D.C., 1966), p. 422.
[15] U.S. Congress, House Committee on Government Operations, *Air Force Project LITE (Legal Information Through Electronics),* 90th Cong., 2nd sess., 1968, H. Rept. 1133, pp. 15–16.

Circuit Court of Appeals, the United States Code, the statutes of all fifty states, and other federal, state, and municipal legal opinions and rules.

Exclusive files for each congressman also may be established and maintained. Information related to a given issue or bill, including the member's recorded statements, can be stored and made available either through a terminal or regular printout form. It may be useful to file electronically pronouncements on an issue made by national party figures, opposition spokesmen, outside opinion makers, and leading newspapers. Procedural and equipment safeguards make it possible for the integrity of the individual office file to be assured.

Each member has files on certain groups of constituents, and the maintenance of these in a current fashion requires following a procedure which consumes much staff time. Many congressmen have mailing lists prepared on magnetic tape, sometimes at their own expense and often with the assistance of a party facility (such as the Democratic National Committee ADP center). The retention and retrieval of *key constituent information*—name, address, family composition, vocation, voting record (if known), extent of political activity—are expedited through the use of computers. Certain types of mailing operations also may be performed with computer and ancillary equipment.

There are some basic housekeeping functions, such as payroll preparation and the maintenance of current telephone directories, which are suitable for automatic data processing execution. As the performance quality of the equipment and programs increase, other applications are possible, and the Congress must become knowledgeable about what technology can do. During his visit to the United States, C. P. Snow remarked to the House of Representatives' Committee on Science and Astronautics:

We must get the ideas of what is happening to us because of the computers, and of what is going to happen, right into the open world of the Congress and of Parliament; for it is their duty not to be supine, not to be just carried along dumbly by the technological tide.[16]

PRESENT USE OF COMPUTERS IN THE
LEGISLATIVE BRANCH

There have been three points of developmental activity within the legislative branch insofar as the use of computers is concerned: the Office of the Clerk of the House of Representatives, the Office of the Sergeant-at-Arms of the Senate, and the Legislative Reference Service. In each case, a computer facility has been established, programs for selected ap-

[16] C. P. Snow, "Government, Science, and Public Policy," *Science,* CLI (February 11, 1966), 653.

plications obtained or prepared, and an operational capability established. Similarly, each facility has followed a pattern of growth in terms of size of equipment, number of software elements, and services provided.

The initiative taken by the Clerk of the House resulted in the installation of a small computer in the Rayburn House Office Building in September, 1967, to be used primarily for the purposes of handling payroll, special accounting, and inventory applications. With the installation of a new computer, allowing a five-fold increase in production and greater storage capacity, the Office of the Clerk is in a position to undertake more extensive automatic data processing services. Two major applications are under study:

1. a computerized addressing service, which will allow mailing list conversion, address printouts, and envelope preparation

2. an electronic voting system for the House chamber has been under consideration for more than a year and has included a study of possible display devices capable of presenting statistical data, running totals, and proposed amendments, as well as allowing key House officials to monitor proceedings from remote locations.

The Senate, in undertaking to apply automatic data processing to some of its information handling problems, has focused upon the development of an automated mailing system. With data conversion and programming support by a commercial firm, the Office of the Sergeant-at-Arms has converted more than one-half of the mailing addresses of Senate members to magnetic tape.

The Legislative Reference Service began providing support to congressional members and committees in the information sciences in 1966. Late in 1967, the first application of automatic data processing to a product for the Congress was effected. The *Digest of Public General Bills,* summarizing the essential features of all public bills and resolutions, was prepared by inserting essential identifying information on each piece of legislation (name of sponsor(s), date introduced, bill number, and committee to which assigned), plus synoptic and indexing information into the computer. In addition to these data, published biweekly, certain information on the status of the bill appeared in the five or more cumulative issues each year.

The *Legislative Status Report,* which serves as a handbook of major (i.e., approximately 250 bills and resolutions) legislation of the current Congress, also is prepared with computer support. The ability to add data elements without regard to sequence and to rapidly change obsolete material has proven to be particularly useful. A typical entry in this publication is shown as Figure 1.

FIGURE 1

Legislative Reorganization Act of 1969

H.R. 2185:

To improve the operation of the legislative branch of the government. To provide for: (1) substantial modification in the procedures of the standing committees; (2) improvement of Congressional oversight facilities; (3) strengthened Federal fiscal control; (4) minority staff for committees; (5) strengthening the Legislative Reference Service; (6) removal of postmasters from Congressional patronage; (7) amendments to strengthen the Regulation of Lobbying Act; and other purposes. (Related bills: H.R. 2186, H.R. 2187, H.R. 2713, H.R. 6278, H.R. 7371, H.R. 7372, H.R. 8158, H.R. 8975, S. 844.)

Status: Referred to House Committee on Rules, January 6, 1969.

Another use of automatic data processing within the Legislative Reference Service is the preparation of an index to the several hundred reports and memoranda of general interest to the Congress which are authored and stockpiled by LRS. The range of subjects is quite broad and although monthly notices are sent to each congressional office, it has been found useful to prepare a cumulative index by subject, as shown in Figure 2, and a separate listing by originating LRS division (e.g., Economics, Foreign Affairs).

FIGURE 2

ATOMIC ENERGY, U.S. foreign policy on   F 296

ATOMIC WEAPONS

Non-proliferation Treaty, History of   F 253

Nuclear strategy, Bibliography on   F 199

Proliferation, Bibliography on   F 198

AUTOMATIC DATA PROCESSING

Bibliography on   SP 107 R

Congressional use of   SP 126

Bibliography on   SP 123

Federal center

Bibliography on proposed   SP 107 R

Proposals for   SP 137 R

Cuba (May 20)   F 297

Greece (March 25 and October 28)   F 278

Hungary   F 263

Israel (May 15)   F 272

Latvia (November 18)   F 338

Lithuania (February 16)   F 258

Rumania (May 10)   F 280

Ukraine   F 255

Labor Day   E 296

Pan American Day (April 14)   F 283

BALANCE OF PAYMENTS and foreign aid   E 294

BALANCE OF PAYMENTS deficit and the restriction of private direct investment abroad   S 112

In January, 1969, a modular development project was begun which was designed to give the LRS research staff bibliographic control over all English-language books, government publications, magazines, and private sector (i.e., universities, lobbyist groups) studies related to congressional issues. More than 30,000 items are involved annually. Basic bibliographic entries such as subject and author plus a brief, descriptive paragraph on the contents of the piece, are entered into the computer. Each week separate subject and author catalogues are printed. During the "pilot project" phase, this was done for eleven of the LRS divisions. Perhaps the most valuable aspect of this new service, however, is the establishment of a "Current Awareness" procedure, similar to that found in a Selective Dissemination of Information system. Each research analyst has prepared a list of terms reflecting his areas of interest, and this "profile" has been matched against the descriptors which reflect the contents of the publications entered into the system.

During 1969, the House Committee on the Judiciary and the Committee on Banking and Currency worked with LRS to develop a computer-supported system for the preparation and maintenance of their official calendars. A typewriter terminal in each committee office is linked with the Library of Congress computer, to which the committee has access during any working day. Not only can the committee operator enter, recall, and edit any data belonging to the committee, but, with permission, can call out certain types of information maintained in the computer by LRS, such as the Legislative Status Report.

Emphasis is being placed within LRS upon the development of other automatic data processing-centered services with a high utility factor to the Congress. With a computer-supported network of thirty typewriter terminals, and installation of additional powerful equipment, services are being planned for providing Congress with quick responses to such questions as: "Send me a list of all legislation dealing with 'demonstration cities'." "Provide a selection of articles on 'gun control'." "Which senators have introduced bills on solid waste disposal?" The intention is to replace current manual research with computer searching either of full text material or of selected citations and abstracts. Legislative histories often are needed by the Congress and their preparation was stated as a priority item for LRS action in the final report of the Joint Committee on the Organization of the Congress.[17] The two-fold objective in this area will be, then, to have the ability to search bodies of textual information on the basis of keyword (retrieval) descriptors, and second, to provide current information on where a bill is in the legislative process.

[17] U.S., Congress, Joint Committee on the Organization of the Congress, *Final Report*, 89th Cong., 2nd sess., 1966, S. Rept. 1414, p. 11.

COMPUTER UTILIZATION BY THE POLITICAL INCUMBENT

Numerous applications of computer technology and better planning and decision-making practices—whether on a Congress-wide, chamber, committee, or member basis—have been discussed above, but there is one additional and important facet of congressional life to consider: each member is a legislator *and* a political incumbent. The necessity of being reelected and the resolve to bring this about are an integral part of every congressman's actions. To many members, this resolve takes the form of a diligent concern for the well-being of all constituents. One apocryphal incident reveals that a certain member, upon arising each morning, faced the mirror and said "Now what can I do for the noble voters of my district today?"

Many congressmen use computers and other mechanical devices in coping with the flood of correspondence that comes from constituents, and which of course must be answered. Devices now exist which can quickly type form letters on certain subjects and address and mail such material to the "folks back home." Assistance external to the member office may be provided by a chamber facility, such as that in the Senate, or through equipment located at a party-oriented installation or a service bureau corporation.

For each constituent, the Democratic National Committee computer facility staff will store and maintain the following information as provided by the individual office:

Name	Occupation
Address	Corporate Officer
Constituent Code	Firm Supporter
District	Nickname
County (numeric)	Organization Affiliation
Precinct	Nationality
Ward	Alien
Party	Key Contributor
Registered	Contributions (year to date)
Sex	Income Group
Age	Home Owner
Religion	Number of Dependents
Special Interest	Education
Special Problem	Welfare Recipient
Key Union Leader & Member	Office Visitor (during year)
Party Worker Skill	Dinner Attendee (invitation list)
Party Interest	Legislative Interest
Veteran	Government Worker
Office Holder	Patronage[18]

[18] "Foreword," "Data Processing Support at Democratic National Committee." (Unpublished paper, Washington, D.C., 1965.)

Some members maintain diversified machine readable files which serve several purposes. They may include listings of key newspapers (both within and outside the district), a newsletter mailing list for key contributors and other V. I. P.s, specialized mailing lists for identifiable groups such as teachers and union members, and a master "postal patron" list to be used for newsletter and opinion surveys.

Another file which is receiving a great deal of attention is the "issue" file, containing selected and essential elements of information on priority problems: international, national, regional, or of state and local interest.

For example, the problem of transportation systems is plaguing virtually all areas of the nation. The organization and contents of an issue file on this subject might look like this:

I. Statement of the problem
   A. Presidential statements
   B. Congressional statements
   C. Statements of officials of executive departments concerned with the problem
   D. Statements of officials of state and local governments
   E. Statements of members of the academic community
II. Existing programs
   A. Department of Transportation
   B. Department of Housing and Urban Development
   C. Department of Commerce
   D. Statements of appropriate congressional committees on the programs
   E. List of major programs
III. Other statements
   A. Editorials from newspapers and magazines
   B. Congressional Record articles
   C. Special reports that reflect major findings concerning the problem
IV. Legislation past and present
   A. Content
   B. Status in legislative process
V. Selected bibliography

The congressman in his political role will continue to use every means at his disposal to keep the voters aware of his usefulness, his concern for their welfare, and his willingness to exert every effort on their behalf. Where the computer can assist in these endeavors, and not offend his constituents, it will be used. The congressman will be, as he has been since the first duly elected representatives rode into the capital on horseback, the servant of the people in every sense of the word. The devices and man-machine techniques which he learns to employ can help him, but to do so, they must be used with acumen.

THE POLITICS OF COMPUTER USAGE

Some persons question that systematic planning and machine-oriented information handling will ever play a significant role in the political milieu. Often heard is some variation of the adage that "planning is rational while politics is the 'art of the possible.' " In viewing the political considerations inherent in the use of computers, three broad areas are apparent: the legislative-executive "separation of powers" and how information technology may affect it; the congressional establishment—the chambers, the committees, and the individual members—and the effect of computers on its structure, procedures, and prerogatives; and finally, the determinations which a member must make as he weighs the pros and cons of utilizing automatic data processing.

The consequences of information technology in both the executive and legislative branches and their areas of interaction are not yet fully known. The structure, legalistic checks and balances, and carefully evolved codes of conduct (often unwritten) have led to increasing rationalization of political authority. In recent decades, our government has been accurately termed "executive-centered." This has resulted in important information disadvantages to the Congress. As the departments and agencies of the executive branch have amassed an impressive array of (4,600) computers, the legislators have chosen to rely upon time-honored manual methods.

Congressmen have expressed, over and over again, a growing frustration at the difficulty of penetrating the executive labyrinth. Their search for program rationales and backup statistical information has been thwarted more by the tortuous bureaucratic procedures and compartmentalization than by any design on the part of an agency to withhold information. In testimony before the Joint Committee on the Organization of the Congress, a number of members urged that access be provided to "preliminary budgetary information" and those agency agreements and decisions selecting a certain course of action. It must be recognized, of course, that direct member or committee access to such information, before it had been reviewed at the departmental or Bureau of the Budget level, could throw into total disarray the normal budget presentation and review chain of events. Related to these disquieting possibilities is the role which Planning-Programming-Budgeting System personnel are playing in the executive branch. Some agencies have averred that their goals and objectives cannot be quantified; the Department of State, for example, was granted an exception and has not participated in the PPB System.

The nub of the problem might be seen as the way in which congressional oversight is to function *and be effective*. Not only must the advance plans—featuring concepts, alternatives for experimentation and implementation, and time-resource considerations—be presented in such a fashion that Congress has adequate time to respond sensibly, but there must be a mechanism for analyzing and evaluating the on-going program. The congressman today feels totally unable to affect the course of events on many developmental projects. Numerous bills have been introduced to create, as noted earlier, a separate Office of Program Analysis and Evaluation, with a congressional oversight committee. *Management information* is the key, and the importance of having computerized information respositories to house the essential data and manipulate it according to the needs of the Congress cannot be overstated.

The congressman who would demand for himself or his committee salient budgetary or planning information from the executive branch must be prepared to do certain things:

1. he must define very precisely his information requirements

2. he must see that compatible formats and procedures for accepting, transmitting, and utilizing the data are prepared

3. he must have available to him those devices and staff capabilities which will allow him to use the data from the executive branch, and

4. he must be able to guarantee, through a system of protective legal and data processing procedures, the confidentiality of the incoming information, where that is a factor in its being made available.

Any discussion of the effect of computers and advanced information handling techniques in the congressional establishment must recognize the changes which have occurred in similar environments. Congress is not impervious to some of these fundamental changes, any more than comparable government or private institutions or certain areas of society-at-large. Of course there are some raw political deterrents and problems which stand in the way of congressional use of innovative tools and techniques. The power of certain chamber functionaries or committee (and subcommittee) chairmen is vested, quite often, in the information which they control. Thus, the allocation of new information resources becomes critical. If a capability is to be established which will provide exclusive computer services to the Congress, the leadership must consider *in advance* these important questions:

Will each chamber control its own information resources? Does this automatically imply that the majority party leadership establishes the policies and operating guidelines?

Will independent access to computerized data banks be allowed each standing committee? Or should *all* committees and subcommittees have equal, unhampered entrée to these data?

Will policy committees and other special party-oriented elements participate in the use of the facility holdings?

Will individual members have time-shared access to the central (computerized) files? Will this include being able to obtain heretofore inaccessible committee or non-legislative branch data?

The ramifications are many, and have led to several alternatives for creating a congressional computer facility. One bi-partisan group in the House has urged the placement of the automatic data processing services in the Legislative Reference Service of the Library of Congress, since this is a non-partisan component of the legislative branch. The argument is reinforced by stressing the current use of computers in this organization and the existence in the Library of large bodies of topical research data of value to the Congress. Another legislative proposal, by Representative Jack Brooks of Texas, assigns responsibility for coordinating the development, establishment, maintenance, and operation of data processing systems to support the Congress to the General Accounting Office.

Only quite recently have more than a few members of Congress come to appreciate the latent power connected with control of the congressional computer support system. Not only are inanimate files and equipment involved, but there must be a group of research specialists and information technologists capable of handling chamber, committee, and member problems.

Three mechanisms must be provided for as Congress moves to revitalize its information services:

First, a permanent legislative oversight group will have to be established. Representative William S. Moorhead of Pennsylvania has called for the creation of a Joint Committee on Legislative Data Processing, and this approach has been incorporated into the House revised version of the proposed Reorganization Act(H.R. 17654, 91st Congress).

Second, a group responsible for analyzing the information requirements of the members and designing a computer-supported "system" will have to be established. Thus far, the House of Representatives has taken the lead in accomplishing this by having the Special Subcommittee on Electrical and Mechanical Office Equipment (Committee on House Administration) form a working group to develop an automatic data processing program for the House.

Third, the formation of a professional staff to manage and operate the projected "facility" or "system" will have to be considered in the light of existing legislative branch computer centers.

There are bound to be individuals and groups within the Congress who will oppose the widened use of computers either out of fear of the unknown or because any change is abhorrent to them. Sometimes the argument of increased efficiency alone can justify shifting to a computerized mode of operation, particularly where service has been marginal in the past. Speed of service is an important criterion on the Hill, and all too often sheer "brute force" methods or a damaging compromise in quality have resulted. An example of this might be the *Congressional Record* index, which has been sharply limited due to the overnight publication schedule. And, of course, where a task can be performed *more economically,* opposition to the fledgling computer services will be lessened appreciably. The House Committee on Banking and Currency, as an illustration, reports a reduction in the costs connected with the publishing of its legislative calendar—using a computer terminal and time-shared access—of more than half!

Where information retrieval is emphasized, the key consideration both for committee staffs and members is the *quality,* not the quantity, of the information obtained. Too much information is disfunctional. Information control—by the party leadership, as a prerogative of committee chairmen, or as a result of little known agreements between committee staffs and appropriate executive branch personnel—is threatened when there is talk of building centralized "open" files containing a broad spectrum of program, budgetary, or issue-oriented information. Political power is vested to a significant degree in the control of information, and the nature of that information—that is, how it is selected, stored, processed, and utilized—can be critical in the political machinations of the legislature.

There are also important connotations to the individual member who must weigh the value of using a computer in his operations. He must not, for example, conduct his legislative business in an iconoclastic way, for to threaten the traditional procedures and prerogatives of his chamber can only lead to ostracism and lessened effectiveness. Similarly, his constituents expect to be treated much as they were in decades past—with the "personal touch." The late Representative Herbert L. Bonner of North Carolina spoke on occasion of his diminishing personal contact with his constituency—of the flood of "strangers" and his wish that it could be otherwise.

As the member attempts periodically to improve his situation, and considers the political and "technical" implications of utilizing computer technology, he must ask himself several hard questions:

Will the projected change, for example the placement of certain information in computerized form, actually benefit me? During his tenure in the Senate, Joseph S. Clark actually commissioned a consulting firm to perform a "management audit" of his staff operations. The recommendations ranged from suggested revision of staff responsibilities and better file organization (including use of microfilm and other media) to identifying the need for improved dissemination of committee products to congressional offices.

If a change is instituted, how will this affect the functioning of my staff? Will new skills be required, or can existing personnel be retrained?

Already, where the computer terminals are in operation, requirements for altering job responsibilities have been identified. Whether this involves simple machine operation training or a wider appreciation of the new "system," more and more persons are drawn into the learning process. In essence, the information with which member decisions are made is handled somewhat differently now, and all involved *must* understand the new ground rules and day-to-day operations.

How much will it cost? Can this be borne in part by funds from the chamber—e.g., the House Committee on House Administration funds the terminal-storage expenses of House committees now using computer support—or must the member or committee pay some portion? Could group-sharing reduce the cost to the individual member without introducing other complications? A study prepared by industry for one Midwestern Senator showed alternative costs of handling correspondence files in terms of a single user or multi-users, both in a time-sharing situation and where courier pick up of records was the option. Although some members could afford commercial services or their own computer, only a few go outside for support in processing opinion surveys.

If word of my use of computer "gets around," will there be possible censure from constituent elements? The American populace is becoming fairly blasé about the use of form letters and other computer-produced items. Urban constituents tend to be less unhappy than rural folk when it comes to receiving standardized transmittals. Use of the computer in addressing and mailing letters does not need to be kept quiet, but most members still do not publicize their use of robot-type machines in the preparation of letters.

Can I go beyond just having a computer terminal and storage for purposes of handling my own personal files, and have access to here-to-fore privileged information (either within the Congress or in the executive branch)? This is not easily answered and will depend in large part on the procedures set up for a Congress-wide information support system using computers, or in far-reaching agreements with executive branch departments and agencies.

Now that a transition is in progress from philosophical speculation about the role of computers and their impact on the legislative process to a condition of systems design and implementation, discernible rethinking on the entire subject is taking place. While there is considerable support for various facets of congressional reform, including the employment of automatic data processing, there is a broad range of feeling as to how swiftly and in what ways such innovative procedures should be introduced. Many members on both sides of the aisle have offered the opinion that the use of information technology is certain. Therefore, the question may no longer be "if," but *"when"* and *"how."*

Not enough is known yet about legislators' reactions to advanced methodology as it would be used in the congressional environment to determine the extent of its usefulness. Great expectations, based on observing certain sophisticated industrial or executive branch ADP-oriented systems, often are not fulfilled when the particular needs of a new situation are analyzed and computer involvement actually tested. There will have to be a long breaking-in period, with a good deal of "give-and-take" between the designers of the system, those responsible for operating it and delivering the variety of products, and the user group—the Congress itself.

One member of Congress has offered the observation that the expanded use of computers within the Federal legislature will "demand a good measure of faith, hope, and charity on the part of all concerned." That the United States Congress must attain greater functional effectiveness in the future is clear, and its ability to meet the challenge of the last quarter of the twentieth century may well depend upon the perceptive utilization of applied logic combined with the potency of computer technology.

IV: SOME QUESTIONS

INTRODUCTION

Politicians may or may not be conservative: their position along this particular spectrum is a matter for the voters to evaluate and accept or reject. Planners, though, are almost universally considered to be liberal. Certainly, if not in politics (if they don't back the "liberal" politicians) they generally end up being on the side of liberalism in the broader sense —aware of, favoring, and advocating change.

The word planning used with reference to government or public planning, is rarely seen without a modifier: urban, regional, city, metropolitan, are among the most common. And functional words show up too: water, transportation, social, recreation. Planning is frequently called (whether or not the title is deserved) *comprehensive*. Yet it is apparent that an increasing realization of the relationships between things and people and events in modern society stimulates an even broader definition of comprehensive planning.

Pierre Clavel suggests that severe problems may result as urban development and the attendant technicians, lawyers, and planners move into rural parts of the country. The conflicts generated by the sharply contrasting modes of thought, behavior, and communication may frustrate the efforts of otherwise sincere and well-intentioned planners, politicians, and citizens to plan effectively in an increasingly important geographic area.

Richard Harmon draws to a considerable extent upon his experience with Saul Alinsky's Industrial Areas Foundation to address not so much the conflict between politician and planner as the conflict they *both* face in their roles within government. Harmon is saying what many say today: that the priorities of government and of politicians and planners are out of joint, that they do not define the major problems of our society today. Tough problems are those which do not yield easily to solution: Harmon has raised tough problems. They must be worked upon by politicians and planners. It is obvious that planners and politicians must beware of exclusively academic debates about their roles and relationships. Perhaps the urgency and intensity of the problems at hand will expedite the exploration of a workable relationship with the philosophical niceties postponed to a more accommodating atmosphere.

In the third selection, Kravitz suggests that planners have been something less than their self-image of enlightened innovators during the period of planning professionalization since the turn of the century. Arguing that they have been victims of the value structure of much of the middle and upper classes *and of their own,* his self-acknowledged radicalism questions assumptions of which many planners are totally unaware. Recognizing these assumptions is an initial step in calling their *value* into question, and it is the latter task which deserves greatest attention.

The overwhelming impression that comes from these three disparate chapters is the expansion of the conception of comprehensiveness. A dangerous word in its very generality, Clavel, Harmon, and Kravitz have each expanded, in his own style, the definition as it applies to planning and politics.

The Politics of Planning:
The Case of Non-Metropolitan Regions
PIERRE CLAVEL

Most attention to planning, and almost all concern with planning as a political factor, has had to do with metropolitan rather than rural areas. Here I am concerned with planning in the predominantly rural regions of the United States—those outside the larger metropolitan areas, including small and medium sized cities, but generally no "SMSAs." Such places often have official planning agencies, but in general they are not afflicted with the most obvious urban problems. Often they have not experienced much increase in population or economic activity, they have not attracted large ghetto populations, and they have not encountered the seemingly insoluble problems of over-bureaucratization apparent in the larger metropolitan areas.

These rural areas remain, however, of great interest for those with a concern for the social and political context of planning activity. They occasion a theoretical perspective that is usually missed in studies of the politics of planning in metropolitan areas or big cities. Briefly, it is often argued that planning gets government involved too much and with a heavy hand in the private economy, with damaging effects on entrepreneurship and a pluralistic political system. This selection makes a different though complementary argument. First, in many respects government plans too little, with attention to the wrong factors and the wrong groups; and this, too, has a damaging effect on entrepreneurship and pluralism. This is particularly apparent if we look at rural areas and small cities. Second, the traditional rural and small city social system is being transformed by the penetration of bureaucratic, nationally linked production organizations paralleled by federal and state agencies, resulting in increased heterogeneity of rural populations. Third, it seems that, as a result of these links and the resulting cleavages in social structure, serious obstacles to pluralist bargaining or other forms of competition exist, and consequently public and private entrepreneurship deteriorates. Fourth, from a review of the activities of a number of planning agencies in rural areas of the United States, I argue that there are tendencies in these activities that may reinforce the cleavages and block the development of pluralism. A final section contains some suggestions as to how we might begin to counteract these tendencies.

THE PROBLEM

Most of the writing about the political context of planning has been based on data gathered in the larger cities, and this has denied us a broad perspective. First, in the big cities the public attention that planning has received has been monopolized by public planning commissions or departments. These agencies claim comprehensive responsibility for all public planning, but nevertheless restrict their attention to a few issues of secondary importance. Much real planning goes unobserved. For example, not really noticed as planning problems are these situations: welfare agencies plan their activities and staffing so that minimal probability exists for the reduction of poverty among their clientele, or a large private corporation plans its investment and production process so as to pollute the water, or to alienate if not disemploy part of the urban labor force.

Public planners in large cities have conceived and sold their services as answers to certain classes of the external costs of growth and change initiated by others: for example, the impact of factories on residential areas, the impact of land use on the transportation system. Their concern is *results*. They have attempted to monitor results by criteria based on aesthetic quality or efficiency of traffic-land use relationships. They have not attempted, in most cases, to think about the structure of the primary productive forces that cause the problems they are concerned with. While such an approach may seem superficial, it has had an impact, especially in more recent years, in such institutions as zoning, urban renewal, traffic improvements, public housing, and, in some cities, budget review. To greater or lesser degrees, these institutions are now important factors in the urban political process in our larger cities.

These institutions have formed the context of most studies of the politics of big city and metropolitan planning. Writers on the subject have focused on the potential, in the planners' proposals, for government overreaction to imperfections in the market. They find the solutions proposed by planners to be bureaucratic, and, in the end, perhaps totalitarian. They contrast them with the values of a pluralistic political system which maximizes not government, but individual or group decision-making. They find that planners' solutions work counter to this norm.[1] This has been perhaps the most important general proposition concerning the politics of planning.

This argument has roots in the nineteenth century liberal tradition of hostility to inappropriate government intervention in the economy. Hayek argued this case in detail.[2] A free political system, he said, is one which maximizes individual abilities to make predictions and respond to the market—essentially, entrepreneurship and private sector planning. To achieve this, government activity should be keyed to private sector externalities, effects of entrepreneurial activity which a functioning market could not control. For example, a market would not motivate a producer to avoid incurring a nuisance to the community through pollution (since there is no market sanction such as the non-buying that would occur if the producer were polluting his own output). In such cases, it is reasoned that social costs to the community exceed private costs to the producer, the market will not motivate a socially optimal outcome, and therefore government taxation or regulation is justified. A somewhat parallel argument, less noticed in the metropolitan context, is that the market also fails to motivate the private production and consumption of goods such as roads or public facilities which in most cases cannot practically be marketed except to a collective purchaser, social benefits exceed private benefits, and government investment is thus required. Aside from such activities, which themselves maintain a good climate for private entrepreneurship, traditional liberal economics suggests that government should limit itself to the establishment of institutions that will make the market work and avoid any activity that will pre-empt private functions. To do otherwise would destroy entrepreneurship.

Rural areas and small cities provide a different political and economic context, and lead us to a different theoretical perspective. Compared to metropolitan regions, they are growing but slowly, and planning to control the results of growth has been relatively unimportant. It is the growth rates themselves, in fact, which have been politically important, because of their lagging or sporadic nature; and there has been some professional and public attention to the problems of production and modernization in private firms. Since the 1950's, area redevelopment has been a major national issue reflecting these concerns, with pressure coming mainly from lagging medium-sized urban regions and rural areas, not from the big cities. Recently, planning has become recognized as a major

---

[1] See Martin Meyerson and Edward C. Banfield, *Politics, Planning and the Public Interest* (New York, 1955) and Alan Altshuler, *The City Planning Process* (Ithaca, N.Y., 1965).

[2] Friedrich A. Hayek, *The Road to Serfdom* (Chicago, 1957). See also Milton Friedman, *Capitalism and Freedom* (Chicago, 1963) for related arguments.

instrument in area redevelopment efforts. But this has necessarily been planning of a broader sort than that meant by land use-oriented big city planners. Economic and social objectives are given explicit predominance, and the planning activities are carried out in multi-county agencies supported by agencies such as the federal Economic Development Administration, the Appalachian Regional Commission, and the Office of Economic Opportunity. In these non-metropolitan areas it is common for a single agency to perform multiple planning functions and to receive support from a number of special-purpose federal or state agencies. In addition to the physical planning activities traditionally associated with urban planning agencies are components such as manpower retraining and industrial extension, which bring these agencies directly into production processes. The major emphasis is on the stimulus rather than the regulation of public and private economic activity. This contrasts with big cities where such activities are more apt to be handled within the private sector, or, when undertaken by public agencies, they are more apt to be performed by specialized agencies.

This picture of planning in the rural context suggests an aspect of the traditional liberal economic argument concerning the effect of government planning on private entrepreneurship, different from that which springs from the big city context. Rural areas may be subject to a distinct kind of government policy error, also indicated by the criteria of liberal theory: government failure to act when, theoretically, it should act to provide collectively demanded goods and services. In these areas, I shall argue, entrepreneurial inadequacies exist as in the cities; but in this case the predominant cause is not government over-response but under-response to the needs of a viable competitive private sector and the failure to provide sufficient physical and institutional support to let the private economy function at its optimal level. This hypothesized association between governmental and private-sector under-response implies quite a different picture from that of the big city case; there is suggested a reinforcing relationship, in which, in parallel fashion, both public and private sectors suffer from the same malady: inability to respond strongly or quickly to opportunities. Thus, beyond a real low level of opportunities, the problem is compounded by the inability of local governments and private entrepreneurs to seize such investment opportunities as do exist.[3]

Such parallel inadequacies are quickly seen to carry over into the political system and to have implications for the kind of political analysis appropriate to the rural context. Private and public entrepreneurial inad-

[3] This thought is elaborated in Barclay G. Jones, Gordon H. Jacobs, Emil E. Malizia and Phaichitr Uathavikul, *Sectoral Response to Secular Change: Indications of Opportunity Loss in a Regional Economy: Cayuga, Cortland, Madison, Onondaga and Oswego Counties, New York* (Ithaca, N.Y., 1967).

equacies reflect widespread lags in the development of organizations and institutions, scarcity of leadership, and an inability to manage sustained political competition. While in the big cities, government over-response by well organized public agencies is met by all organized business firms or competing public bureaucracies, in the rural areas the situation is much different. In rural areas, whatever attempts at planning are made will contrast sharply with the institutional machinery available to implement them, whether this entails local government efforts at public works and services, private sector expansion of firms, or the response to new markets. For the analyst, the big city case is amenable to a focus on the mechanisms and outcomes of conflicts among groups already organized. In the rural case in which planning is introduced to a largely unorganized and unresponsive public, the major issue is modernization of parts of the public and private sectors. One certainly cannot assume conflict to exist as a point of departure for analysis in these cases. One is led to focus on the growth, change, and development of firms, government agencies, and interest groups, rather than primarily on their interaction and conflict.

The above is, however, but a simplified version of the context of planning in rural areas. The picture of under-response is complicated by the appearance of private and public bureaucratic influence in such areas. This has become increasingly important in recent years. This both intensifies the demand for government planning for the provision of collective goods and at the same time makes it problematic whether such planning will result in an increase in entrepreneurship or pluralism. Briefly, the question is whether the appearance of nationally linked, sophisticated bureaucratic organizations in areas of low institutional development will result in an increase of local entrepreneurship and pluralism, or will, instead, overwhelm local institutions to the point where very little such development occurs. The introduction of large organizations in rural areas results in great inequalities between them and existing organizations, particularly with respect to specialized knowledge. The supply of local persons with the time, training, or experience to deal with large organizations or specialists is limited. This inequality whenever contacts occur may well be a pathological situation in the further development of local institutions. There may be a loss of communication in both directions. Bargaining among parties, one of which holds most of the important resources, is largely impossible. Substantively, nationally linked organizations, public or private, tend to serve objectives set elsewhere rather than those of the local community. In the case of private corporations, an example of this has been the development of increasing ratios of capital to labor in most economic sectors. This has resulted in higher profits and growth nationally and has served the public interest of the nation by making it able to compete more effectively with other nations. In localities, on the other hand, the direct results have often been an increasing burden of retraining, welfare programs, and cultural change for the community. Since this burden is usually not picked up by the firm, the result is a widening rift between the corporate world and other segments of the local community.

These developments suggest a revision of the "under-response" hypothesis stated above. That hypothesis suggests that the development of local entrepreneurship is a function of government's ability to supply publicly consumed goods and services when the market does not motivate their production by the private sector. Thus, such collectively consumed goods as roads, bridges, sewers, and education—ordinarily undersupplied in rural areas—should require the attention of rural planners. The development of large scale organization in rural areas suggests an additional concern. If these organizations, through their tendency to overwhelm local institutions under some circumstances, form an inhibiting factor on the development of entrepreneurship and pluralism, then perhaps these organizations themselves should be regarded as the objects of government action and planner attention. Thus government action to regulate their distribution, their internal structure and their relations with local institutions might come within the bounds of reasonable planner concern, if the development of local entrepreneurship and pluralism is an objective.

TRANSITIONS IN RURAL SOCIAL SYSTEMS

Rural social organization is undergoing marked changes, and this has implications for the role of planning in these areas. Rural regions and stable or declining smaller cities have always been, in most senses, low-resource areas. They are low on economic resources and capital, and above all they lack a diversity of institutions and large numbers of persons with experience in complex political or administrative operations. They are at opposite poles from the densely populated metropolitan regions, which are richly endowed with these social resources.

Economically, these areas have in the past depended on the primary industries—extractive activities usually related to an extensive rather than concentrated resource base: agriculture, mining, and forestry. Towns and cities functioned as trade centers and were usually limited in size. At a later date, moderate-sized, locally-owned manufacturing activity spread through these cities. But despite the diversity of goods produced, the scale of productive organization was usually small. Localities came to be dominated by what may be termed a traditional or old middle class based on small-scale capitalism. (In modern census terms, the occupational category of "managers, proprietors, and officials" roughly encompasses this group.) Whatever differences existed in the economic interests of various specializations, they had in common this middle class dominance. Moreover, the middle class dominance was usually limited to the local community, and the community operated as a major integrative mechanism, assuring linkages to the less well off and providing them a share in local institutions that stood against the rest of the world.

Rural and small-city political systems have in the past reflected the limitations of small-scale, old middle class organizational forms. With a lack of concentrated economic resources in the private sector, rural political systems have not developed centers of bureaucratic power independent of the private sector. They have primarily supported town or county offices which, scattered over the countryside and not concentrated at one place, subsist on low salaries by satisfying localistic needs for personal responsiveness. Power is not aggregated on a scale capable of managing big projects. In the small- and medium-sized cities in most rural areas, similar localistic attitudes and institutions prevail, although concentrations of resources sometimes make for at least the trappings of modern administration. Even so, the smaller rural cities seem to have little impact, politically, outside their boundaries.

Rural administration can be characterized as under-developed. Officials tend not to have specialized roles. Recruitment is difficult, and part-time service is the rule, with the few competent or trained executives available being used in too many capacities to acquire real expertise in any one. Competition of office is often low or non-existent, and administrative appointments are correspondingly long-term. Control is stable and hierarchical.

Major changes are now occurring in economic and social organizations in rural areas and small cities, both in the private and the public sectors. These occur both in the stable and the declining areas. They are essentially organizational changes, involving a shift from horizontal, intra-community relations to vertical, inter-community links from smaller to larger centers.[4] First, farming is being replaced by industry and various tertiary activities, including tourism and recreation and second homes, as the major economic activities in rural regions. Second, locally-controlled activities are being replaced by corporate enterprises operated on a regional or national scale and subject to bureaucratic controls emanating from metropolitan areas. Third, small-scale agriculture is being replaced by intensive commercial farming operations, operated in an industrial manner and linked vertically to regional and national marketing and supply organizations. Finally, government operations in rural areas

---

[4] An early and comprehensive characterization of this shift is provided in Roland L. Warren, *The Community in America* (Chicago, 1963).

—which are among the growing tertiary sectors—are increasingly linked via grants-in-aid or direct administration to state and national decision centers. These transitions are occurring not only in medium-sized cities but also in very small centers, to the extent that they virtually cover the map of rural areas in the United States. Insofar as these activities are concerned, it is not possible to think of part of the nation as rural in the traditional sense, distinct from a growing urban area where most change is taking place. The formerly rural areas are being transformed, too.

Perhaps the most significant characteristic of these transitions is that they constitute a penetration of regions previously dominated by the traditional middle class—largely localistic in outlook and small scale in production and organizational capability—by organizational systems that operate on a national or regional scale and which are operated by a new technically and managerially oriented middle class with significantly different managerial attitudes. Their common characteristic is a tendency to plan production and distribution by techniques of prediction and analysis developed mainly since World War II. While the old middle class is best approximated as "managers, proprietors and officials," the new middle class is closer to the category of "technical, professional . . ."[5] Although the public sector tends to lag behind the new organizational forms in the private sector, there are tendencies toward this technological orientation here too, particularly in the new multi-county planning agencies now developing.[6]

With the introduction of the new middle class and technical large scale organization, the hegemony of the traditional middle class is destroyed and rural social organization is split, at least potentially, in two ways. First, the traditional middle class of small businessmen is alienated from the organizational world. Their small industries are made subservient to large-scale suppliers or buyers, and their farms become unprofitable. Only the retail merchants remain viable economically, but their political dominance is now threatened by the emergence of large-scale orga-

---

[5] This is only the roughest of characterizations, limited to the occupational subsets described in the broadest census breakdowns. Some managers and officials, those employed in large organizations, would be included in my definition of new middle class; and some professional and technical persons, particularly those who are self-employed, are old middle class.

[6] A distinction needs to be made between what are formally termed "planning" organizations, and the activity I am calling the "planning process." By the planning process I mean activities undertaken to calculate and evaluate the possible consequences of alternative investments over a long period of time. Planning bodies are usually set up by local governments to oversee the quality of the environment and sometimes to contribute to the effectiveness of public spending programs; planning departments may be set up in any private firm or public agency for similar reasons. Actually, there is no necessary correspondence between the formal title and the process as I have described it; the latter often goes under a different name.

nizations with which they must co-exist. Vidich and Bensman describe the mechanisms by which this subservience is made to seem palatable. They are bombarded by propaganda about the "independence" of rural and small-town life, produced by the large-scale organizations of the mass society which dominates them.[7]

Large-scale organization and technology drive another wedge in rural society by shifting the structure of demand for labor. Technological developments have forced a "twist" in the labor market so that shortages in skilled occupations occur simultaneously with increasing unemployment in the unskilled, low-education segments.[8] These are national forces because technology and the skilled and managerial parts of the labor force are highly mobile. But their effects locally, in rural areas, add to the social cleavages noted above as a highly trained, scarce labor segment is juxtaposed with one whose skills and institutions are becoming obsolete. Miller and Sower have noted these shifts in agriculture, forcing the dispossession of a large part of the farming population and a consequent break-up of farmers as a homogeneous political force.[9] Much of the surplus population, of course, hangs on in rural areas, protected by local institutions such as building codes which maintain employment in building trades or in protected government jobs. The skilled segments continue, however, to demand "modernization"—streamlining of government, zoning regulations, housing and services improvements—but each of these comes as a painful wrench to the unskilled segments who are sustained by the traditional ways of doing things.

The heterogeneity of interests generated by the penetration of bureaucratic organization is supplemented by the introduction of retirement and vacation homes in some areas of the "extended fringe" of large metropolitan centers. This increases the level of demand on local institutions and government, and the pressures for services not previously required locally: health facilities, for example, and protection of amenities. Retired persons have contributed to the supply of governmental activities as well by serving on local boards and committees, sometimes in elective offices. In doing this they provide new ways of operating rural institutions and exert pressures for change. Moreover, the transformation to capital-intensive agriculture has forced the transition to other lines of work for many heads of families. In some cases this has meant attempts

[7] Arthur J. Vidich and Joseph Bensman, *Small Town in Mass Society* (Princeton, N.J., 1958).
[8] James C. Killingsworth, "Automation, Jobs and Manpower: The Case for Structural Unemployment," in *The Manpower Revolution,* ed. Garth L. Mangum (Garden City, N.Y., 1966), pp. 97–117.
[9] Christopher Sower and Paul A. Miller, "The Changing Power Structure in Agriculture: An Analysis of Negative Versus Positive Organization Power," in *Our Changing Rural Society: Perspectives and Trends,* ed. James H. Copp (Ames, Iowa, 1964), pp. 127–58.

to exploit the more obvious tourism and recreation potentials of rural areas, sometimes clashing with conservation interests. In a more general way, it has resulted in impoverishment and the creation of an under-employed, undertrained population without real interest in agriculture or in the promotion of amenities.

"MODERN" RURAL POLITICS

This increasing economic and social heterogeneity, brought on as the result of the introduction of new organizations and occupation groups, may be part of a more general modernization process including the political institutions of rural areas. Politically, there may be a transition occurring, from a system of relatively homogeneous localities with minimal interaction apart from trade, to one where larger regions are integrated along industry and voluntary association lines and where political contention among these interest groups is the focus of political decision-making. The degree to which such a transition has occurred, or is occurring, is doubtful, however—an empirical question, at any rate, on which we have little information. My impression is that real interest group competition is rare in rural areas and small towns, that the form of political activity is one of adjustment among participants increasingly unequal in political resources, and that the resulting effects on political institutions are so slow or so indeterminate that it is very doubtful whether much long-term development toward group pluralism in political institutions is in prospect.

Political domination of the many by the few is a traditional characteristic of rural and small-town politics, although it may not have occurred most frequently. Small-town politics has in some areas followed the New England town meeting style, but it has also included the company town and one-industry economic domination. Hierarchical, compared to pluralistic power structures, are apparently more frequent as the size of city becomes smaller.[10] The base of the power inequality in these cases is

[10] John Walton has pointed out that, for communities in general, this relation is not well supported. He suggests that pluralism is associated with such factors as absentee owned corporations, adequate economic resources, and satellite status. In contrast to the argument of this paper, he also suggests that the transition away from a hierarchical power structure occurs as a result of the penetration of external linkages such as are entailed in new corporate facilities and federal agencies. The effect of these new links is the introduction of new power resources, a challenge to the existing consensus on the rules governing political contention, and increased community conflict leading to a dispersion of leadership and power. See John Walton, "Differential Patterns of Community Power Structure," in *Community Structure and Decision-making: Comparative Analyses*, ed. Terry N. Clark (San Francisco, 1968), pp. 441–59. Walton acknowledges, however, that his hypotheses may not apply to the very small community and his model does posit the existence of "adequate economic resources" and "satellite status," and he suggests that further theorizing is called for. My

generally held to be economic dominance or legal control over political resources, such as jobs and property. The shifts in institutions described in the preceding pages is, however, different. It is a shift in relative capacity to solve problems, process information, do technical jobs, and organize. Hawley did an analysis of communities' success in initiating urban renewal projects in which he attributed major responsibility to low conflict among elites, as indicated by a relatively low proportion of "managers, proprietors and officials."[11] The shifts I am describing, however, reflect another dimension better characterized as technical personnel or bureaucratic staff functions. These latter roles would be equally rare in the company-owned coal camp and in the New England village. It is due to them, however, that the inequalities that characterize the "new" rural politics arise.

The following analysis does not attempt to be exhaustive, to generalize for every rural community or small- or medium-sized rural center.[12] It presents examples which are suggestive and for which I know of few greatly contradictory cases and which I think define the *typical* pattern of the new rural politics, the deviations being matters of degree for further empirical investigation. The pattern has the following characteristics:

1. *rural politics operates under a scarcity rationale.* Rural regions are generally low on economic wealth and productive capacity; to the extent new organizations have been established, there is new capital equipment, but this may have little impact on the generally available wealth locally. Psychologically, people in rural regions tend to accept a scarcity premise, even to the point of underestimating the resources and opportunities that do exist. This legitimizes much rural political behavior, including a slowness to organize and react, and an unwillingness to tax and spend or make public capital investments. Reliance is placed on existing institutions rather than on innovation

2. *politics becomes a consumption item, rather than a process in which local political personnel and representatives participate for real stakes.* Attention thus is directed to national political issues through the mass media, while serious attention to important local issues is usually

---

analysis is concerned with small places, places with low resources, and places too far away from big cities to be satellites. In these situations, the hierarchy-size relation does seem reasonable to assert, as does the assertion of blocks to pluralism resulting from external linkages, made in the following pages.

[11] Amos Hawley, "Community Power and Urban Renewal Success," *American Journal of Sociology,* LXVIII (January, 1963), 422–31.

[12] The generalizations presented here are drawn partly from experience, partly from research I have been engaged in, relevant to the points made. An additional interpretation and report is available in Pierre Clavel, "Planners and Citizen Boards: Some Applications of Social Theory to the Problem of Plan Implementation," *Journal of the American Institute of Planning,* XXXIV (1968), 130–39.

lacking. Locals withdraw from major political skirmishes at home. Vidich and Bensman document this in detail[13]

3. *on major issues involving confrontation between the new organizations and other elements in the community, the typical form of interaction is what might be termed "producer-consumer" politics with the major initiatives being "technical" proposals on the part of the organization in response to relatively unorganized political demands by the community—usually made by members of the old middle class.* This form of interaction arises out of the inequalities in technical knowledge and organizational resources among the participants. A typical sequence of events in this interaction can be described.

First, at the outset of the tenure of a large firm or other bureaucratic organization in a rural area or small city, the "consumption" pattern noted above holds. The new organization is a complex production process and the object of attention without being well understood. It lists its attributes for the community in the form of press releases and verbal statements, but very often does not engage in extensive personal contact. It advertises the number of employees it will hire, the gross business it expects to do, the value of its capital assets and the related tax benefits to the community. Any possible harmful effects, if perceived, are smoothed over. The new organization capitalizes on its command of modern technology in answer to any possible problems—e.g., pollution—it may create. Other local interests are usually not in a position to take the initiative and question the newcomer, since they do not have the technical knowledge, the funds to hire technical consultants, nor the organization to persistently attend to the situation. These comments are meant primarily for the case of the new industrial organization, but they apply also to many external government agencies, as in the case of road-building plans by the state highway department.

Second, contention of some sort may occur as the new organization comes into overt conflict with other parts of the population. Air or water pollution is a common issue of this sort. But typically, neither side pushes very hard for a solution despite frequent and extended costs and hardship on the part of the community participants. On the part of the new organization, a habit of minimizing internal costs is perhaps the controlling factor and little tradition of attention to costs to others (as in the case of pollution) exists. The cheapest thing for the producer to do is to try to placate the community in the easiest possible way. This may entail payments to those most directly affected so as to preclude any cohesive opposition; more frequently a protestation that the injury was accidental —often true, of course—and a promise to "do something" suffices in the short run. A temporary settlement, it should be emphasized, is enough to

[13] Vidich and Bensman, *Small Town.*

deflate whatever organizational response has built up on the part of a normally unorganized political contestant. Often it takes six months to a year to organize opposition once a temporary assurance has been given.

This was the pattern in a series of disputes between large-scale poultry producers and local residents in an upstate New York county in the mid-1960's. In that case, residents and businesses suffering from water and air pollution showed extreme sluggishness responding to these nuisances. The typical pattern was to resort to the simplest traditional institutional technique of handling such problems, agree to pursue it, find the technique a failure, then resort to the next simplest technique. First, appeals to simple neighborliness were made, then in turn to town health officials, town boards, state health department, then litigation in court, and town zoning regulations. In each case, the industry took the initiative in supplying technical ideas necessary in the response since none of the opposing participants had the ability to do so. During the time required to discover the inadequacies of each technical solution, the poultry operations kept producing and the threat of pollution remained. (Of course, *constant* nuisance might have resulted in much stronger reactions, but such cases are probably rare and it does not take continuing nuisances to permanently damage neighboring interests.)

It is difficult to explain the relative passivity of the neighboring interests on grounds other than the psychological costs of competing against forces with an overwhelming technical and organizational superiority. This explains both the relatively easy victories (temporary though they were) of the poultry industry and the failure of local interest to build more effective institutional and political machinery to deal with them (zoning, for example). This raises the possibility that unequal political systems of this sort may lead to adjustments of an unequal nature, with exploitation a normal facet of the system, persisting for a very long time, rather than to a transition from the traditional rural, localistic situation to the pluralism of well-organized groups.

4. *on some issues, the old patterns of pluralistic competition involving the political system dominated by the traditional middle class persist.* However, these are less and less frequently the most important economic issues; they are limited to those issues within the technical and organizational competence of the old middle class, and some of the vigor with which this competition is reported may simply reflect attempts to compensate for the loss of jurisdiction over more important matters.

The Role of Planning in Rural Politics

Given the picture of rural social organization and politics presented above, it is clear that there are great obstacles to the development of entrepreneurship and pluralism. Possibly, the introduction of rural planning institutions could mitigate or overcome these obstacles. They can perhaps be seen as indigenous responses to the changes in the national economy which affect them. They have often been advertised and promoted in this way. But the activities of planning organizations in non-metropolitan areas are at best mixed in this regard. County and town scale planning has not usually flourished in rural areas.[14] The major recent phenomenon in rural planning is the multi-county planning and development agency, which has multiplied rapidly since the middle 1960's. These, like their predecessors, are often described as indigenous organizations. They certainly do reflect local concerns over several kinds of changes including the increase in inter-governmental transfers of funds, a demand for coordination of various government activities, demands for community and regional economic development, and demands for environmental protection and improvement. On the other hand they are not generally well

---

[14] Examples of the latter have been the county agricultural land use efforts established in the late 1930's under Department of Agriculture auspices, the "Urban Planning Assistance" programs under Section 701 of the Housing Act of 1954, and the local development committees of the Area Redevelopment Administration of the 1961–65 period which were charged with the formulation of "Overall Economic Development Programs." The first of these, the county land use planning program, seems to have been largely a federally sponsored program which never received much participation locally. See Neal C. Gross, "A Post Mortem on County Planning," *Journal of Farm Economics,* XXV (1943), 644–61.

The "701" plans usually were, and are, consultant-staffed operations with small impacts on political institutions. They do sustain part-time planning boards during the one- or two-year planning period, and in cities which already have planning staffs, they sometimes increase the scale of these operations. But such planning operations are usually epiphenomenal in local government: the more so, the smaller the community. This is not so much a matter of financial support as it is of the kinds of interests served, even if the finances are available. They have generally been aimed at the production of zoning ordinances, and ultimately the protection of property values and aesthetics for landowners. These hardly go to the roots of the political process in local government.

Where planners have succeeded in becoming institutionally entrenched and important in the politics of smaller cities, this seems to be the result of a long period of involvement in the management of government. The concerns with the aesthetic and property values come later and "701" programs do not last that long. On this process, see Robert Daland and John A. Parker, "Roles of the Planner in Urban Development," *Urban Growth Dynamics,* ed. F. Stuart Chapin, Jr., and Shirley Weiss (New York, 1962), pp. 188–225.

The Area Redevelopment Committees were usually made up of town or county-wide representative businessmen, whose main object was in getting an ARA sponsored public works project or business loan subsidy for a prospective or existing firm. The plans produced were often done by consultants or even federal or state agency field men, often with a minimum of local participation, and thus did not result in changes in local decision-making machinery. It does seem, however, that the ARA committees as well as the "701" experiences have served as valuable though unintended training institutions, readying localities to accept the complexities of federal-state-local interaction and motivating them to cooperate with other localities in the newer, larger scale agencies.

institutionalized in local or state government and depend on outside support. In addition it is difficult to predict whether they will have lasting effects in bringing about changes in the capacities of local political institutions. It seems equally probable that, by maintaining a natural alliance with the newer technically oriented bureaucratic elements, they will widen the splits described above. This is, however, largely a matter of technique and professional orientation on the part of these new agencies and the outcome still seems to me to be in doubt.

Multi-County Agencies

During the 1960's there was a great increase in the number of multi-county planning and development agencies. This resulted in the extension of planning organizations with professional staffs into rural areas, a largely unprecedented event.[15] By joining a number of counties together, it became possible to obtain sufficient local support—a minimal financial contribution, usually, plus at least some political acceptance—

[15] Examples of the multi-county agencies formed are the Rural Conservation and Development districts supported by the U.S. Department of Agriculture starting in the late 1950's, the Local Development Districts and Economic Development Districts established by the Appalachian Regional Commission and the Economic Development Administration since 1964 and 1965, and multi-county rural Community Action Agencies established by the Office of Economic Opportunity since 1964. More recent legislation has fostered additional multicounty jurisdictions including agencies for comprehensive health planning under the Department of Health, Education, and Welfare, and for comprehensive planning under the Department of Housing and Urban Development. In addition to these agencies receiving a major part of their funds from federal programs are Councils of Governments—cooperative associations of elected officials—which are often given authority to review intergovernmental programs. There are also multi-county planning agencies sponsored by state governments in some states.

A 1968 survey of some of these types of multi-county agencies indicated 184 organizations making responses. Of these, ninety-two had been created since the beginning of 1966 and all but twenty-nine since 1959. Many of these organizations are completely outside metropolitan areas, and probably most counties included in them are rural or non-metropolitan area counties, even in those cases in which the organizations have headquarters within a metropolitan area.

The organizations are those responding to questionnaires distributed to all of those listed in the 1968 *Directory of Regional Councils* (Washington, D.C.: National Service to Regional Councils, May, 1968). A few of the agencies listed were single-county agencies serving more than one *local* government. In an examination of fifty-three such "regional" organizations based partly on the data mentioned above for a 364 county area in eight Appalachian states, it appeared that the newer organizations were the Economic Development Districts and Local Development Districts; these tended to include more counties, were more rural, and carried on a broader variety of functions than the older agencies. The latter tended to be located in SMSAs and to specialize in such activities as land use and transportation planning, capital budgeting, and review of local plans. This is included in Pierre Clavel, Robert W. Lewis, and David Povey, "Institutional Factors in Economic Development: Approaches to Measurement and Analysis," Mimeographed (Ithaca, N.Y.: Department of Rural Sociology, Cornell University, 1969).

to hire one or more professionals with the training and inclination to tap sources of federal and state aid and contact potential investors at the national level. Most of the funds still come from federal and state government sources, however, and despite varying degrees and styles of local involvement, the most obvious cause of this increase in rural planning activity has been massive support by the federal government. The federal agencies have their own reasons for giving this support. The most obvious reason is the new problems at the federal level occasioned by the very marked increases in transfers of funds from the federal to the local level during the 1960's. Federal aid to state and local governments increased from 7.0 billion dollars in 1960 to over 20.0 billion in 1969.[16] Moreover, an increasing share was transferred directly to localities, bypassing the states, and other shifts occurred away from capital improvement to redistributive human resources programs.

These shifts put various pressures on federal agencies; multi-county programs were seen as at least part of the response. First, the technical and political difficulties of allocating funds among localities and among programs increased. Technically, each additional dollar is more difficult to justify and politically, each additional program—particularly if it is redistributive in nature—takes on greater visibility and is subject to more public criticism. Second, as programs become more numerous, complaints of "overlap," and demands for coordination increase, while at the same time coordination in Washington or in field offices becomes more difficult. Finally, expansion of programs into areas where they are not only new but where nothing similar has been seen before raises problems of local response: there is a need for persons or agencies with the ability to generate projects, fill out applications, and pursue the intricacies of inter-governmental relations.

One major federal response to these problems has been the delegation of planning functions to multi-county agencies. A Bureau of the Budget memorandum indicated an increase from 162 million dollars for planning grants distributed by all federal agencies to states and localities in 1966 to 309 million dollars proposed for 1969.[17] Accompanying the increase is a trend to send a greater proportion of these funds directly to localities than in the past. One reason for this increase in planning funds is that they represent a *minimal* threat to either federal or local institutions. For the federal agencies, they promise increased flows of informa-

[16] "Special Analysis J: Federal Aid to State and Local Governments," *Special Analyses, Budget of the United States, 1968* (Washington, D.C., 1967), pp. 147–48, and "Special Analysis K: Federal Aid to State and Local Governments," *Special Analyses, Budget of the United States, 1969* (Washington, D.C., 1968), p. 161.
[17] "Federal Grant Programs Assisting State and Local Governments in Functional and Comprehensive Planning," mimeographed (March 26, 1968).

tion upward and the implantation of a local bureaucratic apparatus—both developments which reduce the uncertainties accompanying any local initiative. For the local governments, planning agencies have only advisory formal powers. The threat of usurping local political access to federal funds may be a problem, but this is mitigated by the fact that many programs are new ones, so that no existing funds are actually cut back. In any event, federal agencies generally prefer to keep open any access route that exists, bypassing the multi-county agency if necessary.

Agency Performance and Political Impact

The heavy federal bureaucratic involvement in multi-county agencies raises the questions of: (1) whether they are simply extensions of the trend toward penetration and dissolution of rural social structure by nationally oriented bureaucratic organizations; and (2) whether or not this is so, do they offer a prospect for lasting change toward pluralistic local political institutions. Here, I will review some evidence indicating a "yes" answer to the first question and a "no" to the second, though these cannot be generalized for all rural areas and only a very qualified answer to the second question is really possible. This analysis is mainly based on case studies of a number of multi-county agencies in the Northeast.[18]

First, many multi-county agencies are, by virtue of their technical resources, new middle class oriented. This tends to separate them—by their style of thought—from the old middle class and the poor who make up the bulk of the rural population. Even if they are not as technical as their urban counterparts, they seem technical to their rural clientele. Planning agencies will probably always have this tendency and their technicians will find it more comfortable to deal with others used to technical thought than with groups who reject this style. By itself, this need not separate them if they conceive their task as one of linking up the newer styles with the old. This is a matter of ideology—a rationale or "philosophy" guiding agency leadership in its efforts to co-opt support and clientele, pacify or overcome competition.

Unfortunately, there seem to be more ideologies channeling the attention of multi-county agencies to state and federal levels than there are ideologies directing their attention locally. For one thing, professional reference groups tend to be regional or national in scope, not local. Moreover, the dominant economic rationale for these agencies is one of modernizing public and private management with the aim of maximizing gross economic product for the area. This is mainly the interest of the

---

[18] These are reported on and cited in detail in Pierre Clavel, Harold R. Capener, and Barclay G. Jones, "Alternative Organizational Models for District Development," mimeographed (Ithaca, N.Y.: Department of Rural Sociology, Cornell University, 1969).

new middle class and the large-scale corporate interests. The typical motivation for the multi-county organizations is production, and they are sold to the public with the claim that an increase in gross product for an entire region will benefit everyone. Localism and competition, on the other hand, will not support the scale of activities and services necessary for modern industry, or for the attraction of highly skilled professional and technical persons to the labor force.

There are several issues in which the technical new middle class can use public planning organizations. One is public works and housing—the establishment of infrastructure necessary for the attraction of technical and professional personnel. Another is industrial development and promotion of tourism. There was widespread disenchantment with the local and county committees set up in the early 1960's under the Area Redevelopment Administration; even more scorned are local chambers of commerce. In both cases, the reason is impatience with these local committees' inability to deal with large-scale, non-local investors. Partly this reflects the predominance of the old middle class on these committees, partly the notion that they are "small time." It is said, for example, that local chambers are unreliable in many cases in handling potential sites for industrial prospects, letting information leak out prematurely. Also, some facility for research, or at least the ability to transmit reasonably accurate economic data to prospective investors, was often beyond the local organizations, which often indulged in fancifully optimistic assessments of their communities.

These tendencies seem to be harbingers of modernization, and in fact the addition of new services and administrative capacity in local government is often an aim of the multi-county organizations. But local government remains one of the major employers, a haven for the old middle class, and in addition it commands overwhelming political power in most rural areas, political competition being relatively infrequent. It would seem that modernization will have to include these elements, since they are numerous relative to the new middle class, and since, even though neither middle class group seems to be closely linked to the poor, the old middle class is perhaps in a better position to form coalitions with them. This raises the ironic prospect of policies to support the old middle class to keep it in a position where it can interact and bargain with the technical and organizational forces on the one hand, and with the poor on the other. This is clearly a redistributive kind of policy, since if grants and aids were given to those most able to turn an economic multiplier, all would go to the technical middle class and the large organizations.

In addition to the new technical middle class and the traditional middle class interests, a third increasingly large but only potentially organized segment exists. These are the poor, whose numbers are large and whose proportion is apparently growing in many rural areas. If the new planning organizations have difficulty in linking themselves with the old middle class and entrenched power, possibly they could reach out to the poor. Such links seem to be exceptional rather than frequent, however. If there are gaps in organization and technique between corporate and planning professionals and local officials and boards, the gaps are even greater when they face the poor who, in rural areas, are notoriously lacking in organization.

Moreover, there are often similarities in ideology, at least, between technical and traditional middle class. The new multi-county organizations, though more technical than their local counterparts, are generally no more redistributive in their intent or programs. At best they operate on a crude "trickle down" premise, assuming that any growth at the top will adequately filter through the local economy. For example, an industry-supported foundation in a small upstate New York city is putting priority on new middle- and high-rent apartment housing for executives, despite the existence of higher vacancy rates in high-rent categories and greater shortages in the low-rent categories. Most multi-county economic development districts and regional planning agencies also seem to set priorities in this way. The development plan for one in West Virginia stressed coal as the key to revitalization of the area, despite the fact that employment would be primarily in high-skill occupations and the area boasts thousands of unemployed, uneducated miners. Many professional planners and developers have little idea what to do about such human resources problems; they continue to focus on technical economic requirements for increases in gross product.

Furthermore, it has been argued that even if the aims of the multi-county operations were redistributive, they would have a middle-class bias in practice because, generally, it is the middle class rather than the poor who have the resources or the time to operate at more than a local scale. People without cars, for example, or those who work at night when meetings are held, cannot sit as representatives in such organizations.[19] To counteract this, the federal Economic Development Administration and the Office of Economic Opportunity encourage or require representation of minorities or the poor on boards of directors of these bodies. But the success of such requirements is quite spotty.

[19] These points are made in a preliminary research report by Robert Warren, "Alternative Governmental Structures for Area Development," presented at the Economic Development Administration Research Conference, February, 1968, and in Robert Nathan Associates, Inc., *Findings of a Study to Identify Criteria for Determining the Appropriate Unit of Organization of Rural Community Action Agencies,* prepared for the Office of Economic Opportunity, Washington, D.C., September, 1967.

The Results of Inter-governmental Influence

These tendencies inhibiting agency linkages with the old middle class and with the poor are generally reinforced by the pattern of federal-state-local interaction. These external sources of funds sustain the agencies and at the same time direct their attention away from local interests. They operate in this way even when other federal or state policies explicitly require horizontal links with other segments of the community. The usual complaint against the higher level bureaucracies is that they pursue relatively narrow goals compared to the needs of the localities they serve, and that they demand that their resources serve only these goals, even when local circumstances vary. Particular programs have their own planning and representation requirements, meaning that extra time must be spent on planning activities that duplicate material and seem arbitrary to local directors, and two or more separate boards of directors must be mobilized. Commonly much of this is avoided by informal agreement with the agencies' field men, but time is still drained away from local concerns. Such a "market" of federal programs, each sold with its individual requirements to local authorities, could be justified if each locality had a choice which it was freely capable of exercising among a wide variety of programs. But such choices typically do not exist in small cities and rural towns. Agencies create their own demand, and once a community sinks its meager institutional capital into one program, it may be years before it is ready to embark on another.

These local failures of federal programs do not always result in a cutting of losses and retraction of federal influence. There seems to exist, in at least some cases, a tendency to encourage the continuation of programs proven inappropriate by low local response. This raises questions from the standpoint of the use of national resources, but it can also be harmful to the development of local response in the long run. Hopes are raised by a program, then a segment of the local community stays with it while others lose heart. As local energies wane, the outside agency takes on an ever-increasing role and once more local public and private entrepreneurship is displaced. These problems are made worse by the newness, number, and uncertain life-span of many programs. This has been a handicap for the initiation of the new multi-county agencies, and the response of local interests has been very slow to develop in many rural and small city localities. Passive support rather than active involvement has been the rule in many areas.

These localities may be overestimating their risks; on the other hand, the psychological costs of interaction with a national economy and federal system may be higher than most analysts suspect. Old-style entrepreneurship entailed the ability to combine local factors of production in order to produce and the ability to operate in a risky but rather simple market. Modern entrepreneurship requires the ability to deal with regional and national sources of capital and markets and suppliers and the ability to obtain and process not just economic but also political and bureaucratic information. The public sector may not be so much different from the private now in these respects; existing political personnel are equally lacking in ability to cope.

With federal and state agencies demanding particular responses and with localities slow to respond to *any* stimulus, the multi-county agencies are in a difficult middle-man role. On the one hand, their first concern is to build a local clientele. To do this they offer all the resources at their disposal: (1) special access to sources of outside funds, mainly for public works projects and service programs; and (2) the presumed benefits of cooperation and collective planning. Most rural towns are not at the stage where they are "ready" for the second kind of incentive, and as a result the distribution of "projects" is the most important sustaining activity for most multi-county agencies. This in itself can be an important modernizing factor, for it puts local governments in contact in a new way and it generates demands for adjustment mechanisms in which questions of prediction and priorities can be raised.

But federal influence on this process can cut down the maneuvering room for the multi-county agency. In the extreme case, competing programs bypass the multi-county agency to give direct access to localities in project application and review. There is motivation for this in that the bypassing cuts down the number of steps in the review process and at least gets "inputs" (if not outputs) to the localities faster, helping maintain the federal agency politically. Bypassing and support of the multi-county agency can even occur simultaneously by two different parts of the same federal agency. One result of this is to help isolate the multi-county agency—often the only locally responsive agency with the expertise to deal with the larger firms and federal and state agencies in the area—from its localistic old middle class clientele. Conversely, where multi-county agencies have been able to maintain the adherence of the old middle class elements dominant in local politics, they have done this by convincing localities that they can best serve as a representative vis-à-vis the large variety of programs potentially available.

A DEVELOPMENTAL APPROACH TO RURAL PLANNING

In the preceding argument, I have noted a number of obstacles to the easy spreading of planning technique and technical ability to the non-technical segments of rural society, despite the introduction of rather impressive expertise in multi-county agencies. In effect it has been an elaboration of the hypothesis stated at the outset: failure of government to act and plan for the preconditions of entrepreneurship will result in the inhibition of entrepreneurship in the long run. The major extension of the hypothesis has been in the introduction of an institutional factor. Without denying the value of new private sector activity, it is argued that new activity can be overwhelming. Thus, the appearance of large corporate activities tends to incur costs on the local social and political system—a training and technical skill imbalance, in effect—that must be rectified by government activity to supply an institutional and political infrastructure locally that will make pluralistic political interaction possible in rural areas. A corollary proposition is that a simple extension of federal or state presence in rural areas will, in the national course of things, simply duplicate and reinforce the overwhelming effort of private sector bureaucratization. Thus, the promotion of local pluralism is, by this argument, a difficult problem.

This essay has reviewed some of the obstacles to solving it. It is disturbing, in fact, to see the paucity of counter balancing policy options now available for overcoming them. Some suggestions, somewhat speculative, can be made, however.

Organizational Pluralism

Probably the aim of national policy should be the development of a degree of organizational equality within rural regions—at the scale of, say, labor markets. A natural distribution of organizations may be more like a normal curve with technical complexity on the vertical axis than like a pyramid or a case with gaps between the most complex and the next most complex organizations. For any large organization, there ought to be others with nearly equal complexity (and presumably ability) to compete politically. Economic development policy might be the first place to apply such a principle. Instead of promoting *any* new productive activity for an area, it should first be evaluated for its organizational complexity. Similar principles should be applied in the case of public agencies or other institutions. Of course, this is the roughest of criteria. It suggests research on the political development process and the formulation of indicators to measure institutional change in localities. Neither type of analysis is much in use now.

Real vs. Phoney Pluralism

I noted earlier that, even in places where great inequalities in organizational development exist, there may often be the appearance of pluralism in communities. Rancorous conflict on such issues as school bonds and fluoridation may be more frequent in towns dominated by the new middle class than in places where organizational strength is more evenly distributed. There also may be a good deal of conflict on some issues which involve little interaction with national political and organizational forces and hence for which little is at stake for the community in many cases.

Unfortunately, this may be a case of noise with little effect. The kind of pluralism that will help the rural area is interaction and bargaining at the greater than locality scale and that probably means activity through a well developed secondary organization in which local people have control. Grass-roots activity, in the usual sense, does not necessarily provide this. If a grass-roots movement is read as real political capacity by federal and state administrators, it will tend to inhibit them from differentiating among communities along the lines I have suggested. Ironically, the attribution of "equality" when only the surface manifestations of equality really exist is no favor to the weaker localities. It leads to an unintended lack of selectivity among communities in the allocation of program inputs. As a result, the impacts on local institutional development will tend to be random, at best.

Redistributive Administrative Ideologies

Despite the formal authority vested in existing governmental positions which are mainly occupied by the old middle class, the growth of organizational capacity in some sectors requires a redistributive program to maintain a balance. At present, the major force for such a policy exists in the beliefs of some federal and state agency personnel that participation by non-technical persons is essential for a federal-local partnership to work. It is believed that without local initiative at the "end-point" of administration, information and ideas will not flow upward or downward. These ideas have existed in such agencies as the Tennessee Valley Authority, parts of the Department of Agriculture and some newer agencies such as the Economic Development Administration and the Office of Economic Opportunity. These ideals are implemented not only in formal representation requirements but in the day-to-day interaction to which local organizations are subjected. Despite my concern with the effects of vertical local-state-federal linkages in turning local agencies away from their old middle class and low income clientele, I think this particular aspect of these linkages is valuable. My suggestions above concerning institutional indicators, in fact, are made with the hope that their use will reduce some of the undesirable effects of vertical interaction on local institutions and politics and will increase the sensitivity with which the interaction occurs.

Split-Level Casbah:
The Natives Are Restless

RICHARD HARMON

August 30, 1968, that last night: Humphrey's speech finished, the TV floormen's insect headsets removed, bland and obvious "commentary" wrapped up, the set flicked off—millions of Americans sat out a moment of roaring silence, trying to recover from a four-day TV siege of violence, frustration, and banality that in itself climaxed five months of blasting events which turned every living room into a special forces camp under continual mortar shelling. With one difference: the rounds came in over TV.

My own mind, reeling, reached back and out, collecting events, digging for patterns and relations which could give this siege some sense beyond the obvious, that the country had lost all humane direction and was careening out of control: the war's grotesqueness finally giving LBJ a severe beating in the polls; McCarthy's "children" stunning everyone as they swarmed New Hampshire; on March 31st, LBJ announcing he would not run; on April 4, the King assassination, and large blow-ups in most cities, goading Mayor Daley to issue the "shoot to kill" order; my wife and I and two friends running into a brief but nasty taste of National Guard power at a hidden night road block outside Durham; on April 24th, the Columbia student revolt paralyzing the University; two weeks later, French students fighting police from behind barricades in Paris; on June 4th, the Kennedy assassination, followed by yet another nationally-televised funeral procession; Spock, Coffin, Goodman, and Ferber expecting to get heavy sentences; the opulence of Miami Beach mocking the agony of Miami's ghetto; Humphrey and Johnson and Nixon masquerading back and forth on the war; on August 20th, Russian tanks treading into Prague (over TV: What would be next—watching World War Three from our living room?); the shaping up of a confrontation between Irish police power and Yippie hair power in Chicago's streets, against the backdrop of near-gleeful anticipation among Wallace operatives; and then the actual events of Chicago, a maelstrom whose fascination over TV was equaled only by the battering our physical senses took—images and sounds of those four days filled my dreams for weeks, might remain in the national subconscious for many months or longer.

Personal events seemed, over the next few days, to take on new meaning in this context.

In the late summer of 1957, having fled the cultural and physical chaos of Los Angeles three years before to go to college in upstate New York, I found myself hitching rides across the country back to southern California. In retrospect, it was clearly a trip for touching the bases of my earlier life—suburban Chicago, rural Nebraska, small-town Colorado, Los Angeles—to try to carve more clarity not just out of my own personal history, but equally important, out of the total American environment of the late fifties.

In Maywood, a working class suburb of Chicago, my parents had operated a small business during World War II out of an old frame building that leaned over the street corner where I learned to handle a ball and glove, memorized the names and years of all of Detroit's products, and, sitting on the stoop, passed countless hours floating in boyhood fantasies. Coming back with hopes of recalling and redigesting some of those memories, I found something else: the entire corner had been levelled for a used-car lot.

So I went further out on Chicago's outskirts, to Hillside, where the family had bought, in 1943, a large old German basemented home on an acre of land. The place became special after my mother brought home one night an extra-tough piece of veal, bartered from the meat market with ration stamps. My step-father blew up, and swore we would eat well during the remainder of the war. In an orgy of labor, he built sheds and fences for 250 chickens, fifty ducks, twenty-five turkeys and two lambs; later two Airedales were added. It was hard work, but a menagerie of never-ending fascination for a small boy. This place, too, was gone: the "zoo" was now the outside lane of the Congress Expressway, and the house's foundation was hidden in the weeds of the embankment.

A few days later, car after car passed by me in remote southeastern Nebraska, an area which had always been famous for its hospitality and warmth. I learned when, exhausted, I reached my uncle's farm, that two convicts had escaped a local prison three days before, and the state police had broadcast warnings against picking up riders. My uncle's house, a hundred years old and long-filled with the familiar odors of hard farm work, coal space heater, and aging wood, stood in growing isolation. Most of the surrounding farms were abandoned, grey-black and weedy, their families, after three generations of work, victims of exhausted land and remorseless economic force. My uncle and aunt, once tied into an elaborate social network, now spent their evenings watching TV; their friends and family were gone, there was nothing else to do.

Two weeks later, on the outskirts of Greeley, Colorado, the town where I was born, I was picked up by the police: hitching rides was against the law. They insisted I take the miserable bus ride into Salt Lake City.

Los Angeles remained chaotic—only more so. Government seemed impossible to locate. Certainly no one took clear responsibility in the kaleidoscope of conflicting municipal powers. So stucco shacks for the new affluents marched row on row up and down stripped and amputated hillsides, smog lay smothering everywhere, freeways ate up the land and drove up the pace, women turned more and more into mannequins, tanned but brittle shells. As the plane, heading back to New York, climbed over the neon valley, the millions of L.A. lights yielded no patterns—except, in my mind's eye, the elemental direction of a massive lava flow, glistening and fascinating, flaming at key intersections, rolling off the hills to spill into the ocean.

The nation has lost a sense of place, where return and refuge and re-creation of the relation between self and society can work their way.

Or, a year earlier, in the fall of 1956, a debate in the University chapel on Stevenson *versus* Eisenhower: My opponent was a well-dressed if not very bright classmate who had wangled his way into Nixon's entourage; his "duties" seemed to consist of flying around the country lining up college supporters at airports—or at least that was the way it struck me because he was full of confidence about the way America looked from the air; he said little else. As for me, I had worked up a good head of moral steam and drove through the Eisenhower record like an ironsides through a whistle stop, smashing home point after point on foreign policy, inflation, race. At some particularly vulnerable point (so it certainly seemed at the time), when I was thrusting my well-documented stiletto through my opponent's flabby defense—into the chapel strode the University President.

The President was tall, at ease with himself and his movements, a member of several top corporate and foundation boards, a close friend of Stevenson. He was known as a liberal eastern Democrat, and as a man who seldom attended student affairs. So I was, after momentary surprise, determined to speak my mind on what I thought was wrong with the country and why Eisenhower should be defeated. On I went; what it came down to was that the nation lacked purpose, that what we needed in the White House was a man who would mobilize the nation's dormant energies into new, human directions, evoking the people to construct the new society of equality, creative leisure, and citizen decision-making.

When I stopped, I turned to my opponent, who was due a rebuttal. He shook his head, went to the mike and said, "I have nothing to say to that." It was over. The small crowd applauded, and we stepped down. The President approached. We shook hands, and he took me slightly aside. He said: "It was good, but you were too hard on him, too hard on the rules."

Stunned, I looked at him and walked away. *Too hard on him! Too*

hard on the rules! We were debating *the country* and *the White House!*
At that point, although it became clear only three years later, mainstream liberal university education and politics fatally slipped; they held
no vividness, no risk, no challenge.

Much the same conclusion came out of twenty-eight months of sem-
inary study at the University of Chicago, where the obsolescence of the
institutional church and the powerlessness of the ordinary Chicagoan before his crumbling environment became overpowering facts of enraged
life.

*The nation has lost more than geographical and architectural sense
of place. We have lost institutional sense of place—politics, religion,
family, community.*

So when the opportunity emerged to organize a community, in the
spring of 1961, it was an opportunity to help build a new institution
where citizens could overcome their gnawing powerlessness, where refuge and re-creation of meanings and relations could happen, where, out
of that, citizens could re-create a sense of geographical and architectural
place.

The Chicago Convulsion evoked these meanings, and more: millions of Americans turned away from their TV sets with a sense of helpless outrage, a sense that there was nothing they could do about it all; a
sense of—Who *asked* us if we wanted a war in Viet Nam? Who asked us
if we wanted these particular candidates? Who asked us if we wanted
unsafe streets, filthy streams, dying lakes? Who asked us if we wanted
our youth marching in the streets, if we wanted the police to go beserk?
Who asked us if we wanted all those missiles, that little black box following the president anyway? Who asked us if we wanted conglomerate corporate behemoths? Who asked us if we wanted madhouse expressways,
dirty trains, clogged downtowns? Who asked us about any of this mess
we're in? We don't remember making *any* of those decisions.

Adding to the sense of no control over our lives was the effect of
TV, especially in that August, with both the Russian invasion of Czecho-
slovakia and the Chicago seizure exploding in our living rooms. TV has
flooded us with events and data from around the globe and beyond. It is
as if we are daily pounded with answers, thousands of them—yet we
have not asked their questions; the inundation of answers permits no
time, no place, no privacy for developing thoughtful questions. Beyond
that, TV, along with rocketry and computers, has flooded out the foundations of the old industrial society and swept in the still-undefined forms
of the electronic society; TV has collapsed the traditional refuges of time
and distance, shrinking the world to a "global village." Yet at the same
time the world, to the ordinary citizen, has become incomprehensibly

vast. The world has simultaneously shrunk to a village and expanded to limitless space. For the ordinary citizen, standing isolated and remote because he is cut off from meaningful mediating institutions, the world has become too crowded, too complex, too "big" to understand. For many of us, our sense of powerlessness rises out of more than just public issues—crime, blight, taxes, race, war—that are too unwieldly to be handled. Our sense of powerlessness flares up from the awareness that we stand *alone*, fragmented, isolated, before this torrent of data and events driving in on us at almost the very moment they happen. And we stand alone before this tidal wave of information because the institutions of the industrial society, institutions which once helped us to *interpret* events and information, no longer provide meaningful feelings or images or concepts. The standard religious interpretations of the industrial culture are wiped away for most of us. Science has become increasingly remote (though we know its political, economic, and military power as an institution), obscure, providing no common understanding of nature for most of us. We feel betrayed by the political "wisdom" offered to us, most acutely since 1964. So we are left with meager, if any, tools for understanding. We compensate for TV's collapse of outer space and distance by forcing up inner walls, to preserve some small area of inner space. (Okay, it is happening, we saw it on TV. But it's only a *TV program*.) The reaction: panic quietude ("castration without representation") exploding intermittently into police riots; or deep retreat into raw experience, of drugs, alcohol, perhaps sports.

And in our panic or retreat we evade or repress our adolescents' expressions of their enormous psychic energies, their life force. We run away from, or stomp down on—in family, school, community, political party—the profound spirit, the elemental energy flow of our young people at precisely the time in their lives when they seek to authenticate and legitimatize that life-spirit with identities they can discover only in relation to adults. Adults, psychically battered by the transformation into electronic culture and swept by floating powerlessness, fear the massive spontaneity of that energy moving in and through our young; so adult society does not lead the young through the all-important rites of passage which all young people require. In fact, American adult society *exploits* its young by removing them from meaningful work, locking them into educational uniformity, removing adult legal rights in "juvenile" courts, forcing them into the draft. And the adult work roles we offer them require, for the most part, *repression* of the life-energy that flows in them. Without an adult social reality they respect, in relation to which they can carve identities and roles that *utilize* that spirit, they turn, floundering and in rage, to each other: they will seek their *own* risk and vividness, their *own* social reality, their authentic and legitimate roles in *isolation* from adults. Repressed or evaded by adults and adult institutions, the young flow with rage, and swear to destroy those institutions.

Underlying the shrieking agonies of 1970 America—underlying race, poverty, youth, purposeless politics, pointless war, pollution of air, water, and food, blight, dirt, overcrowding and sprawl—is powerlessness. Without power in millions of new hands, the electronic culture will never yield its profound possibilities for purpose, spirit, and creativity. Without major redistributions of power in America, the electronic culture will flame out into cinder.

*   *   *

"What can we *do?*"

That cry rose from many middle class American whites in the spring and summer of 1968, following the bombardment of the Kerner Report, the King and Kennedy murders, and April's black uprisings. Out of that cry of conscience, anguish, and fear flowed volunteer tutoring forays into the ghetto, committees on "white racism" in the white community, and renewed efforts to bus black children into lily-white suburbia. Most have failed to hit the mark. Why?

Inside the black community a major reawakening of consciousness has produced the ideology and strategy of black power and black pride, directed primarily (where it is real and not rhetoric) into the black community, not outside to whites. This turning inward to strengthen the black community, to develop its institutions and black control over those institutions is as natural as breathing and growing. For blacks, in demanding community control and self-determination, are simply following the *actual* pattern of social movement of America's white ethnic groups (as opposed to our civics book fiction). None of those groups were *integrated* as a group into the wider society. The Irish first had to take control of police forces and the political machines before they were "accepted" by the English, Scottish, and German-American establishments and could become desegregated, or open the doors to wider American opportunities.[1]

Furthermore, many of the whites who have been so insistent upon

---

[1] For the Irish, this is called the shift from shanty to lace curtain. Italians were forced by the Anglo-Saxons and the Irish into politics, organized crime, and food processing and food producing; once the Italians took control of these institutions in their own neighborhoods, they were able to move out into the suburbs. Jews moved into politics, retailing, and smaller financing, and took power in these fields before they were able to move out of their American ghettos. Both these groups and some German elements have used primary and secondary education, especially since World War II, to climb up and out of the "old neighborhood." The Poles, further "behind," are just now using politics, union posts, and lower level management jobs to move out in large numbers, often to suburban enclaves, such as Cheektowaga, outside Buffalo.

integration, as opposed to desegregation, are actually assuming that "white is right" and "the way to solve the race problem is to make the blacks like us, so there will be no differences." Only people who are frightened, who can in fact make a quick transition to fascism, insist that "everyone is really the same." Why be frightened of a multi-cultural society where there are genuine cultural differences, accepted as real and healthy by all sides? What is basic human equality without physical and cultural variety?

The "white is right" assumption has totally collapsed within the black community because of the failure of the Anglo-Saxon value system to work for the great mass of blacks. Not only has the economy failed the blacks, but the Anglo-Saxon values of "individual effort" and "melting pot" have in fact mocked the black struggle in America for three centuries.

Finally, the civil rights-integration strategy used by whites failed to address the root grievances of the masses of poverty blacks. That strategy was really addressed primarily to middle class and upwardly mobile blacks, who either had made it or were well on their way. Black power, in contrast, is addressed, at its best, to the broad base of the young and the most poor, and really says, "none of us makes it until we all make it."

The other set of reasons for the failure of the "What can we do?" drive has to do with the nature of political reality in *white* America. From the sit-ins of 1960 to the urban uprisings of 1967, those who believed in civil rights, both black and white, assumed that bringing injustice to the attention of white Americans would arouse their conscience, and would produce the rapid, basic change that the country required. That assumption has been blasted into America's domestic Hiroshima: America has very little conscience, as the collapse of the traditional civil rights movement so eloquently testifies. Most unions, either trade or industrial, are rigid guardians of the racial and economic status quo. The churches, while active at the upper staff levels, seem to have stalled badly of late, as the depth of the situation produces vast irritation and frustration.[2] Until the ghettos exploded, in 1966 and 1967, business did next to nothing. Suburban groups which have sprung up around the country to desegregate suburban schools for the most part have been clobbered into oblivion by their own neighbors.[3] Recent experience shows that when

---

[2] A recent United Church of Christ survey of 24,000 Protestants in the Middle West showed that they ranked the churches' commitment to racial justice *last* in "important" church program areas; only 7½ percent ranked this area as most important.

[3] Exceptions exist, as in suburban Boston and Hartford, but Boston's small success is due, finally, to a remarkable State Education Department headquartered in Boston; and Hartford's program is so small as to barely touch the large black student population.

suburban groups surface publicly on school bussing or transfer programs, all hell breaks loose, in what appears to be overwhelming opposition, forcing those groups to retrench, rethink strategy, go nearly underground—or go out of existence.

Many of these suburban groups discovered a central fact about American political life when they tried to talk with their neighbors about the Kerner Report and "white racism." Most members of the broad middle class—or, for that matter, blue collar workers—simply won't look at "white racism." Why not?

At one level, this response touches on the kind of rationalizing we all have to do in order to survive. Just as the black community has been forced to develop a set of psychological responses in order to live in a brutal society, so have whites—in order to endure a floating sense of meaninglessness, the pressure of economic and social competition, the seldom-admitted sense of being regarded not as persons but as consumers. I contend that, if we took a hard look at the *actual* history of this country, at what it has *actually* done to blacks, to Indians, to blue collar workers, to white consumers, most of us would go out of our minds; we couldn't stand it.

For the fact is that America's great economic success rests on immense injustice, from our founding to this day. The great colonial commercial companies of the seventeenth and eighteenth centuries took two tragically intertwined and contradictory directions. On one hand, they laid the base for our democratic institutions and habits, by selling stock to an increasing bloc of settlers and giving stockholders the vote; this practice of power spread into the Colonial assemblies and on into the early congresses, giving the founding fathers their actual experience in self-determination.

In complete contradiction, the economic base of those early commercial companies rested on seizing land from the Indians and slave labor from blacks. And each subsequent expansion of economic and political opportunity has contained the same contradictory seeds. As a nation, we have always had an escape hatch—the frontier, the industrial explosion, the arms race, and now the space race—to draw us in fascination away from grappling with our central contradictions.[4]

---

[4] Jackson extended political and economic benefits to the towns and to the settlers west of the Alleghenies, but he also extended slavery and shoved the Indians across the Mississippi. The Civil War laid the basis for a national, political and industrial infra-structure, but also resulted in the final drive against the Western Indians and a willingness to sacrifice black citizen rights, in the Compromise of 1876, as less important than bringing the Southern Bourbons back into the Democratic Party and into the frantic industrial development following the war. The New Deal may have addressed the economic and political grievances of the white union movement, segments of industry, and Southern agriculture, but it certainly did little of real substance for blacks or unorganized poor whites,

One of the major reasons for our inability to face these tragic contradictions at the deepest center of our national life lies in the role of the schools, colleges, and universities. The values and perspectives of our educational institutions have been controlled, consciously and unconsciously, by those in economic and political power. Time and again, teachers or writers or artists who try to raise basic questions with our youth about these national contradictions have been hounded into isolation, unemployment, and exile. The power elite of the nation, whose power has rested upon stolen Indian land, or slave labor, or brutal working conditions, or weapons contracts, or manipulating consumer "needs," have everything to lose from a rigorous widespread analysis of the basis of their power. The deepest cultural, political, and economic assumptions of those power elites have been disseminated through the schools, colleges, and universities, which have *not* generally encouraged root analyses of our great issues. Teachers' colleges have trained hundreds of thousands *not* to question operating national assumptions and structures, *not* to encourage controversy. Textbooks at all levels are bland and superficial (in the guise of being "balanced"). Administrators and teachers, whose status depends on riding along with current assumptions, generally have *not* raised basic questions with their institutions or students.[5] The result amounts to brainwashing, especially in the social sciences. So most of us wind up deeply ignorant of the social, political, and economic reality of American life. We may be well trained to become blue collar workers in the factories, or new class white collar workers in management, law, education, or health. But we have been very badly trained to think critically about our real roles as workers and consumers—blue *or*

---

except to offer unrealistic hope; in fact, through the development of the farm subsidy program for cotton plantations, the Roosevelt-Truman era actually drove millions of white and black poor to the cities, laying the groundwork for our current urban crisis. And the current tide of prosperity, beginning in 1941, has rested fundamentally on spending for armaments and mass media seduction of consumer "needs"; in fact, over-reaction to the Cold War, Viet Nam, and now the space race has drained billions away from use for critical domestic requirements, especially to enable 20 percent of the nation to rise out of poverty and become productive citizens.

[5] I do not buy the overly rigid conspiracy analysis of "the establishment" now current in SDS. The elite of the nation vary enormously in intention, capability, and consciousness. A fair amount of what I ascribe to the elite flows from their deeply subconscious myths and from their political incompetence. Much of "the system" is not so much deliberately unjust as lethargic; its real immorality lies as much in its half-conscious decisions *not* to act, and in its lack of political skill, as in its deliberate exploitation. This is especially true of large organizations. This qualification however, does *not* mean you don't move against decision-makers in order to redistribute power; in fact it makes realistic victories much more likely because it removes ideological blinders and permits specific analyses of *actual* power patterns, not patterns we wish-dream into existence.

white collar—or to think through to the roots of our economic and political system so that we can carve out full meaningful lives for ourselves. Out of this half-consciousness, millions of white Americans, blue and white collar, share a tremendous sense of alienation, rootlessness, and powerlessness. This has been accentuated by the new electronic culture provided by TV, computers, missiles, pop music, and drugs, especially as adult and youth square off in the "generation gap."

Politically, this sense of alienation and powerlessness (shared with blacks) came out clearly in the 1968 Presidential campaign:

from a Wallace supporter in Oklahoma: "They have never paid any attention to *us,* but they will if enough of us vote for him."

from a McCarthy worker in Indianapolis: "The McCarthy campaign is just a way to give politics back to people."

from Senator Robert F. Kennedy in countless campaign speeches: "The individual *can* make a difference in moving the country."

from black leaders in Brooklyn: "The white-run control system for the schools has failed to educate our children, so blacks must control our own schools, to change the system."

Three highly different constituencies—Wallace supporters, young white Democrats, and Black Power spokesmen—agree on one fundamental requirement: American political and governmental institutions must be decentralized. (Many Republicans also agree, except that they often mean that power should be restored to local banking and industrial elites.)

While there are major differences in what these constituencies want from political decentralization—whether it is called "government by the little people," or "participatory democracy," or "community control"— the shared alienation from the big institutions of government, business, and labor may be one of the few remaining bridges, if not the only bridge, across the continually widening ethnic, political, and generational chasms of the nation.

Where do we go from here? The strategy of "conscience" has failed. White groups trying to talk about "racism" to their neighbors have lost effectiveness. Blacks, Puerto Ricans, Mexican-Americans, and poor whites have lost most of any "trust" they had left for white "liberals" because when the going got rough, middle class whites could—and did— walk away from struggles whenever their mood changed. So the blacks, Puerto Ricans, Mexican-Americans, and poor whites have declared, with rising militancy, "Go do your own thing in the white middle class community. Don't exorcise your guilt on us." Finally, the strategy of "conscience" simply turns off threatened blue collar whites who see blacks as their prime enemy.

If we are concerned to make a social change toward an open society, yet agree that for all practical purposes America has no "conscience," then we must take a hard look at just what *will* move white America—the America tangled in cultural and political crisis, with major constituencies agreed on little except the necessity for institutional decentralization.

* * *

The great source of untapped power in America lies in what we can call the new class—the nearly 30 million families that have an income of $7,000 or more, the two-thirds of the nation that is white and not poor. This population includes segments of the blue collar work force, especially foremen, auto and steel workers with seniority, and big-city construction workers. (Recent construction contracts call for $9 an hour, or $13,000 for a nine-month work season.) It includes most of the 35 million white collar professionals, managers, clerks, and salesmen, and sections of the 9 million service workers. It includes most of the 67 million suburbanites. Educationally, most of the new class has graduated from high school; it certainly embraces the 11 million college graduates, who were 28 percent of the 1968 electorate, and will be 35 percent of the 1972 electorate, over 40 percent by 1976.

The people of this new class will be the carriers and molders—indeed many already are—of the electronic culture because they have enough money to buy into the new experience of that culture. Their money, leisure, mobility, information, and education are bringing them face to face with the immense possibilities and terrors of that new culture, moving them at almost blinding speed out of the industrial culture.

What is the self-interest of the new class? What are the issues to this constituency?

Some reply that there *are* no issues which affect this group. Some maintain, for example, that only the poor and the blacks are caught in the middle of urban crisis, and that the job of the white middle class is to develop programs which meet the needs of the poor and the blacks—of *others*.

I believe it is incontestible that the new class is highly victimized and is in fact itself "caught in the middle of the urban crisis." This new class shows countless signs of alienation from its work, from its institutions, from its culture, from its youth; it is, in fact, searching for new forms of community and creativity.

The problem, as I see it, is to organize around issues which do not require new class members to commit psychological suicide, issues which make sense, issues which can tap the enormous reserve of creativity and energy present in the white, middle class communities. It is more than clear, by now, that "meeting the needs" of *others,* either blacks or poor whites, is not such an issue. Men simply do not organize mass, permanent organizations to "help" *others,* even in the crisis created by urban warfare, not in the real world, where organizing must begin.

First, let's be frank about why many whites have gotten "concerned" about race in America; the ghetto explosions of the last few years scared hell out of a lot of people. Just plain fear of urban warfare is a major moving force for many white activists worried about the ghettos. Fear—of personal, bodily harm, of complete disruption of the social fabric—is a natural element in white self-interest.

But beyond that, on the positive side, self-interest for the new class should be seen in a broad sense—in the fundamental relation between persons and their environment. We live in a befouled, inhuman environment—as one scientist recently put it: "We stand knee deep in rubbish shooting ourselves to the moon." I mean environment in the broadest sense—political, economic, esthetic, physical. And I mean the person's relation to this environment in each of the fundamental modes—political, economic, esthetic, physical.

Self-interest to the new class, then, is not just bread and butter. Self-interest for the new class must be seen much more broadly, extending into the areas of values, creativity, significance, meaning, and must tap a self-image that is much larger than just economic man. That is the major implication rising out of the transition from industrial to electronic culture.

Specifically:

1. in the primary and secondary schools of the new class communities, education has turned into programming. Our schools attempt to make robots of our children, training them, unthinking, for roles as uncritical consumers of gadgets, passive consentors to public bureaucracies, and dutiful drones, repressing spontaneity, in the mass organizations of industry, education, health, and war. As a suburban mother recently said to me, "Our schools train my children to compete, not think. That robs them of all human feeling." A major function of the schools seems to be to kill human spirit and creativity. The best sign that this system is failing badly is in the burgeoning numbers of underground high school newspapers, in the use of drugs, in the revolts against school dress codes, and in the demands by high school students for basic curriculum revision. The *best* students are rejecting the schools—and the adult values which underlie them

2. higher education has taken the same fundamental direction. In biology, chemistry, and physics, the academics in large measure have provided "services" for the arms industry, the Defense Department and civilian junkware companies. Economists and business school professors

have made great contributions to motivational research which loads the nation with gadgetry through media manipulation. Much of what passes for "scholarship" in literature and the social sciences is really aimed not at raising life questions but at training apprentices for the academic guilds. This "scholarship" is irrelevant to the national political and cultural crisis, and amounts to the same kind of blindfolded "scholarly work" pursued by the pre-Nazi academics of the Weimar Republic, oblivious to the nation's agony. In the academies, as in primary and secondary education, the question is: *"Education for what?"* In the current wave of student unrest, the issue is not academic freedom, but guild monopoly. And the reason, fundamentally, why students reject the faculty claim to a monopoly on which questions should be asked and which answers given goes deeper than just the depersonalization of large campuses; it lies not only in the attempt of universities to maintain the remote yet all-pervasive regulatory atmosphere of elementary and secondary schools, which rests on the repression of adolescent life-force. At bottom, student unrest rises out of rage over the alternating evasion and repression of that life-force, by a generation of academics and administrators which has *not* proven its moral strength; for the professors and administrators have *not* forced the universities to challenge the domestic and overseas brutalities of the nation. Why should students respect the "professionalism" of people who, in the name of intellectual "disinterestedness" and "objectivity," have "educated" the economic, political, and military leadership that has brought the nation to its present agony? And why should students accept the life-view of academic leaders who are emotionally incapable of escorting the youth through its desperately-sought rites of passage?

3. the best of new class youth is revolting against many of the contradictions between professed beliefs and actual performances in the nation—on the war, on race, on the deadly lock-step of secondary and higher education, on marijuana vs. alcohol, on the lack of adult influence on the public environment across the board. The "generation gap" is an important issue for new class organizations to meet and deal with because countless new class adults just don't see opportunities for moving closer to their own adolescents and young adults. One recent example of how this could happen lies with the San Francisco mother who told her son's draft board that she had advised her son not to report for induction. She was as much against the draft as he was, and since he was still her ward, if they wanted to jail anyone, they should jail her. She lost, partly because she did not organize a large force of parents caught in the same situation. Fifty to one hundred new class parents moving against a local draft board could set off long-delayed changes in the draft laws,

and could go a long way toward restoring the "generation gap" with their own sons. Strong multi-issue organizations could amass the power and intelligence to address some of the hypocrisies which enrage the young

Another example where the battle over an issue bridging the "generation gap" is developing is in states where the legislatures are cutting back higher education budgets and raising tuitions. In Indiana and Wisconsin, students are going into their home communities to organize adults to pressure legislators, on an issue that cuts deeply into the pocket books of both adults and students. To win on this issue, the students need not only their own parents, but also blue collar parents whose youth will be kept out of college by high tuition and cut-back facilities. In addition, this issue raises basic questions about how tax dollars are used— what *are* national and state budget priorities? The same crunch is coming now in our big-city public high schools, following the closing of many Catholic schools, with the same opportunity for joint parent-student political education and action

4. the women's liberation movement is tapping into a significant new class source of energy, especially among single and young married women.[6] The issue is more than unequal wage and salary levels, more than rank job discrimination in most firms and universities. The movement for women's liberation really rises out of the confused picture of womanhood abroad in the transitional culture, and out of the collision between an educational system which asks women to compete, and a social system which asks women to remain tied to children and home isolated from the city centers of creative employment and self-expression. New class organizations can tap the great creativity and energy of concerned, educated women who want to change their own role and give their life public significance. Beyond that, new class organizations can develop new legitimacy for first-rate day care centers, upgrading child-care as a full-time occupation, which will have enormous impact on public education and will free large numbers of women for different work and political roles. And work on this issue will surely raise in many minds the dilemma of suburban flight, which isolates women from central city career opportunities. Women who take their potential seriously may demand that their families move back into the city

5. federal tax policy, with its loopholes for oil companies, real estate investors, bond holders, and large stock holders, has become a public scandal in the past year.[7] The American ability to collect taxes rests

[6] For statistics, see the U.S. Labor Department's *Handbook on Women Workers.* On the psychological and sociological issues involved, see *Daedalus,* "The Woman In America" (Spring, 1964), especially Alice S. Rossi, "Equality Between The Sexes: An Immodest Proposal" and David McClelland, "Wanted: A New Self-Image for Women."

[7] Between 1961 and 1965, municipalities in this country floated $400 million in

on the citizen believing the tax structure is fair. The present structure is patently *not* fair. In fact, the tax policies of the nation are further concentrating wealth in fewer hands, so that while the *level* of wealth is higher for more people, their *share* of the national wealth is smaller now than at any time in the nation's history. Here is a fine opportunity for strong coalitions between new class organizations and groups from the lower middle and upper lower classes, coalitions resting on fundamental economic self-interest; and the interaction between these organizations can raise the basic budgetary questions about the nation: how *are* we spending the tax dollar, and why? Which opens a hornet's nest of questions about the Pentagon, the big-farm lobby, the highway lobby and many other special interest groups drinking at the public fountain

6. local tax policy usually benefits large industry, which turns around to pollute the community's air and water. But the most disastrous implication of local tax policy is in its encouragement of slums and blight by penalizing rehabilitation and new construction.[8] Several European

---

federally-exempt industrial development bonds. Banks have gotten interest rates on these bonds as high as 6 percent, compared to non-exempt bond rates of about 3½ percent. Industries, under this scheme, get what amounts to free plants, for they don't have to invest in construction; they simply *lease* plants (built to their specifications) from municipalities, which enables them to escape most property taxes. The only other expense is the cost of buying out local politicians so local governments will vote for the bond issue. Stanley Surrey, Assistant Secretary of the Treasury, told these two stories to Urban America, an organization in Washington, D.C., on October 28, 1968: One group of thirteen real estate developers reported capital gains of $1 million on new construction. They used the depreciation allowances so effectively that nine of the thirteen reduced their federal taxes to zero, and two others to less than $25. Another developer with a total income of $7½ million was able to reduce his tax rate to 11 percent, which is the same rate paid by a married wage earner with two children and an income of $10,000. How? Accelerated depreciation claims. Surrey estimated that this real estate tax shelter costs the Treasury $750 million a year, $250 million from residential real estate alone. Former Treasury Secretary Joseph Barr estimated that $50 billion a year is lost in tax loopholes, almost completely for the benefit of the rich.
[8] Major repairs very seldom add to the level of rents a landlord can charge, nor do they bring an actual higher value to the property. An assessor's decision that major repairs require an increased value, and hence an increased assessment, is actually for the most part arbitrary and unreal. In addition, many local property taxes are based on the cost of construction of a building. Therefore, an apartment house built in the 1920's is taxed at a much lower rate than a comparable new building, although the owner of the older building may receive nearly the same amount in rents. The fair way to tax office and apartments would be to base the tax on the structure's gross income. New York State farmers have just received what amounts to a single property tax on land, for the 1968 session of the legislature exempted for five years any new or rehabilitated farm buildings on which work starts between January 1, 1969 and January 1, 1979. That is, farmers will *not* have to pay taxes on improvements for that period, provided the improvements are new construction of sizeable rehabilitation. This is exactly the policy which should be adopted in the cities.

countries have removed *all* taxes on buildings and improvements, taxing only the land. The result: continually self-renewing cities, and no slums.

Federal tax policy reinforces this local incentive for slums, because "accelerated depreciation" encourages a slumlord to sell in a hurry; and IRS regulations call many major repairs capital improvement rather than maintenance, which means that deductions can be taken only over several years—hence, major repairs don't get made.[9]

The local-federal tax tangle does more than discourage rebuilding the cities. More ironically, it flies in the face of the elaborate array of federal and state housing and development programs. Citizen experience with urban renewal or FHA programs is embittering, before the incredible delays imposed by the staggering pile of paper work and red tape that grinds along between local, state, and federal bureaucrats. If we had designed a system geared *not* to rebuild our cities, we could not have done a better job. How much more easily the cities could be rebuilt, and slums eliminated, if the natural flow of dollars was directed, through a sane, equitable tax policy, toward continual rebuilding and rehabilitation. As it stands, the flow of dollars is blocked from effecting an essential social and physical change, and is directed, instead, to non-essential areas whose lobbies make it increasingly difficult to reorder our public priorities. This constipation has gone on long enough to spread poison and paralysis throughout the urban system.

Add to this the huge amount of church, government, and railroad property which contributes nothing to the tax rolls, yet requires municipal services, and a picture emerges of a tax policy geared to benefit only special lobbies, geared to victimize new class whites, blue collar whites, and blacks

7. federal contracting and subsidy policies benefit the economic and political giants, at the expense of unorganized constituencies.

Most prominent in the public mind currently is the defense industry, whose largesse, along with the Pentagon's internal spending, now consumes $80 billion a year, 60 percent of the national budget. Of course the basic question is, what does "security" mean when we appear at the brink of a domestic civil war brought on by long-standing

[9] One reason this tax shelter is used so widely is because local tax policy discourages rehabilitation and new construction. There are a number of remedies under discussion in Treasury:

   a. Consider any major maintenance item, up to a certain percentage of a building's total cost, as maintenance rather than capital improvements, so it can be fully deducted from taxes the year it is done.

   b. Disallow a portion of the currently allowable depreciation deductions unless they are matched, dollar for dollar, in repairs and maintenance.

   c. Disallow special accelerated depreciation on buildings, and require full recapture of deductions claimed when an owner claims depreciation that more than reflects the actual loss of value of a building.

neglect of crying domestic needs? What does it mean when 3.5 million persons are on the Pentagon payroll, and the Pentagon has $80 billion a year at its disposal? What does it mean when many congressmen are dependent upon defense contractors and unions for political support? It means that the nation attempts to solve critical political and social problems, both domestically and abroad, with military force—a course which fails disastrously, as in Latin America and Viet Nam, and which tears the nation away from its founding political and historical purpose.

Aside from the fundamental policy question, virtually all major defense contracts do not require competitive bidding, and permit profits to be "renegotiated"—in most cases upward, to the company's benefit.[10] Waste is incredible, payoffs to politicians and bureaucrats enormously lucrative.

FHA, which has benefitted not the poor so much as white middle class homeowners, has removed all the risk to banks and mortgage houses by insuring much of America's new housing. This policy, in effect, has channeled money away from central city housing and commercial rebuilding, at the same time paying for suburban sprawl.

Huge subsidies to the cotton-growing giants have taken great quantities of land out of production.[11] "Vertical" farming has increased sharply, with rapid mechanization. Add to this the ability of rural interests to escape paying farm workers minimum wages, and their successful pressure on state legislatures to avoid decent welfare allotments.[12] All of these forces, combined, have driven millions of poverty blacks and whites off the farms, into the cities.

This farm subsidy issue is as good a place as any to lift up the incredible, contradictory set of federal, state, and local policies which have produced the current urban disaster. Federal rural policy has driven millions of unskilled workers into the cities at precisely the time when unskilled workers are no longer needed in the cities.

In the urban areas themselves, federal policy for the most part either has hurt the incoming poor, or has done nothing to alter local self-destructive policies. For example, FHA has financed the flight of whites to the suburbs, where low population densities drive up costs of municipal services and force the construction of expressways instead of rapid

---

[10] See Sanford Watzman, "The Tax-Court Peephole," in *The Nation* (January 27, 1969), for a summary of renegotiation procedures and defense profits.
[11] The average federal subsidy for each of the 322 largest cotton farmers is $113,000. Senator Eastland received $157,930 for not planting crops in 1967—$437 a day. In 1967, 9,952 farmers received $408 million.
[12] In Mississippi, a mother must feed herself and twelve children on thirty-three cents a day. In 1968, $9,774,260,000 was spent by government for welfare grants to the poor. Contrast this with Barr's estimate (see note 7) that the wealthy of America are getting $50,000,000,000 in welfare grants, in the form of tax loopholes.

transit. In turn, the FHA-financed white flight has stripped the cities of crucial tax resources and leadership. FHA also, from 1935 to 1950, refused to insure mortgages in racially mixed neighborhoods;[13] the effect of this FHA policy, obviously, was to cater to (even create) block-busting during the period of heaviest migration of poverty blacks, contributing fatally to the cities' rigid ghettoization. Federally-financed urban renewal programs have displaced far more poverty blacks than they have housed, spreading slums, creating white hysteria and black bitterness. Federally-financed public housing has been jammed into poverty ghettos, a policy which increases the spiral of rising municipal costs in these areas, while their tax base continues to deteriorate.

No federal redevelopment program has been made conditional on reform of local tax laws, which fatally curtail rehabilitation and rebuilding. Nor are federal welfare payments conditional, most critically in the South, on meeting a decent national standard—which drives poverty populations into states such as New York, where higher allotments are paid. Nor have the billions of federal subsidy dollars going into suburbia —for schools, FHA insurance, sewers, expressways, etc.—been conditional upon opening the suburbs to scattered low-cost housing.

Even if, for the sake of the argument, you ignore the incalculable damage to poverty groups wrought by these federal, state, and local policy contradictions; even if you ignore the entire matter of race—and look just at the straight economic implications of these policies, what emerges is this: the federal government has paid Southern plantation magnates and Bourbon state governments to drive impoverished farm workers to the Northern cities, where the same federal government has paid middle class whites to flee outward, stripping city governments of essential tax revenues. Meanwhile, the federal, city, and suburban governments have jammed the unskilled into continually deteriorating enclaves, driving up municipal service costs and driving down tax revenues. A drunken Bolshevik couldn't have designed a more expensive and wasteful policy.

Not to mention, for example, that this economic mess creates the conditions first for do-nothing politics, then repressive politics as frustrations grow on all sides. Nor to mention that the federal tax dollar collected from city dwellers goes first for weapons, second for farm subsidies, third for suburban subsidies, last for city programs: so that the city dweller permits the federal government to use his tax dollar to destroy his environment.

[13] FHA went so far in its manuals as to draw up sample restrictive covenants, advising that white children in desegregating neighborhoods go elsewhere to school and urging that zoning be used as an instrument of racial exclusion. How did this happen? The National Association of Real Estate Boards placed several hundred of its members in key FHA posts shortly after FHA was created. Profits to the real estate industry, from block-busting and suburban "sprawlments," have been mammoth.

These ruinous policies—misplaced subsidies, discriminatory taxes, destructive housing programs—have created a grotesquely irrational urban situation, the result of well-organized lobbies fighting to line their pocket: farm blocs, black-hating politicos from both North and South, highway contractors, auto and petroleum associations, banking associations, real estate groups. Their untold benefits have been gained at the expense of the cities, specifically at the expense of the unorganized constituencies—blue and white collar whites, and blacks. But most of these lobbies have local tentacles, and are subject, at least indirectly, to one of several types of counterpressure: grass roots political campaigns, stock proxy fights, depositor or consumer withdrawal campaigns[14]

8. air, water, and land pollution are nearly out of control: Americans dump 142 million tons of smoke and noxious fumes into the biosphere every year. In Chicago, 40 percent of the sunlight is cut off, most of the year, by pollutants. We annually junk 7 million autos, 20 million tons of paper, 48 billion cans and 26 billion bottles and jars. The American mining industry throws away more than 3 billion tons of waste rock and mill tailings every year. And we pour into our rivers and lakes some 50 trillion gallons of hot water and unknown millions of tons of organic and chemical pollutants from our cities, farms, and industrial plants. Cleaning up Lake Erie will cost, at the least, $1–3 billion; Lake Ontario $300 million. Polluted air causes $11 billion a year in *property* damage alone—spoiled paint, eroded metal, crumbling masonry. The cost in public health cannot even be estimated. The effects on basic weather and wildlife changes will be great. Already the millions of tons of kerosene dumped by jets across midcontinent has sharply changed cloud patterns.

New class organizations, aware of the inter-related effects of pollutants on our ecology, can move hard against public and private violators,

---

[14] Citizen education on all of these issues, and especially advocate planning of counter-proposals, has been carried out very successfully in a number of communities. For example, The Woodlawn Organization hired a planner to demolish the city's urban renewal plans in the fight with the University of Chicago, and later, with that battle settled to T.W.O.'s satisfaction, the urban studies department of the university helped translate T.W.O.'s Model Cities Program, developed in dozens of community hearings, into technical jargon. In Rochester, FIGHT retained a fine architect, Robert Macon, who listened for months to FIGHT member groups express what they wanted for FIGHT Square, and Xerox worked for nearly a year with FIGHT in training a technical and management team to run FIGHT's new wholly-owned factory, turning out transformers and metal stampings. Metro-Act, the white new class organization in Rochester, is developing counter-proposals for low and moderate cost housing on city-owned land. BUILD in Buffalo brought in health planners when Erie County decided to move the county hospital away from the ghetto out to the suburbs; that technical knowledge enabled BUILD's members, massing against the county, to stop the hospital move. This kind of mass citizen counter-proposal—the finest kind of genuine citizen education—can be developed in all areas of public and private redevelopment, health, taxes, pollution, education, etc. It offers one of the most exciting opportunities around for professional planners who want to see their efforts come to fruition.

through economic boycotts, stock proxy battles, pressure on the media, and election fights. The law can be used in many situations: the Federal River and Harbor Act of 1888 and the Federal Refuse Act of 1899 provide for fines from $125 to $2,500 for convictions on specific violations; half of any fines collected for these convictions go to the person who reports the violation, which amounts to respectable bounty hunting! The law also declares that the U.S. Attorney has responsibility for prosecution, and if he doesn't act, he can be sued

9. in the health field, millions of federal and state dollars are given to the states for projects over which citizen organizations have little or no control.[15] One result is that many "research grants," for example, benefit a group of health bureaucrats but may not touch basic public health needs. Medical costs are soaring out of sight. The medical profession ignored warnings over the past twenty years to develop a different sort of financing plan for medical education in order to expand the number of doctors; now we face a critical shortage of medical personnel. Hospital planning has been notoriously short-sighted, permitting the administrators and trustees to build parochial little empires, without maximum dollar benefit to the public.

The American Medical Association and its local organizations have not thrown their enormous power against the root causes of bad public environmental health services for a simple reason: the economic self-interest of organized medicine has been to cure people already ill, not to prevent mass illness. The former course makes more money immediately for many individual doctors, who find themselves, often unconsciously, caught up in a system that makes them wealthy, so they don't try to analyze the roots of the system. That is why the AMA doesn't lend itself to eliminate slums (which breed rats, TB, and high infant mortality) or industrial pollution.

Furthermore, new class whites pay through the nose for medical care because they accept the premise of paying the doctor every time they visit him. The alternative to this is not necessarily government-run health plans. Mass-based organizations can fairly easily organize private prepaid group plans large enough to guarantee doctors excellent salaries[16]

10. the highway lobby is just beginning to run into opposition from citizen groups questioning the mainlining of cities—the physical disruption of communities—for the sake of materials companies, con-

---

[15] Federal law now requires every region to establish a Comprehensive Health Planning Council, which must include both health service dispensers and health service consumers. In both Buffalo and Rochester, citizen organizations are fighting for representation against opposition from entrenched medical bureaucrats and lobbyists who have had this preserve to themselves for years.

[16] The Kaiser Foundation plan in California starts its doctors at $18,000; pay goes up to $50,000.

tractors, oil companies, and Detroit. It is clear that countervailing forces can be developed to change basic transportation policy. The new forms of mass transit must be utilized if cities are to have any sense of place about them at all, for the glut of cars—their noise, their pollution, their supporting facilities—disintegrates cities, and encourages suburban sprawl in unplanned directions. New class organizations will have to carry out rigorous research on the power figures who, in both public and private arenas, make transportation decisions. For example, in New York State, many major bankers sit on the transportation authorities; these authorities are autonomous state corporations which even the state legislature cannot effectively influence. But new class organizations can use the economic power of their membership against the banks and businesses of the authority board members to influence public decisions

11. the consumer issues that Ralph Nader and others have raised represent a major area of activity for new class organizations. Detroit will never change phony warrantees, planned obsolescence, or rotten repair policies until organized groups of new class car buyers threaten—and carry out the threat—to deprive dealerships of their livelihood. Utilities companies not only pollute the air and water, but generally charge far more than is necessary for their services, and ignore critical areas like gas pipeline safety. A simple tactic like folding thousands of the computer cards that accompany payments, or paying slightly more or slightly less than the bill requests, can seriously cripple a giant utility company's operations. New class tactics can also be used against companies that sell disinfectants, detergents, and pesticides which damage health; or against companies that sell the faulty heating plants that injure 125,000 people a year; or against casualty companies that raise auto rates arbitrarily instead of pressing Detroit for meaningful safety devices. Or action can be directed against units of government which don't enforce consumer protection laws; if congressmen see strong grass roots organization for consumer protection, they will start raising hell with so-called regulatory commissions which have been taken over by the very industries they are supposed to regulate

12. television would do a much better job of entertaining, advertising, analyzing, and reporting if it received strong local pressure, even on the local level, from strong new class organizations. This could mean holding up license renewals, support for educational TV stations, proxy campaigns against publicly-owned media companies, or economic pressure on advertisers.

This is important because TV is critical to the mode of sensibility of the young. In using sex and love in advertising, TV digs into some of our most precious and private areas of feeling to manipulate us into buying products—which amounts to pornography, tying together sex, violence, and the possession of gadgets as the single most powerful image of what life in America means. What an impact this has had on most of us, in our search for ourselves, for love, for meaning. As one friend puts it, "You want to sleep with the girl, so you wind up buying the Dodge."

13. politics—the parties and candidates—require basic changes in almost every area of the nation. We can no longer afford politicians who hold power *only* for patronage, or delegations to state capitals and Washington who remain ignorant of the fundamental economic and social agonies of their constituencies.

However, the basic weakness of most reform-minded movements is that they tend to view politics as some grand moral crusade. Hence, the collapse of most WASP-inspired city-reform campaigns. Even where liberals can get local councilmen or an occasional congressman elected, the fundamental right and need of citizen participation in on-going political decisions goes by the board; once elected, the "reform" candidate very seldom faces a permanent grass roots organization to which he must remain accountable. A major contribution of new class organizations, either urban or suburban, would lie in the organization of periodic district conventions, say every six months, to which the relevant officials would have to report and project coming issues, taking general instructions from the organized people of their district massed in convention. This would offer politicians a major opportunity to educate large numbers of people about the complexities of legislative and executive power and it would give significant numbers of citizens a role in electoral politics *between* elections. Local electoral politics could take on high vividness in this context, a genuine politics of accountability.

Beyond this, however, given the fact of highly varied constituencies in the metropolitan areas, the first rule of politics must be obeyed, if *lasting* changes are to be made. As Murray Kempton formulates it, "Politics is property." That means organization is more effective than moral purity (which is only phantasy anyway); that the only way to beat local know-nothing machines is to create rival machines, which is difficult and tedious work. It also means that these organizations must develop programs which increase bread-and-butter opportunities for blue collar whites, both in and out of unions.

One of the greatest weaknesses of many McCarthy-type "liberals" in the last Presidential campaign was their tendency to dismiss the blue collar Wallace voter as some species of unspeakable, savage beast. But the fact of life, in most metropolitan areas, is that there will be no winning for new class types unless they develop programs which meet the legitimate economic and social grievances of blue collar workers. This does not apply to the hard-core Wallace machine, which is fascist. But it does apply to most of the workers, especially in the Northern industrial centers, who voted for Wallace: they are strapped with heavy debts, often two jobs, clobbered physically and psychologically by assembly-line labor, worried stiff about their children, tired of having no power (witness the many wildcat local revolts), and deeply envious of the rise in status and attention of new class whites and blacks. Wallace recognized this clearly in his platform, which, beyond the "law and order" appeal, was full of standard Populist planks.

To win over Wallace voters, the political strategy should be to recognize clearly their grievances and develop programs which offer opportunities to *them* as well as to blacks and new class whites. This should be done to neutralize the fascist leadership which tries to use blue collar insecurity and frustration to climb into political power.

Specifically, this strategy means strong pressure to create new industry and new public construction projects, so that *both* blue collar white and black job opportunity is vastly increased. As the administration cuts back in Viet Nam, slack employment in the defense industry can be picked up through rebuilding the cities, the schools, the hospitals, the mass transportation that we must have in a new, humane environment.

Or take schools. Blue collar white schools are in terrible shape. And when school boards, which over the years have ignored pleas from blue collar white parents to improve their schools, bring in black kids in busses, another needless conflict develops. A small pie is cut into even smaller pieces, and the whites wind up blaming the blacks. The way out is to vastly improve *all* the schools, not just with money, but, more important, with radical changes in teacher selection and training, which is atrocious. That can be done with pressure from all sides—blue collar white, new class white, organized blacks.

Another idea with which to break the school impasse is using "magnet" schools. These are top-flight schools into which *all* the students are bussed. Whites send their kids there because they are the best schools around; the black kids come for precisely the same reason. Blacks and whites meet there as cultural equals (not because "they should sit next to white kids to get the right values"). These schools could prove that desegregation works, taking the steam out of local Wallace-type politicians. They could provide a place for suburbanites who want their children to have an inter-cultural education, but who can't break the overwhelming suburban opposition to desegregated schools "out here." And they could prove what education *can* be in an urban scene, as, say, what the Bronx High School of Science does in New York.

Taxation is another self-interest issue around which coalitions of organized blacks, new class whites, and blue collar whites could develop. New class owners are not only demoralized by a city which cannot, because of a penalizing property tax, rehabilitate and rebuild; they are also discouraged from improving their own homes. Blue collar whites, heavily saddled with debt, are also penalized every time they want to make major repairs. Black home-owners are in the same bind. Black tenants are exploited by slumlords for whom it is economically sound, with present tax regulations, to make no repairs and to get out in a hurry. Once again, a pie can be sharply expanded by attacking the economic root of the issue. And that expanded pie can free sizeable groups from deep insecurity, thus preventing ethnic and class tension from growing into urban warfare.

None of this should suggest that new class organizations should simply *ignore* race issues. Certainly there are plenty of openings in the white casbah for desegregation, and for technical and financial assistance to the organized black community on a negotiated basis. But in most white communities, raising the race issue directly is the surest way to lose. However, attacking local issues of mutual concern (such as duplicated water systems, crazy zoning and assessment patterns, high school curriculum changes, recreational facilities) can establish productive working relationships, *shared experiences* for citizens who would oppose, under ordinary circumstances, any desegregation measures. Once a working relationship is established, race is easier to talk about, more information can be provided, easing fear and insecurity, and work on nonracial issues can continue. This approach may not be "morally pure" but it so happens that most whites, in most communities, will oppose desegregation and won't have it shoved down their throats by a tiny band of "morally pure" supporters of desegregation. The alternative to the approach I've suggested may be "morally victorious," but it won't produce any desegregation.

As for those new class whites who just cannot bring themselves to attack local issues in their own communities, but find themselves forced to run into the ghetto for tutoring programs or "field trips," I would say that they are really operating with an unconscious need to remain "superior" to blacks ("they need us, the poor devils"). And they find it strangely self-assuring to "help" the black "disadvantaged" on an individual basis. On the other hand, for this type of person, it is often deeply frightening to confront his white neighbors, especially those neighbors in local power positions, with issues close to home, for that means going up against his self-acknowledged equals, or even superiors, whose status he is struggling to attain.

To those persons who declare, "But there must be integration, or we'll wind up separatists," I would reply that the Kerner Report was obsolete before it was written. We are not "moving toward two nations, one white, one black." This country has *always* been two nations, from its founding, and the only people who would deny that reality are those who buy the story of America peddled in the school civics books. Now, in its rapidly-sharpening self-awareness, the black community intends to develop itself so that it can deal with the white community, which has broken so many promises, from a basis of power. Current and future promises will be kept—not because of "morality" but because of a lack of political and economic alternatives to do anything else. Only from a negotiated basis of power can the black community get a long-range economic change and desegregation. In this course, the black community is only doing what every other ethnic group has done in America—becoming a tight, well organized lobby.

Why should whites assume that blacks will "trust" them as allies on issues that whites are free to walk away from? Organizations "trust" each other when each knows the other's self-interest, when each knows the other is *locked into* the alliance, when each knows the other has a great deal to lose from breaking the deal.[17]

Furthermore, the most "helpful" thing white organizations can do for the black community—aside from standing aside to permit black skills to develop, and making available specific technical skills and money on a negotiated basis—is to attack the root grievances of the new class and blue collar white environment. Why? Because underlying the tangle of race in all our metropolitan areas is the powerlessness of *all* victimized classes—blacks, blue collar whites, new class whites. Nothing of basic importance to justice in the metropolitan areas will happen until all three of these victimized constituencies gain far more power, far more ability to change their environment, than they have now. The key to the new situation lies in the new forms of alliances that can be developed between new class and blue collar whites, and between them and the black mass organizations. The key to those alliances lies in bringing to the consciousness of the new class the awareness that its members are victimized and therefore must organize out of self-interest (exactly the process that the black community has gone through). Then, they must sit down with organized blue collar representatives and democratically-elected black leaders to analyze their common victimization, moving into issues which can mean *mutual benefit for all three constituencies*. Once we are acutely aware that we are *all* caught up in the middle of the urban crisis—and not just "those poor devils over in the black ghetto"—then

---

[17] Look at the new alliance between the University of Chicago and the Woodlawn Organization against Mayor Daley on model cities as an example. Or the alliance between Xerox and FIGHT to establish a black-owned factory. Or the deal between BUILD, the Buffalo Board of Education, and the State University College to establish the Black Academy.

we can get down to the business of defining our *real* opposition, and organizing to get what we must all have to be fully human: control over our own futures.[18]

* * *

As new class organizations develop more consciousness of the forces which are destroying our environment—and the relationship between their members and that environment—several basic organizational implications become clear:

1. there must be a clear understanding of the meaning of the word "issue," not just as a noun, but as a *verb*: "Issue" must be understood as a *changing public relation* between power groups which involves action/reaction and hence controversy. And organizations must keep in mind that issues depend on the relevant arena of power. An issue exists only when the organization can do something about it; an issue must be immediate, specific, *actionable,* and realizable

2. self-interest as the prime motivating force means more, in the new class, than grievances. It taps the powerful urge to positive creativity —which can mean new institutions, new schools, new health organizations, new symbols, new organizational forms, new environments. New class organizations can be, if they are developed with this vision, instruments through which adults escort their young through the sorely-missed rites of passage

3. new class organizations can also become the vehicles for moving away from our current massive privatism, which is the loss of the sense of *relation* among persons, and between persons and meaningful institutions. Through new class organizations, we can rediscover the knowledge

---

[18] At one level, the movement toward self-analysis of the new class situation can be seen in the history of Friends of FIGHT in Rochester. FOF was organized shortly after FIGHT was organized, primarily as a white appendage to FIGHT, to help buffer opposition within the white community while FIGHT got on its feet. It has become absolutely clear that FIGHT is here to stay, that its legitimacy is well established, and that it needs no protection from within the white community. At the same time, FOF began to look to the white community for more membership and for ways of tackling issues within the white community which had little if anything to do with race. FOF found that its name got in the way, and that it was viewed by many whites as simply an arm of FIGHT, without its own mind or autonomy. So in order to be effective within the metropolitan Rochester area, FOF changed its name recently to Metro-Act. It has not thrown off its alliance with FIGHT on specific issues. But Metro-Act is now free to build a genuine grass roots power base around legitimate nonracist grievances within the white community, such as lack of housing, recreation, taxes, quality of schools, pollution, etc.

The same process can be seen, at least to some degree, in Buffalo, as CAUSE dropped its initial name, Build Us Too. If real power is to be developed in white Buffalo, both CAUSE and BUILD must have genuine autonomy, with their own programs—without an umbilical cord leading in either direction.

that the highest creative potential of *individuals* is realized only within *relation; that* is where the vividness of life emerges, that is where the word "public" again becomes meaningful

4. organizing the energy of the new class will enable government to do its job. Orderly public administration has lost its effectiveness because of its isolation from citizens, energy, and creativity. Consent can once again become active, not just passive, which means that our public alternatives no longer need swing between "law and order" and "anarchy"

5. *multi*-issue organizations can provide a continual flow of intellectual excitement, bringing a continual infusion of new ideas, new issues, new tactics. With that electricity in the air, new class organizations can develop new symbols, new meanings—meeting, in part at least, the need for a new semi-church, where new hopes and accomplishments emerge

6. these new class organizations are in reality new power institutions, which can re-create the critically important sense of architectural and geographic place: *institutional place can create architectural and geographic place.* Traditional planners come at the problem backwards, by trying to develop architectural and geographic place in an institutional dehumanized vacuum. Architectural and geographic place are robbed of their meaning unless they are created by people whose moral purpose, self-interest, self-image, and actions are centrally expressed in creating that environment. For re-creating the *relation* of persons to a humane environment, the thrust must come from the bottom up, from the experience of the people to the conceptions and then the creations of new architectural and geographic places.

*   *   *

What can we *do*?

For whom?

Who is the victim? Are there some of us *not* caught in the center of the urban crisis of metropolitan America?

The black casbah has awakened, is on the move. The white split-level casbah is just beginning to awaken to its *own* victimization and to the *actual* social reality which produces its purposeless privatization and impotence. To solve the new class crisis, the white casbah will have to spring to full consciousness, remove the illusions, heal the split psyche by careful self-analysis—which will open up no end of issues, no end of tactics.

Move out of schizophrenia, if you will.

Split-level casbah, or a place to live?

Mandarinism: Planning as Handmaiden to Conservative Politics

ALAN S. KRAVITZ

In a technology-dominated age such as ours and as a result of forces and attitudes that have brought about this dominance, "can," a conditional and neutral expression of feasibility, begins to be read as if it were written "ought" which is an ethical statement connoting an imperative. Thus feasibility, which is a strategic concept, is elevated to a normative concept, with the result that whatever technological reality indicates we can do is taken as implying that we must do it. The strategy dictates its own goal. The action defines its own *telos*. Aims no longer guide invention: inventions reveal aims.[1]

. . . studies reveal a profession complexly identified by the exigencies of its times and the condition of the environment, by the availability of pertinent tools, and the evolution of its own ideas.[2]

Something is, indeed, very wrong when planning goes unplanned; when planners tolerate a situation where "strategy dictates its own goal. The action defines its own *telos*," and they allow their profession to be "identified by the exigencies of its times and the condition of the environment." Yet, the rhetoric of the profession notwithstanding, planning practitioners and theorists alike have allowed their profession to be defined by its environment. Conditioned by both the profession and the larger society, they have learned to adapt to their environment, to take its stimuli literally, and to accept traditional perceptions of it. They are unaware that their entire environment is based on a set of assumptions implicit in the dominant ideology and serving different ends than those articulated by the ideology. As a result of this lack of awareness planners have not felt the need to question the ultimate ends of their actions. They remain enslaved by the ideology to a course of action that is not of their choosing and does not reflect their aims.

A great deal of thought has been devoted to the development of planning, most of it concerned with the means or immediate ends of planning activities. Little or nothing has been done to probe their ultimate ends with the result that planners have lost sight of their aims and lost the capacity for foresight. They have become myopic and, in turn, allowed themselves to become mandarins to a liberal ideology that seeks

---

[1] Hasan Ozbekhan, "Can Implies Ought," in Stanford Anderson, ed., *Planning for Diversity and Choice*, (Cambridge, Mass., 1968), p. 210.

[2] Ralph A. Gakenheimer, "The Planning Profession: Retrospect and Prospect," *Journal of the American Institute of Planners*, XXXIII (1967), 290.

social reform through democratic pluralism. I have used the term "mandarinism" to describe their condition in much the same way as Chomsky has used it to describe the role of liberal intellectuals in the setting of American foreign policy in an era marked by "The End of Ideology."[3] To me, "mandarinism" is the condition of acting or behaving without being aware or conscious of the role *really* played, the function *really* served or the objectives *really* pursued. In the vernacular of existentialism and "negativism" it is being "one-dimensional," "other-directed," "unauthentic," or "technical." From the phenomenological perspective it is neither intentional nor purposive and, therefore, must be viewed as non-rational at the existential level although it may be rational at the pragmatic level. Put into a positivist vernacular it is allowing role to be externally defined, functionally or operationally, with respect to the maintenance of a given system, an established reality, or a set of ends which are not of one's own choosing. In the humanistic sense, it is not being a man and, thus, the very antithesis of planning. With the problem of definition removed, it becomes feasible to ask what it means to accuse planners of mandarinism and to attempt to justify the accusation.

IDEOLOGY AND POLITICAL REALITY

Prior to the heightened interest in planning which emerged in the latter part of the nineteenth century, most planning had been practiced privately and on an *ad hoc* basis. The precursors of the planning movement were technicians, skilled professionals hired to exercise their ability to solve certain kinds of previously defined problems. These technicians were caught up in the rhetoric of "professionalism" and in their own ethic of "amenity." It was neither in their temperament nor their interest to concern themselves with the broad social and political implications of their professional role. Whatever time they did devote to thinking about their role was given over to further development of technical skills and to promotion of them.

It was the legitimization, institutionalization, and professionalization of city planning as a governmental function that presaged the development, during the twentieth century, of a vast body of thought about planning practice. A majority of this thought or "planning theory" focuses on the scope or content of planning, its methodology, and its organizational or institutional setting. These aspects of planning theory are based upon presuppositions, often only implicit, about the relationship between planning and politics. However, this relationship is seldom dealt with either in regard to any of the other aspects of planning or in the abstract. In its place we find some work on the relationship between planning and gov-

[3] Noam Chomsky, *American Power and the New Mandarins,* (New York, 1969). For the origin of the title, see his essay "Objectivity and Liberal Scholarship," in the collection. In this work he traces its use to a paper by Ithiel de Sola Pool.

ernment which is variously termed the planning "process," "function," or "strategy," as the central element of planning theory. Because governmental form and process is a reflection of the dominant political ideology, the element of ideology is not totally obscured from the planner's purview. However, ideology itself is not subject to critical review with the result that the presuppositions of the ideology remain obscured as do the political interests or politics served by them. These are the *real* "politics of planning."

Over the years planners have come to recognize that ideology, governmental form and process, and politics are, with methodology, the major determinants of planning, but they have remained unaware of the latent politics, the politics of ideology that lurks beyond. Gans may view planning as "politicized" because planners have not only adapted to liberalism but also adopted a variety of viewpoints within its scope.[4] Wilson may say that they have become responsive to "how deeply embedded in politics the planning process is."[5] However, the planners are unaware of the degree to which they have been politically socialized to serve as mandarins to a liberal ideology the ultimate objectives of which are not only unchosen but also unknown to them.

If planning is to be "planned," then the profession must examine more than the range of alternatives prescribed by liberalism. A "critical" examination of this type would raise many difficult ethical and metaphysical questions that go beyond planning to the model of man upon which it is based.[6] If this examination were combined with "normative" thinking it might lead to or make important contributions to the development

---

[4] Herbert J. Gans, *People and Plans* (New York, 1963), p. 73.

[5] James Q. Wilson, "Planning and Politics: Citizen Participation in Urban Renewal," *Journal of the American Institute of Planners,* XXIX (1963), 249.

[6] The term "critical" is used here in much the same way as it is used by Herbert Marcuse in the introduction ("The Paralysis of Criticism: Society Without Opposition") to *One-Dimensional Man* (Boston, 1966). For Marcuse, a critical theory is one which "analyzes society in the light of its used and unused or abused capabilities for improving the human condition" (vol. x). In any such analysis, the established way of organizing society is measured against other possible ways, which are held to offer better chances for alleviating man's struggle for existence; a specific historical practice is measured against its own historical alternatives (*Ibid*).

For a slightly different but equally provocative definition of the idea and the role of critical thought see I. C. Jarvie, "Utopian Thinking and the Architect," in Stanford Anderson, *Planning,* pp. 8–31. Perhaps the best account of the death of critical thought in the American intellectual community is found in Chomsky. He is able to trace it back, through Bell's "End of Ideology," to Dewey and the glorification of pragmatism and its elevation to the level of ideology. The most important attempt to trace the influence of American pragmatism on planning may be found in John W. Dyckman, "Introduction to Readings in the Theory of Planning: The State of Planning Theory in America," (unpubl. manuscript, n.d.). The basic argument against the development of a "critical" approach to planning is found in Robert A. Dahl and Charles E. Lindblom, *Politics, Economics and Welfare,* (New York, 1963).

of new models of man, theories of social and political organization and new political strategies for their realization as well as new concepts of planning. These developments are crucial steps on the way to fundamental social reconstruction but are clearly beyond the limited scope of this essay which is limited to a prior step, a radical analysis of the relationship of planning to liberalism. Planners have become handmaidens to liberalism without understanding the conservative politics which that ideology really serves. It is as though they failed to heed the caveat of Manheim who cautioned that "there is implicit in the word 'ideology' the insight that in certain situations the collective unconsciousness of certain groups obscures the real condition of society both to itself and to others and thereby stabilizes it."[7] It is this "collective unconsciousness" that must be removed. Then the "real condition of society" will be revealed to the planners and their responsibility for that condition exposed. Then, for the first time, planners will be free to choose whether they wish to continue to stabilize it or to begin to contribute to the reconstruction of the human condition.

This ambitious task may be accomplished through an analysis of the relationship between the three basic theories or models of how planning *should* be practiced and the various perspectives on liberalism out of which each developed. In doing so I should be able to clarify the historical significance of each in the development of liberalism and to expose the latent politics of liberal political ideology. These three "normative" theories dictate how planning should be practiced under varying perspectives on what is wrong with the city, which, in turn, stem indirectly from "scientific" analysis of the urban condition and directly from political perspectives which fall within the spectrum of liberalism. These theories, although considered normative in terms of planning practice, must be viewed as operational at the political level as they have been functionally defined with respect to the maintenance of an accepted political reality.

In the pages that follow, the subordination of planning to liberalism is demonstrated. Firstly, the "classical model" of rational planning was a basic element in the reactionary efforts of the "political reform movement" to establish corporate or welfare liberalism. Secondly, the two contemporary models of planning practice, policy planning and advocacy planning, are linked to an established liberalism through the efforts of "professional" and "activist" reformers, respectively, to live with it.

REFORM AND THE CLASSICAL MODEL

There is widespread agreement among those who have studied the history of planning that the development of the modern American concept of city planning was triggered by a series of reactions against the physical and social conditions in the crowded, industrialized cities of

[7] Karl Manheim, *Ideology and Utopia,* (New York, 1936), p. 40.

mid-nineteenth century America.[8] Most would agree with Hancock that "the haphazard physical growth and social disorder accompanying American urban development . . . stimulated increasing demands for amenity, systematic physical reorganization and social reform which preceded and helped shape the modern planning movement."[9] While it is possible to trace early manifestations of a widespread demand for urban reform as far back as the end of the Civil War, the actual "birth" of modern city planning is usually traced to the last decade of the nineteenth century and, more precisely, to the opening in 1893 of the Chicago World's Fair.

"The Fair's vital lesson was the supreme 'need of design and plan for whole cities'."[10] It was the culmination of a series of developments in the physical design professions. The concept that it was possible to create a design for the major physical elements of an entire city which, if implemented, would accomplish its physical reorganization was put across by the Fair, disseminated by those who had visited it, and widely accepted by civic booster or civic improvement groups throughout the nation. In the "City Beautiful" concept these groups saw an opportunity to alter the visible image and improve the quality of life in their communities without incurring any of the costs or complications of social reform. As they would ostensibly improve the quality of life, the plans would be attractive to the growing middle class. Furthermore, they might even placate the working class and their middle class sympathizers who were demanding public action for social change by creating an image that the whole spectrum of the society was concerned with the condition of city life and committed to changing it. With a concept that promised all this, a nationwide "City Beautiful Movement" was easily launched.

It has been frequently argued by the critics of planning that these booster and improvement groups believed in an "environmental determinism" which had developed out of the preoccupation of the design professions with the physical environment. Hancock writes that these groups were "convinced that physical order equalled social order,"[11] and others have suggested that they equated improvement of the physical environment with social change.[12] To do so is to assume that that meaning-

---

[8] See for example John Reps, *The Making of Urban America* (Princeton, 1965); Arthur B. Gallion and Simon Eisner, *The Urban Pattern* (Princeton, 1968); Roy Lubove, *The Urban Community: Housing and Planning in the Progressive Era* (Englewood Cliffs, N.J., 1967); and John L. Hancock, "Planners in the Changing American City, 1900–1940," *Journal of the American Institute of Planners,* XXXIII (1967).

[9] Hancock, "Planners," p. 292.

[10] Lubove, *Urban Community,* p. 9.

[11] Hancock, "Planners," p. 293.

[12] See for example Gans, *People,* p. 2, and David C. Ranney, *Planning and Politics in the Metropolis* (Columbus, 1969), p. 23.

ful social change was the ultimate objective of plans and the programs which emerged from them. With rhetorical and ideological evidence to support this argument, there is good reason to believe that, perhaps, planning had an entirely different objective and that what appears to the critic as "environmental determinism" developed as a means of rationalizing that objective to its proponents and of obscuring the true objective from the scrutiny of others.

Equally difficult to accept is the argument stated earlier—that the development of planning was caused by a sincere, reform oriented reaction to the conditions of urban life. The argument is not false; it represents only a half-truth. Such a reaction did exist and did provide planning with its physical content and its reliance on government intervention. However, the actual shape of the planning function, its governmental setting, and its ultimate objectives were more the result of the reactionary efforts of a powerful segment of the population to spread both the myth that gradual social reform was all that was necessary, and the ideology of corporate liberalism.

It was during the infancy of the planning movement, a period from 1893 to 1910 which coincides with the City Beautiful movement, that planning was discovered by the establishment and subordinated to their developing ideology of corporate liberalism with its ultimately conservative ends. Through the early interest of the civic improvement groups they gained a toehold on planning. As they came to recognize that government intervention could be made to serve their interests, planning came to be a major component of this elitist effort to maintain power through the establishment of a new liberal ideology of reform through government intervention. In the face of revolutionary ferment, these efforts to establish an ideology based on government intervention and to control that intervention so that it might stabilize the status quo can only be termed reactionary.

The literature describing the development of planning credits the social reform movement with having instilled in planning a "a proud tradition of service, an egalitarian ethic, and a pragmatic orientation to betterment . . . ."[13] Statements such as this abound and are typical of the failure to distinguish between rhetoric and reality—in this case, the misconception stems from a failure to distinguish between liberal rhetoric and the reality of the planning experience. It has been compounded by a tendency to lump together all of the factions involved in the political struggle out of which liberalism emerged and to view liberalism as a kind of national consensus beyond ideology.

It has been suggested that there were as many as five factions in-

[12] Melvin M. Webber, "Comprehensive Planning and Social Responsibility," *Journal of the American Institute of Planners*, XXIX (1963), 241.

volved in this struggle. Among these was a "revolutionary" faction which sought to achieve radical change in all spheres of American society and saw it necessary to go outside legitimate political channels to accomplish this. This faction centered on the International Workers of the World and was made up of a wide spectrum of revolutionary groups, most of which had Marxist-Socialist leanings. To their right was a labor-oriented "radical" faction (typified by the Knights of Labor) which sought basic social and economic reforms through independent but legitimate non-revolutionary political organization and action. Both the Marxists and the radicals viewed social and economic conditions as intolerable. There were two factions that viewed conditions as bad but felt that they were not intolerable. The first of these was the "progressive" faction which urged the use of governmental intervention to ameliorate social and economic inequities which they felt were the result of unfettered capitalism. They hoped to save the political and economic system by political action to check the unintended or undesired consequences of private activities. To their right were the "philanthropists" who felt that the problems were more fleeting, perhaps, the result of rapid immigration and economic development, and that they could be solved by organized private activities directed at the socialization of the poor to the values and attitudes which would make it possible for them to succeed within the system. Finally, there were the "conservatives" who saw no need for change.[14]

Thus we see that it was the "progressives" who were initially responsible for suggesting the use of government intervention to attain social reform. But was it the progressives who formulated that concept into an ideology and harnessed it to the preservation of the status quo? To answer this it is necessary to first determine who the progressives were and what they sought to accomplish.

The vast majority of the progressives were drawn from either the upper class or upper middle class business and professional community. They advocated reform for two reasons. First they were pulled by a threatened or perceived loss of their status or power to either the new, corporate-oriented element of the upper and upper middle classes or the revolutionary working class and their lower middle class friends. Then they were pushed, or, rather, driven by their community-regarding ethic rather than by their self-regarding Yankee-Protestant ethic. If they were to maintain their status and satisfy their conscience they had no choice but to suggest a middle road.

The phrase "to clap a rational democratic harness onto an expanding American industrialism" seems to express the attitude of these progressive reformers

[14] Thomas H. Logan, "The Birth of Zoning in the United States" (Chapel Hill, N.C.: unpub. manuscript, 1967). The primary source is Daniel Levine, *Varieties of Reform Thought* (Madison, Wis., 1964).

quite well. The problems they saw were grave, but not endemic to the political system. This cherished system they sought to use to bring the economy under control and to "mitigate its worst effects."[15]

Thus it was that the progressives created a concept of government intervention to achieve social reform. However, this concept was seized upon by reactionary forces and turned into an empty ideology which could gain the necessary political support by promising social reform, but be controlled and made to serve primarily to preserve order, stability, and economic development. This is not to say that social reform would not occur, but that it would become a secondary or instrumental objective. Progressive or reform liberalism thereby became corporate liberalism. Once in the political arena, a sincerely liberal concept became the basis of an ultimately conservative ideology.[16]

Just as the progressives provided liberalism with its basic concept and means, they did much the same for planning and there again provided the basis for an ultimately conservative governmental function. In terms of influence on local government the most important of the progressives were those concerned with housing reform. They played a major role in the development of zoning and its subsequent adoption as the principal tool for plan implementation. Nonetheless, from about 1910 on, the reformers played an increasingly reduced role in the development of the planning function and its subsequent institutionalization. One frequently cited indication is the history of the National Conference on City Planning and the Problems of Congestion. The Second National Conference, which was convened in Rochester in 1910, was dominated by representatives of conservation, civic improvement, or municipal efficiency groups and their architect-planner collaborators.[17] The social reformers or progressives who had brought their concern for health, housing, and public welfare to the 1909 conference were no longer in evidence. Furthermore, the portion of the earlier conference's title dealing with "The Problems of Congestion" had been deleted and a new National Housing Association formed around the Committee on Congestion of Population in New York, which had been the nucleus of the progressive-reform contingent.[18] From 1910 on, the progressive-reformers remained outside the mainstream of the planning movement and its key organization. This organization, the National Conference on City Planning, was later to become the basis of the professionally-oriented American City Planning In-

[15] Logan, "Birth of Zoning," p. 7.
[16] There has been a vast debate over the origins and control of the Progressive movement. For a survey of many of the viewpoints see Part 1, "The Progressive Era," in Barton J. Bernstein and Allen J. Matusow, eds., *Twentieth Century America: Recent Interpretations* (New York, 1969).
[17] Hancock, "Planners," p. 294.
[18] Logan, "Birth of Zoning," p. 12.

stitute which separated from the National Conference in 1934 to become the American Institute of Planners.[19] The reformers focused their attention on certain substantive areas such as health, housing, and public welfare while also devoting a great deal of effort to the development of the social sciences. They did not totally abandon planning but continued to pressure the profession to adopt the standards which they were developing in the substantive areas and to adhere to the goals of social reform. It was not until the mid-fifties that the tide began to turn.

If Webber and those who follow a similar course can be interpreted as saying that contemporary planners have inherited only an empty ideology from the progressive reformers, then they are correct; however, if, as seems to be the case, they mean that actual planning practice served liberal, egalitarian ends, then there is sufficient evidence to indicate that they are sadly mistaken. To do so is to confuse ideology and rhetoric with actual performance. The heritage of the progressive-reformers consists of the concept of government intervention and the tool of zoning, perhaps the two basic elements of the planner's rhetoric, a rhetoric which obscured "the real condition of society" and rationalized the development of a planning model which served as a conservative force in the society.

With the reformers out of the picture, most of the support for planning between 1910 and World War I came from the Municipal Reform or Political Reform movement. With this new base of support came a major shift in the priorities and self-image of the profession. Amenity and order, which had been its explicit objectives, were replaced by efficiency, and what had been viewed as an "Art" quickly became a "Science" in spite of the fact that previous efforts to move in these directions had been frustrated by the successes of the City Beautiful movement. Hancock notes:

By 1911 president Charles Mulford Robinson called it the "science of city planning"—a decided shift from his earlier views (see *Modern Civic Art*, 1903). Beautification was not discussed as a major NCCP topic between 1910–20 but "planning" (rather than "plan" or "plan-making"), "system," "efficient and intelligent public controls," the "ordinary citizen" and the "common welfare" became commonplace in the idiom.[20]

This new "idiom" was directly drawn from the rhetoric of the Municipal Reform or Political Reform movement. Why the sudden shift? Was it, simply, as has been suggested, the result of the fact that both the Planning and Municipal Reform movements had "occurred simultaneously" and tended "to share a similar set of attitudes . . . about the evils of ma-

[19] Hancock, "Planners," p. 294.
[20] Hancock, "Planners," p. 294.

chine politics and the way cities ought to be run,"[21] or were the Planning and Municipal Reform movements more intimately related in a much different way? Many of the men who had been members of the civic improvement groups which had sponsored "City Beautiful" plans were now moving to the forefront of local municipal reform groups. As Lubove points out, the early planners wanted to be technicians and professionals, and, above all, to influence the development of cities.[22] This opportunity was offered only by those concerned with municipal reform. It would have been simple for the planners to adopt and even to rationalize a new idiom consistent with the rhetoric that was now issuing from their old clients.

It is commonly argued by liberal historians and political scientists that "the main motivation of the reformers was not to overturn the machine (or generally take control of government) but rather to make government more effective and more democratic,"[23] and that " 'good government' was a class ideal" which meant that "from the standpoint of the middle-class ethic, characteristically that of native Yankee-Protestants and Jews, the task of government is to serve the 'community as a whole.' "[24] It has been demonstrated, however, by Hays and many others[25] that the political reformers acted more out of self-interest than their rhetoric and ideology would have us believe. Time and time again they took the opportunity to utilize "liberalized" government intervention to protect the value of their own property, to serve their interests, and more, depending on the extent to which they had been successful in their efforts to wrest control of local government away from the lower classes who were coming to dominate city politics. Perhaps they were after "municipal efficiency" and "effective government," but they wanted to be the ones with the power to establish the criteria against which these would be measured and thus establish governmental priorities.

Although documentation is lacking, it seems that the basic political strategy of municipal reform was formulated by a rich and powerful coalition of the old elite and the new upper class. It is known that much of the financial support for the building of a national movement came from the Rockefeller and Russell Sage Foundations.[26] This strategy called for

[21] Ranney, *Metropolis*, p. 35.

[22] Lubove, *Urban Community*, pp. 14–15.

[23] Edward C. Banfield, "Good Government: Introductory Note," in Edward C. Banfield, ed., *Urban Government: A Reader in Administration and Politics* (New York, 1969), p. 268. Banfield does not support or refute this view, but finds it articulated in Don K. Price, "The Promotion of the City Manager Plan," in Banfield, *Urban Government*, pp. 286–98.

[24] Banfield, *Urban Government*, p. 267.

[25] Samuel P. Hays, "The Politics of Reform in Municipal Government in the Progressive Era," in Bernstein and Matusow, *Twentieth Century*, pp. 34–58.

[26] The Russell Sage Foundation supported both the NCCP after 1910 (Hancock, "Planners," p. 294), and the National Municipal League which was, very much, the research and public information center for the Municipal Reform movement.

an alliance with the propertied portion of the middle class to be based upon a common concern for improvements in transportation, protection of residential property values and community, and stabilization of governmental costs. Furthermore, the alliance was based upon a commitment to whatever social reforms were necessary to guarantee social and political stability. The major element of the strategy was the effective disenfranchisement of the lower laboring class through a series of specific reforms in the structure of municipal government.

These political reforms were an ideal instrument, for they could be implemented at the state level where the balance of power was still in favor of the reform interests. The reforms would remove local politics' traditional control (or a large degree of control) over urban policy. Moreover, they could be justified as mechanisms which would facilitate representation of the "community as a whole,"[27] or "the interests at large, rather than 'specific interests.' "[28] According to the rhetoric of the Municipal Reform movement, these proposals would lead to more representative and, hence, more democratic government which would permit "rational," "efficient," or "effective" management.

The key element in the rhetoric of the movement was the concept that:

there is a public interest that can be applied to all of the issues of local government. The public interest is that course of action which best serves the public as a whole. Private interests . . . must take a backseat to the public interest . . . "politics" involves the serving of private interests and should, therefore, be kept out of government.[29]

Out of this basic concept the reformers deduced "three principal political ideas" which were reflected in "three fundamental principles" of "good government." These were:

First, there was the idea that the most capable and public-spirited citizens should serve on the governing body as representatives of the city at large, to determine policies for the benefit of the community as a whole, rather than for any party, faction or neighborhood. This idea was embodied in the nonpartisan ballot and in the system of election at large of a small council.

Second, there was the idea that municipal administration should be delegated to a thoroughly competent, trained executive, who should get and hold his job on his executive ability alone and should be given a status and salary comparable to that of an executive in charge of a private corporation. The idea was embodied in the concentration of administrative authority in the city manager.

[27] Edward C. Banfield and James Q. Wilson, *City Politics* (Cambridge, Mass., 1963), p. 41.
[28] Robert Agger, Daniel Goldrich, and Bert Swanson, *The Rulers and the Ruled* (New York, 1964), p. 21.
[29] Ranney, *Metropolis,* p. 40.

Third, there was the idea that voters should hold only councilmen politically responsible and should give the city manager a status of permanence and neutrality in political controversy. This idea was embodied in the unification of powers in the council as a body comprising the only elected officials in city government.[30]

Planning was not quite on a level with this trinity, but the trinity was a major factor in the legitimization of planning as a governmental function and in the shaping and implementation of that function. The "Classical Model" of "Rational Planning" which emerged between the end of World War I and the late twenties was consistent with the trinity and based upon the same concept of a public interest from which it had been deduced.

Bolan offers this concise summary of the salient features of the classical model:

1. The planning commission (with its professional staff) is an advisory body which assists government in formulating policy. Its view is comprehensive in that no aspect of community development is asssumed to be beyond its responsibility. It is also comprehensive in the sense that the planning commission is the guardian of the *whole* public interest rather than any particular social interest.

2. From this, it is assumed that the planning commission is both capable and responsible for establishing long-term development goals which provide a broad perspective and give substance to short-term particularistic community decisions. Planning is construed to be the antithesis of nihilism and is thus responsible for developing the broadest and highest aspirations to give meaning and purpose to the community's day-to-day activities.

3. These long-term goals are expressed by a long-range comprehensive or master plan whose salient features include a map of what the pattern of land development will be at some distant point in the future and some general policies as to how the community should be guided as it attempts to strive for that end state.

4. With this, it is assumed that short-term, small scale development decisions are to be measured against the yardstick of the master plan. The master plan would essentially eliminate debate on goals and on general means so that debate could focus on relatively narrow grounds of particular means.[31]

According to the model, the ultimate objective of the planning function was to facilitate policy-making that would be rational (comprehensive in scope, scientific in method) and in the public interest. The function would be carried out through the operation of an advisory, quasi-independent planning commission which would guard the public interest and

[30] Don K. Price, Harold A. Stone, and Kathryn H. Stone, "Three Fundamental Principles," in Banfield, *Urban Government*, p. 266.
[31] Richard S. Bolan, "Emerging Views of Planning," *Journal of the American Institute of Planners*, XXXIII (1967), 234.

would be aided in its efforts by a professional staff with a comprehensive viewpoint and a scientific approach. The efforts of both bodies would center on the development and implementation of a comprehensive or master plan which would be a physical expression of the public interest and would include program or policy guidelines consistent with it.

It is somehow typical for critics of this model, including Altshuler[32] and Gans,[33] to assume that the explicit objectives stated within the model reflect its real intent and its real political function. Starting from this assumption, they collect overwhelming evidence to prove that planning failed to influence public policy in the direction of either rationality or a "public interest." According to Gans:

In terms of its impact, however, the master plan has been a failure. Although individual recommendations have often been implemented, no master plan has ever become a blueprint for the development of the city.

The failure of the master plan can be traced to the ends and means emphasized by the planners and to their view of the city, its growth processes, and the politics of planned change.[34]

He goes on to support this assertion, but fails to recognize his initial assumption that the explicit objectives of the model which he uses to evaluate it are representative of its real intent. This failure is strange coming from a man who has recognized that the political reformers behind the planning movement were

attempting to maintain the cultural and political power they had held before the arrival of the immigrants by imposing on the city the physical and social structure of the Protestant middle-class, particularly as it then existed in rural areas and small, preindustrial market towns.[35]

It seems rather likely that if the "Classical Model" was derived from the ideology of the Political Reform movement, it would not reflect its real intent any more than that ideology did. To assume that it would, as Gans does, is simply naive. To observe such clear-cut failure without also observing a serious reaction to it should have made him aware of the possibility that planning served a hidden agenda. Based on Gans's own observations, it appears that the actual intent of the "Classical Model" was to facilitate the maintenance of upper class control over urban policy. What was ostensibly a liberal, reform-oriented approach to planning was, in reality, part of a conservative effort to maintain the political status quo and to serve the interests of the powerful and propertied.

Contrary to much of the literature, the "Classical Model" has not

[32] Alan A. Altshuler, *The City Planning Process: A Political Analysis* (Ithaca, 1965), p. 299.
[33] Gans, *People*, pp. 60–65.
[34] Gans, *People*, p. 61.
[35] Gans, *People*, p. 58.

fallen from grace and power. In this literature, the "fall of the Classical Model" is usually attributed to the "attack on the Classical Model" by the behavioral scientists in their studies of local politics and administrative processes. What was under attack was, precisely, the *model,* an abstract conceptualization of the planning function. To the best of my knowledge, none of the attackers were aware of the latent function it served, thus, they attacked it rationally, on the grounds that political and administrative reality made the model both obsolete and unworkable. They succeeded in convincing many planners that planning was a process within a decision-making environment, that this environment was not assumed under the "Classical Model," and that planning must adapt to this environment. They also succeeded in convincing many government officials that planners might be of service to them, but they have failed to alter to a significant degree the day-to-day reality of planning. The attack created a split reality for many planners but like good mandarins they continued on.

PLANNING FOR REFORM: POLICY PLANNING AND ADVOCACY

As early as 1923 the dynamic leaders of the Regional Planning Association of America were planting the seeds of a new planning that would serve a society committed to some degree of social reform. The leadership group consisted of such men as Clarence S. Stein, Henry Wright, Frederick L. Ackerman, Benton MacKay, and Lewis Mumford who were ideologically connected to the social reform movement, but were more concerned with the amelioration of the conditions of the middle class than their predecessors had been.[36] In part, this concern was a function of the prosperity of the times, but the overriding factor behind their orientation was a sincere optimism about the quality of life that a reform-oriented liberalism could bring. Because of their desire to see significant improvements in the quality of urban life, they reacted strongly against the evolution of the professional planner, in the years after World War I:

into a technician who minimized normative goals—structural or institutional innovation—and became the prophet of the "City Scientific" or "City Efficient."[37]

In accordance with their viewpoint they developed a program which combined native traditions with European influences. From the progressive era they borrowed "conservation, landscape architecture and park planning, the Garden City, housing betterment," and combined them with Howard's new towns and regionalism, Unwin's cellular or organic

[36] Lubove, *Urban Community,* p. 17.
[37] Lubove, *Urban Community,* p. 14.

approach to the design of residential communities and Geddes' ecological approach and utilization of demographic analysis.[38] Finally, they added a measure of the City Efficient's concern for rational allocation of scarce public resources that took the form of capital budgeting. The net result was, perhaps, less a new planning than the beginnings of a new planning in the roots of the old. They succeeded in creating a synthesis of social reform (in terms of improved living conditions), municipal efficiency, regionalism, environmentalism or organicism, and new analytical tools that resulted in a planning that was better equipped to deal with basic functional problems of cities.

Unfortunately, the society was not quite ready to do what had to be done to accomplish the planners' new objective. It was unwilling to do more than remedy some of the most obvious difficulties caused by private activities or the lack of public action. The economy was booming and to a great many people the entire nation was prosperous. There was little public sentiment for governmental action while it was felt that anything that needed doing could be done by private enterprise at a profit. It would take a severe depression to force the emergence of a new political ethic with a sincere commitment to social reform and social welfare, and an additional decade for it to emerge in the form of federal assistance aimed at improving the urban condition.

During the Depression, valuable insights into planning were gained as a result of national level tests of the innovations proposed earlier. By the late thirties, Robert Walker, Wesley Mitchell, and others were attempting to reconnect planning and politics through a focus on the policy-making process.[39] They argued that the master plan was a static, Neo-Platonic concept while society was dynamic, that planning had remained attached to a marginal institution, the quasi-independent planning commission, that was limited to an advisory role in the policy-making process, that the locus of power had shifted to the executive while planning remained detached from him, and, finally, that the planning profession had clung to a set of internally derived norms, standards, and objectives rather than adopt an analytical, procedural, problem solving approach. What they were calling for was a "policies planning" which functioned by providing information otherwise lacking in the decision-making environment, thereby facilitating a *greater degree of rationality* in the policy-making process. Gone was the emphasis on the rationality of plans, in its place was a rational process for plan and policy-making. Since policy-making was the recognized responsibility of elected officials, especially the executive, planning should be directly attached to the policy-maker, thus affecting the desired reconnection of planning and poli-

[28] Lubove, *Urban Community*, pp. 17–18.
[39] Robert Walker, *The Planning Function in Urban Government* (Chicago, 1950).

tics. As this was an era in which social science was dominated by a positivistic attitude, there was little concern for the particular politics to be served.

During wartime, experiences in the nation, like those during the Depression, did a great deal to strengthen the emerging model. In 1947, under the direction of Rexford Tugwell and a group of social scientists, a new program of graduate education in planning was put into effect at the University of Chicago. In their curriculum they managed to achieve a synthesis for a new planning model of many of the disparate developments of planning and the social sciences. Although their efforts met with failure in the short run, it posed a major challenge to the profession and, in the long run, produced the men with the ideas and ability to bring the Chicago approach into a position of dominance. This transformation was aided by a variety of significant changes in the environment within which planning occurred.[40]

Planning practice in the prosperous decade between the end of World War II and 1956 was preoccupied with the problems of rapid growth and development in suburban areas and with the concomitant decline of central cities. In many communities the focus of planning activity shifted from the preparation of master plans to both staff and line activities concerned with controlling urban development. This was a move in the direction suggested by Walker; however, it was a matter of expedience rather than principle. The new emphasis of planning reflected the priorities of the time, it tended to be adaptive and pragmatic even in those communities where rapid development pressures were to fundamentally alter the shape of the environment. The reality of planning practice fit neither of the models, although it had begun to lean in the direction of the newer one. This situation prompted many observers to accept the dictum that "Planning is what planners do."

Although a great many efforts had been made to develop a critique of planning practice and to come up with a workable model of the new planning, it fell to a Chicagoan to complete the task. Combining a reaction to opportunistic, programmatic planning for housing, urban renewal, and suburban development with a University of Chicago approach, Martin Meyerson in 1956 called for planning to focus on policy-making by building a "middle-range bridge" between the goal-oriented master planning of the "Classical Model" and the *ad hoc,* adaptive project planning that had become typical of the profession in the years after the war.[41] He described the new policies planning in terms of the activities and procedures which planners could undertake to accomplish the desired objec-

---

[40] Gans, *People,* pp. 65–72.
[41] Martin Meyerson, "Building the Middle Range Bridge for Comprehensive Planning," *Journal of the American Institute of Planners,* XXII (1956), 58–64.

tive. His model was a direct development of the approach developed by the Chicagoans who

approached planning as a method of rational programming. Briefly, they argued that the essence of planning was the deliberate choice of ends and the analytical determination of the most effective means to achieve these ends— means which make optimal use of scarce resources and, when implemented, are not accompanied by undesirable consequences. Ends, the Chicagoans argued, are not imposed by planning ideology or by a priori determinations of the public interest, but by political and market processes and by other forms of feedback from those affected by planning. Means and consequences are determined through predominantly empirical analysis and by other studies which test the fit of means to ends and predict the consequences of these means.[42]

Before turning to the political implications of the new model it is important to clarify the differences between it and the "Classical Model." These changes include a shift in the level of the ends, the definition of comprehensiveness, and the function of planning.

The practice of planning had culminated in actions which were, at best, remedial and adaptive as opposed to the normative ends of the "Classical Model." The ends proposed for policies planning were to be ameliorative actions which would lead to improvement in the urban condition. These ameliorative actions would be midway between the normative and the adaptive and would focus upon the elimination of functional problems easily within the realm of legitimate government action. This shift in the level of ends was the result of the growing analytical emphasis on systems and on cause rather than symptom, basic political changes which made possible a broader range of local programs, and the failure of past practice to have a lasting impact of development problems.

In place of the comprehensive or master plan, the planner was called upon to set up a planning process which would facilitate the development of an "integrated 'policies plan' which would be a mutually reinforcing bundle of policies dealing with all aspects of development . . . ."[43] Comprehensiveness in the old model was end-state oriented, a top down approach to optimization of benefit for an entire urban system. In the new model it becomes a target-oriented (that is, it is aimed at an intermediate, time-specific achievement level), bottom up approach to suboptimization for related sub-systems. Thus, comprehensive is redefined in terms of the operational constraints to holistic rationality which tended to make the classical definition unworkable.

The primary function of policies planning is to provide information

[42] Gans, *People*, p. 71.
[43] Melvin M. Webber, "The Prospect for Policies Planning," in Leonard J. Duhl, ed., *The Urban Condition* (New York, 1963), p. 329.

on means through systematic, scientific analysis. The planner is no longer to be a plan-maker or program-maker, he has adopted "the tactic of pro-gramm*ing*," which consists of methods for the formulation and analysis of "programmatic, goal directed courses of action."[44] This tactic is, pri-marily, information yielding and utilizable in the selection of targets, the design of programs, and the evaluation of alternative strategies. In con-tradistinction to the "Classical Model," the actual selection process is not part of the planning function but left to the policy-maker. Finally, to carry out this function a new analytical methodology was borrowed from the

methods of rational decision-making being developed in political science, public administration, and management . . . . In turn, this has enabled city planning to use the personnel and approaches of other disciplines, including operations research, decision theory, cost-benefit analysis, input-output studies, information theory and simulation models as well as sociological and man-power analyses for understanding the behavior, attitudes, and ends of the clients of planning.[45]

The net result of these shifts was a new model that might well be termed "neoclassical" because it continues to pursue technical rationality as its primary objective. What has changed is the nature of that rational-ity, and it is a change of degree rather than kind. In the "Classical, Model," rationality is defined in the holistic, Bergsonian sense which makes it total, absolute, and perfect. In the policies planning model it is situational in that it has been bounded by both the cognitive and political constraints to perfect rationality discovered as a result of behavioral study of political systems and administrative decision-making. The need for a planning process aimed at bringing a degree of rationality to the policy-making process was based upon certain assumptions about the na-ture of the policy-making environment. These assumptions had been val-idated by the behavioral studies which put an end to perfect rationality and rational plans as anything more than an ideal type, and, possibly, something to aim for. With the use of an "objective" analytic methodol-ogy firmly established, it was inevitable that the question of political neu-trality of the planning model be raised, but quite unlikely that the answer would have much influence on the nature of planning practice. However, something was beginning to happen outside the profession that was to have a very great effect on it.

The middle and upper classes were made aware of poverty and seg-regation in the late fifties. The widespread public response in the early sixties triggered an active, heated debate within the planning profession.

[44] Melvin M. Webber, "The Role of Intelligence Systems in Urban-Systems Plan-ning," *Journal of the American Institute of Planners*, **XXXI** (1965), 292.
[45] Gans, *People*, p. 71.

In the course of this debate, which focused upon the ultimate objective of the planning function, the question of political neutrality seems to have been answered at the cost of a political schism in the profession. This debate was, by no means, a new one. As we have seen, it had been smoldering since the earliest days of the planning movement in spite of numerous efforts to ignite it on the part of social reform oriented planners and others. Among those who made significant attempts after World War II were Issacs in 1948, Bauer in 1951, Meyerson and Banfield in 1955, and Gans in 1958.[46] It was not through any weakness of argument that they failed, rather it was a mark of the times. It was to take fifteen years of post-war affluence before the society was to become secure enough and sufficiently liberalized to discover inequality and even to begin to think about taking action against it.

As long as the debate remained general, dealing with such broad issues as the social and economic impact of physical planning, poverty and segregation and what the society should do about them, and even the possibility of social planning, it seldom became overheated. However, when it focused on the social and political implications of policies planning, things got hot. The intense debate surrounding this issue seems to stem from the fact that the rational programming tactic of policies planning was widely regarded as the most advanced development of "methods-oriented" planning.[47] This particular issue has not been resolved and it is unlikely that it ever will because it reflects two fundamentally opposed political perspectives on liberalism. Instead, it has resulted in a split of the profession into two camps, the first conservatively oriented and concerned with serving the public interest, the second liberally oriented and concerned with the elimination of racial and economic inequities and the realization of equality of opportunity. The adherents of policies planning are split between these two camps to a much greater degree than those who still hold to the "Classical Model" and fall, for the most part, into the conservative, public interest oriented camp. I will refer to the conservative policies planners as the "rationalizers" and the liberal policies planners as the "equal opportunists."

[46] Reginald Issacs, "The Neighborhood Theory, An Analysis of its Adequacy," *Journal of the American Institute of Planners*, XIV (1948), 15–23 and Catherine Bauer, "Social Questions in Housing and Community Planning," *Journal of Social Issues*, VII (1951), 1–34 are both cited by Gans (*People*, p. 76). Also to be included in this literature are Martin Meyerson and Edward C. Banfield, *Politics, Planning and the Public Interest*, (New York, 1955), and Herbert J. Gans, "The Goal-Oriented Approach to Planning," in Gans, *People*, pp. 78–83.
[47] In his "City Planning in America: A Sociological Analysis," (*People*, pp. 57–77) Gans tells us that rational programming was a form of "goal-oriented" planning because of its problem-solving emphasis. I, however, hold that it was means-oriented and was restricted to problem-solving by the very nature of the means employed.

Let us briefly dispense with the issue of value-free, politically neutral planning. The work of Davidoff and Reiner,[48] Webber,[49] and a great many others both inside and outside the planning profession virtually eliminated any attempts to invoke scientific positivism within the profession. They have demonstrated that, although the methodology of policies planning may be scientific and objective, the application of this methodology carries with it certain assumptions which have important political implications, including the acceptance of certain structural elements as given, which may, in political reality, be variable. They have also demonstrated that the selection of priorities and the definition of problems to which the methodology will be applied is a political act as it amounts to an authoritative allocation of values. In the words of Webber:

The scientist, no less than the politician or the merchant, is *inside* the system, and his work affects its workings. None of us can escape the fact that our facts are instruments of change.[50]

With the possibility of a value-free planning eliminated, it became necessary to select a role consistent with either the conservative or the reform approach.

The split of the policies planners into two camps has been noted by Gans:

It appears that the profession is being split into progressive and conservative wings, the former calling for social planning to reduce economic and racial inequality, the latter defending traditional physical planning and the legitimacy of middle-class values. The rational programmers are a third wing, seeking to develop an approach that makes it possible to plan for all interest groups, but they, too, are split over the issue of working with or against the establishment.[51]

The rationalizers are those rational programmers who work with the establishment, accept the legitimacy of middle-class values, are optimistic about the ability of the political system to make the "right" ethical decisions for by definition the decisions produced by the "democratic process" are right, and who want to see the basic elements of the system preserved. They are Dyckman's "political right" and they accept the two basic presuppositions of our "pragmatic, conservative, democratic ideology," which are:

one, the structure of power cannot be changed from below, and *two,* behavior and taste cannot be changed from above. Under the first, not only are revolutionary *means* excluded, but radical ends are ruled out as well. By the

[48] Paul Davidoff and Thomas A. Reiner, "A Choice Theory of Planning," *Journal of the American Institute of Planners,* XXVIII (1962), 103–15.
[49] Webber, "Intelligence Systems," p. 292.
[50] Webber, "Intelligence Systems, p. 295.
[51] Gans, *People,* pp. 73–74.

canons of presupposition *two*, democracies must resist the imposition of preferences upon the weak by the strong.[52]

Thus, they insist "on confining operations within the alternatives of the status quo."[53] It is not that they fail to recognize that political problems exist, it is just that they see these problems as resolvable within the status quo and, therefore, as secondary to what might best be characterized as the technological problems of a crowded, complex, urbanized, technologically based society.[54] For them, the most difficult task is the training of rationalizers and the development of techniques of rationalized decision-making. They are most concerned about the ability of a technocratic elite to come up with an analytical, problem-solving methodology which would allow the ultimate decision-makers to make correct, pragmatic decisions about resource allocation. They accept the "if" of the democratic process, and want to be the ones to provide the "then." Moreover, to do so, they seem to be willing to forget about "presupposition *two*" and allow the strong to impose their preferences on the weak as long as that imposition is through manipulation of the environment rather than direct, authoritarian manipulation.

It is worthy of note that few of these most conservative of policies planners exist within the confines of the planning profession. Most of them identify more with their methodology than with the rhetoric of the profession. Until 1968, most of the rationalizers were trained in planning schools, especially in their doctoral programs, but more recently there has been a trend away from planning towards "policy sciences," systems analysis, and operations research programs where the methodology is more advanced and the rhetoric more constrained.

The equal opportunists are those rational programmers who, having escaped from a "methods-oriented" planning, are committed to planning for equal opportunity. Although they are "goal-oriented," they draw their goals from middle class values and their means from within the range defined as legitimate by the system. They are very close to Dyckman's "administrative right" in that their concern for inclusion in the reward system and participation in the "political" process is based on both equity and the belief that if the poor and the blacks are allowed to "transform themselves . . . the whole game will work more smoothly."[55] Because they identify "equality of opportunity" as their objective rather than absolute equity, they are not concerned that the primary benefi-

[52] John W. Dyckman, "Societal Goals and Planned Societies," in H. Wentworth Eldredge, ed., *Taming Megalopolis* (Garden City, N.Y., 1967), I, 262.
[53] Dyckman, "Societal Goals," pp. 262–63.
[54] Donald N. Michael, "Urban Policy in the Rationalized Society," *Journal of the American Institute of Planners,* XXXI (1965), 283–88.
[55] Dyckman, "Societal Goals," p. 263.

ciaries of a smoothly functioning game are the more powerful, a group which happens to include themselves.

This group of policies planners, although more open to change and more liberal than the rationalizers, remains committed to a technical rationality and as such remains covertly political. The equal opportunists are committed to an open political objective and, as a result, tend to associate themselves only with those governmental and private agencies which are also committed to similar ends or are likely to be susceptible to pressure from within. Their primary tools are still analytical, their politics limited to the selection of appropriate points for the utilization of their analytical tools, and they utilize their tools to develop arguments in favor of programs that will equalize opportunity.

The equal opportunists are part of a "professionalization of reform" observed by Moynihan with great favor.[56] Policies planning has come to play a major role in professionalized reform since the advent of the Great Society's "war on poverty." The equal opportunists provide targets, technology, and political support for what is the most significant effort to date to accomplish the objectives of welfare or corporate liberalism. According to Hayden, the role of the planners in professionalized, institutionalized, and, above all, centralized reform is to create "a kind of 'early warning system' for the country's elite."[57] The policies planner, as part of this elite, stands to gain in terms of both security and material rewards for his contribution. The complex rationale of social policies planning as the approach of the equal opportunists makes no mention of self-interest but is openly optimistic about the possibility of achieving whatever institutional reforms that might be necessary to preserve the system, especially the political system. They see no need for fundamental alteration of the representative process or elimination of private enterprise, but view it as a problem of insuring adequate representation and of controlling private enterprise. They see social policies planning with appropriate citizen participation as a way of aiding representative government, by "anticipating or translating the people's needs for government,"[58] and designing programs which will aid government in ameliorating those needs.

The equal opportunists focus on substantive needs under the assumption that it is possible for the society to meet those needs under the current system. They are not aware of the fact that the needs will only be met at levels sufficient to prevent disruption or to coopt the oppressed.

[56] Daniel Patrick Moynihan, "The Professionalization of Reform," in Marvin E. Gettleman and David Mermelstein, eds., *The Great Society Reader: The Failure of American Liberalism,* (New York, 1967), pp. 459–75.
[57] Tom Hayden, "Welfare Liberalism and Social Change," in Gettleman and Mermelstein, *Reader,* p. 487.
[58] Hayden, "Welfare," p. 489.

They do not recognize that the needs they seek to ameliorate are but manifestations of the real condition of society. Instead of dealing with real conditions which demand radical change in the institutions of the society, they have reduced the basic problems of elitism and one-dimensional culture to problems of access to opportunity which can be handled through gradual reform:

> They see a step-by-step transformation of society as the result of pushing for one 'politically acceptable' reform after another. But it appears that the American elite has discovered a long-term way to stabilize or cushion the contradictions of our society. It does this through numerous forms of state intervention, the use of our abundant capacity for material gratification, and the ability to condition nearly all the information which people receive. And if this is the case, then more changes of the New Deal variety will not be "progressive" at all. Except for boosting the relative income of a few, this entire reformist trend has weakened the poor under the pretense of helping them and strengthened elite rule under the slogan of curbing private enterprise. In fostering a "responsible" Negro and labor leadership and bringing it into the pseudo-pluralist system of bargaining and rewards, a way has been found to contain and paralyze the disadvantaged and voiceless people.[59]

Although they advocate significant institutional changes, the liberal, progressive social policies planners accept the constraints imposed by an ideology which serves to help maintain a conservatively oriented political reality and a repressive technology. The ideology of welfare and reform liberalism is a facade covering a more coercive core.

> The need is not to expand the welfare state, not to incorporate the "backward" parts into it, but to replace it with a political economy that serves, rather than denies, the needs of the poor and millions of other people in this country and abroad. But replacing the political economy is not a negotiable issue arrived at through institutional reform. It is a revolutionary issue, resolved by building new institutions to replace the old.[60]

This coercive core is sustained through the activities of both the rationalizers and the equal opportunists. Each makes an important contribution to its continuation. The overt political perspective of the equal opportunists may be more progressive and more liberal than that of the rationalists, but the ultimate political implications of both are the same. Both function to protect our "pragmatic, conservative, democratic ideology."

The past five years have seen the emergence of another group of reform-oriented planners. Unlike the equal opportunists who were professional reformers, this group has adopted an overtly political approach to planning which makes them "activist reformers."[61] Unfortunately, as

[59] Hayden, "Welfare," p. 491.
[60] Hayden, "Welfare," p. 492.
[61] Hayden, "Welfare," p. 489.

will be noted, they have taken "pluralism" too literally and, thus, met with only marginal successes in terms of substantive changes in plans. Rejecting regular planning institutions and professional roles, while at the same time, accepting regular, politically (read ideologically) defined planning mechanisms and processes, these activist reformers are bringing to planning a perspective on politics which may be traced back to an earlier "radical" group. Like the Knights of Labor, they wish to remain within the political system which they hold great hope for (pluralism) as defined through its basic mechanism (party politics) while at the same time remaining outside the traditional institutions (parties) through which the system functions. Like the Knights of Labor and all activist reformers, the advocates want to be the internal outsiders who play by their own rules; however, as is the case with all who attempt this, they have contributed to the continuation of the very thing they set out to bring an end to.

The concept of "advocacy," which provides the means to "plural" or "pluralistic" planning, is a linear extrapolation of the legal advocacy concept as modified to fit the needs of the poor by the Legal Assistance Programs of the war on poverty.[62] According to Davidoff:

Where plural planning is practiced, advocacy becomes the means of professional support for competing claims about how the community should develop. Pluralism in support of political contention describes the process; advocacy describes the role played by the professional in the process.[63]

Thus, the model is both drawn from and embedded in pluralism, a political process which has been demonstrated to be inherently conservative and favorable to dominance by an open, "democratic elite."[64] While the discovery that planners were making a direct contribution to racial and economic inequality led the professionalized equal opportunists to concentrate on substantive problems, the activist advocates focused on the more overtly political procedural questions:

Advocate planners take the view that any plan is the embodiment of particular group interests, and therefore they see it as important that any group which has interests at stake in the planning process should have those interests articulated. In effect, they reject both the notion of a single "best" solution and the notion of a general welfare which such a solution might serve. Planning in this view becomes pluralistic and partisan—in a word, overtly political.[65]

[62] Paul Davidoff, "Advocacy and Pluralism in Planning," *Journal of the American Institute of Planners,* XXXI (1965), 331–38.
[63] Davidoff, "Advocacy," p. 333.
[64] See for example Peter Bachrach, *The Theory of Democratic Elitism: A Critique* (Boston, 1967); William Kornhauser, *The Politics of Mass Society,* (New York, 1959); and Robert Paul Wolff, *The Poverty of Liberalism,* (Boston, 1968).
[65] Lisa R. Peattie, "Reflections on Advocacy Planning," *Journal of the American Institute of Planners,* XXXIV (1968), 81.

This rejection of a "rationalistic" general welfare leads the advocate planners to view both the "Classical" and policies planning models as irrational as they result in a "unitary plan." It is not the plan that is irrational, but the process, which cannot take into account possible alternatives which can only be generated through professionally supported representation of all interested parties. Even with the addition of most mechanisms for "citizen participation," these models are seen as lacking effective representation of diverse interests in their respective planning processes. As a result, the many variations on the basic advocacy model attempt to provide effective representation through some combination of community or interest organization, technical assistance, and advocacy appropriate to the planning context.

The key to the politics of advocacy lies in the view of representation upon which the model is based. The original view of representation saw the planner as advocating or facilitating efforts at advocating for one of the opponents in an adversary proceeding. A more recent view sees the planner as proponent of a plan reflecting the interests of his client to a tribunal which is to judge its merits. In either case:

> The agenda, which the advocate planner has such a large part in setting for the community (his client), is in turn largely set for him by the action opportunity structure. The items for the agenda are presented by the available programs and institutions and their priority must reflect the necessity of dealing with and the possibility of taking advantage of the programs that exist. The advocacy plan thus tends to be more a reaction to than an enactment of.[66]

The representation, therefore, is representation in a secondary political arena, the parameters of which have been set in the primary arena where the "action opportunity structure" is established. It was intended that plural plans in this secondary planning arena would reveal basic policy issues and stimulate "lively political dispute" with the *"alternatives strongly supported by their proponents"* who, in turn, had been politically organized around plans.[67] Unfortunately, the advocates misread the nature of political reality, for their efforts met with marginal success in the secondary arena and seldom were the clients organized well enough to escalate to policy issues in the primary political arena.

Advocacy, then, can be seen as a strategy for representation within the planning arena and, to a slight degree, within the political arena. This orientation is the result of the belief of most adherents of advocacy in the the basic liberal view that pluralism, protected by procedural democracy as embodied in "due process," is the appropriate mechanism for social change and, more generally, the establishment of public policy because it provides for or allows all interests to be represented and given a hearing.

[66] Peattie, "Reflections," p. 86.
[67] Davidoff, "Advocacy," p. 332.

When the activist reformers in the profession attempted to make this "idealized political process" the standard against which to judge the process through which urban renewal, housing, zoning, transportation, and other planning decisions were being made, it became clear to them that something was wrong. Upon closer examination that something turned out to be the "idealized political process" which was not working for certain groups—usually the poor and the black. Moreover, it was not working because these groups lacked professionally supported representation in almost all cases and any representation whatsoever in a large number. Because these activists were also planners, the arena was the planning arena. This perspective led Davidoff to comment:

> If the planning process is to encourage democratic urban government then it must operate so as to include rather than exclude citizens from participating in the process. "Inclusion" means not only permitting the citizen to be heard. It also means that he be able to become well informed about the underlying reasons for planning proposals, and be able to respond to them in the technical language of professional planners.
>
> A practice that has discouraged full participation by citizens in *plan making* in the past has been what might be called the *"unitary plan."* This is the idea that only one agency in a community should prepare a comprehensive plan; that this agency is the city planning commission or department. Why is it that no other organization within a community prepares a plan? Why is only one agency concerned with establishing both general and specific goals for community development, and with proposing the strategies and costs required to effect the goals? Why are there not plural plans?[68]

Where were the results of the behavioral studies of planning which established that basic public policy and the action opportunity structure within which planning operated, were determined within the political arena. Activities aimed at the planning arena could only play a marginal role in the changing of basic policies. Advocacy efforts have met with some success in terms of substantive change in public policy, but have not made any significant contribution to the establishment of "democratic urban government," its own ultimate, explicit objective. Quite to the contrary, it is rather likely that any substantive improvements have come at the expense of basic procedural reforms that could lead to that objective. This occurs when advocacy ties up limited political energy that might have been more effectively utilized in political activity or when successful advocacy efforts serve to reduce pressure for more basic reforms by pacification.

Like most activist reformers, the advocate planner has fallen into a trap which was not so much set as it was just left open. Now that he is in the trap, there is a great deal of money available from the Office of Eco-

[68] Davidoff, "Advocacy," p. 332.

nomic Opportunity and the Department of Housing and Urban Development. As this money becomes available, advocacy efforts meet with more frequent success in altering public policy. This, in turn, results in a decreased effort at political organization and a weakening of the demand for community control over the policy-making process.

As one would expect, very little conflict exists between the equal opportunists and the advocates. Rather than compete for dominance of the profession, they cooperate for mutual gain. After all, they share the same objective, the preservation of liberal democracy. Any existing difference is one of means rather than ends, degree rather than quality. The equal opportunists are more optimistic about the governmental process —they seem to take it for granted that the society has a real commitment to equality and needs only to be shown the way. The advocates are more pessimistic about political reality and have attempted to forge a role for themselves which would contribute directly to political reform. In the end, however, the distinction is rather fruitless. The results tend to be the same in our pragmatic, conservative, democratic society.

TOWARDS A LIBERATORY PLANNING

What is called for is a "liberation" planning serving a radical politics, planning that will play a significant role in freeing us from our pragmatic, conservative, elitist democratic ideology and the perfidious "technological" mentality which protects it. This new planning must help to clear away the old rhetoric and dogma which caught and dominated all the previous planning strategies.

Given the conservative nature of political reality, any radical planning must be pragmatic rather than idealistic in its means. It must serve as a liberating, radicalizing device rather than as a mode of planning appropriate to a radical political reality. It must not focus on policies or institutions or even processes as much as on men's minds. It must serve to free us from the constrained, bounded, technological way of thinking, the pragmatism to which we have been conditioned by an entire cultural milieu based on scarcity, the threat of jungle-like competition for survival, and maximum material productivity. Such a planning would be decentralizing, developmental, and humanizing. It would be a means for people to take power over their own lives.

At the roots of this "liberation" planning might be a new, participatory utopianism that would radicalize individuals by enabling them to create new possibilities beyond those defined as "feasible" by traditional political, economic, or even technological constraints. It would create a demand for the equalization of power and the decentralization and democratization of authority by focusing on the development of new life styles based on individual and shared awareness of authentic intentions rather than externally determined wants. Planning would be from the bottom up, rather than from the top down. People would become the planners; planning would be *by* the people with the professional serving as the catalyst or "actualizer" of a communal planning process.

The best place to start a movement in this direction is at the sub-city, neighborhood, and small-group level, especially in areas or among groups where community or consumer control has already become an issue—with those for whom "Power to the People" has replaced "Equal Opportunity." New methods and techniques must be created or borrowed from radical organizers and creative educators. People must begin to design their own environment, not from a series of narrow options provided for them by someone else's action opportunity structure, but creatively and experimentally utilizing the best available knowledge and intuition to serve one's own needs. If an environment is to be supportive, it must be designed by its users, otherwise they are bound to stagnate in it. What is being called for is more than a new planning, it is a new planning that can serve to facilitate the development and innovation of a new model of man and society. The old, utilitarian, materialistic, technological model imposed on us by our history must be replaced by a new, existential, humanistic model in which man the competitor becomes man the cooperator, man the debator becomes man the dialogist, and man the ego becomes a whole man. Man must free himself from his situation, and planning must be an agent of that struggle. If planning cannot free itself from its present course, if it continues to serve as handmaiden to a pragmatic, conservative, technological, elitist reality then all that is human is lost. "We could be and must be *in creative control . . . trend* is not *destiny.*"[69]

[69] Albert Mayer, *The Urgent Future* (New York, 1967), p. 3.

BIOGRAPHIES

NORMAN BECKMAN is Chief of Governments and General Research Division, Legislative Reference Service, Library of Congress. He was formerly Director of the Urban Management Assistance Administration, U. S. Department of Housing and Urban Development, where he was responsible for programs supporting comprehensive planning and increased public management capability at the local, metropolitan, and state levels. He has also served as Assistant Director of the Advisory Commission on Intergovernmental Relations and has held positions with the Bureau of the Budget, the Public Health Service, and the New York State Government.

THAD L. BEYLE is Associate Professor of Political Science and Research Associate in the Institute for Research in Social Science at the University of North Carolina at Chapel Hill. He received his Ph.D. from the University of Illinois in 1963. He taught at Denison University and in 1964–65 was a National Center for Education in Politics Faculty Fellow in the Governor's Office of the state of North Carolina. From 1965–67 he served as Research Associate to former North Carolina Governor Terry Sanford in A Study of American States at Duke University.

JACK M. CAMPBELL is Director of the Institute for Social Research and Development at the University of New Mexico and President of the Federation of Mountain States. He was Chairman of the Institute on State Programming for the 70's, from 1967–69. He previously was Governor of New Mexico, from 1962 to 1966. Earlier he served four terms in the New Mexico House of Representatives. He holds A.B. and LL.B. degrees from Washburn College, Topeka, Kansas.

ROBERT L. CHARTRAND serves as the specialist in information sciences for the Legislative Reference Service of the Library of Congress. As a political scientist with responsibilities for counseling the Congress on the impact of technology on society, he has prepared such works as *Information Support, Program Budgeting, and the Congress*. Following a Fulbright-Hays appointment to advise the Italian Parliament on the potential of systems technology in its functioning, he received the "Cavaliere Ufficiale" decoration from the President of the Italian Republic.

PIERRE CLAVEL is Assistant Professor of City and Regional Planning and Rural Sociology at Cornell University. He holds a master's degree in Regional Planning from the University of North Carolina and a Ph.D. in Regional Planning from Cornell University. He previously taught in the Graduate Program in Planning and The School of Public Administration at the University of Puerto Rico, and he has consulted and written on city planning, economic development, and administrative organization.

RICHARD HARMON has worked for Saul Alinsky's Industrial Areas Foundation since 1961 in Chicago and Buffalo. He is now on the staff of the recently established Industrial Areas Foundation Training Institute in Chicago, training organizers.

GEORGE C. HEMMENS is Professor of City and Regional Planning at the University of North Carolina at Chapel Hill and Director of the Urban and Regional Systems Program in the Department of City and Regional Planning. He received his A.B. degree from the University of Illinois and his Ph.D. from the Massachusetts Institute of Technology. He has been engaged in teaching, research, and professional practice in the areas of metropolitan transportation, urban spatial structure, residential location behavior, and urban activity systems.

S. KENNETH HOWARD is Associate Professor of Political Science and Assistant Director of the Institute of Government, the University of North Carolina at Chapel Hill. He did his undergraduate work at Northwestern and received his M.P.A. and Ph.D. from Cornell. He did government consulting work and taught at the University of New Hampshire before assuming his present position in 1965. Dr. Howard is co-author of *State Capital Budgeting* and has published articles in *Midwest Review of Public Administration, Physical Therapy,* and *Modern Hospital.*

ALAN S. KRAVITZ is Lecturer in Urban Planning at the New York University Graduate School of Public Administration. He is currently completing his Ph.D. dissertation, an attempt to critically evaluate existing models of the planning process from the perspective of a radical politics and to develop a model of a radical planning. He has taught at Hunter College and at the University of North Carolina where he received an M.R.P. In addition to his contributions to various research efforts in the areas of community organization and planning, he is the author of "Advocacy and Beyond," in American Society of Planning Officials, *Planning 1968* (Chicago, 1968).

GEORGE T. LATHROP is Lecturer in Transportation and Urban Planning and Director of the Metropolitan Simulation Laboratory in the Department of City and Regional Planning at the University of North Carolina at Chapel Hill. He received his B.S.C.E. from North Carolina State University, an M.C.P. from Yale, and his Ph.D. is pending at North Carolina. He has engaged in professional practice and consulting as a transportation planner and continues his major interests in urban systems, systems analysis, urban activity systems, and transportation.

SUREVA SELIGSON served as Director of Publications for the U. S. Department of Housing and Urban Development during 1968–69. She was Director of Research for the Institute on State Programming for the 70's (1967–68) and for the National Endowment for the Arts (1965–67). She was a member of the Democratic National Committee staff from 1963 to 1965, supervising the Office of Research during 1965.

JACK L. WALKER is Associate Professor of Political Science and Research Associate in the Institute of Public Policy Studies at The University of Michigan. He has been concerned in his research and writing with the theory of democracy, models of social change, and the process of public policy formation. He has also written several articles on race relations and civil rights policy and is co-author of the forthcoming *Race and the Urban Community* (Boston: Little, Brown).

DEIL S. WRIGHT is Professor of Political Science and Research Professor in the Institute for Research in Social Science at the University of North Carolina. He has served on the faculties of Wayne State University, the University of Iowa, and as a Visiting Professor at the University of California (Berkeley). He has authored books and articles on public administration, state and local government, metropolitan politics, intergovernmental relations, and public finances.

Index

223

149912